The Dunsmuir Saga

The Dunsmuir Saga

Terry Reksten

Douglas & McIntyre
Vancouver/Toronto

Copyright © 1991 by Terry Reksten
First paperback edition 1994

99 4 3

Douglas & McIntyre
1615 Venables Street
Vancouver, BC V5L 2H1

Canadian Cataloguing in Publication Data
Reksten, Terry
   The Dunsmuir saga

   ISBN 1-55054-070-X

   1. Dunsmuir family. 2. Dunsmuir, Robert, 1825-1889. 3. Dunsmuir, James, 1851-1920.
4. Coal mines and mining—British Columbia—Vancouver Island—History.
5. Vancouver Island (B.C.)—Biography. 6. Businessman—British Columbia—
Vancouver Island—Biography. I. Title.
FC3823.1.D85R44 1994   971.1'203'092   C94-910137-0
F1088.D85R44 1994

Editing by Saeko Usukawa
Design and composition by Eric Ansley
Cover design by Robert Macdonald/MediaClones
Printed and bound in Canada by D.W. Friesen & Sons Ltd.
Published with assistance from the British Columbia Heritage Trust.
Printed on acid-free paper ∞

Front cover photos: Craigdarroch (*centre*), also known as Dunsmuir Castle, was built in Victoria in the Scottish baronial style for millionaire Robert Dunsmuir, who died before it was completed in 1890. Robert Dunsmuir (*top right*) and his wife, Joan (top left). Their two sons, Alexander (*bottom left*) and James, with his son, Boy (*bottom right*). Kathleen Dunsmuir (*centre bottom*) was one of James and his wife Laura's eight daughters.

Cover photo credits: British Columbia Archives and Record Service: *front centre*, HP5445; *front top left*, HP2698; *front centre bottom*, 78930; Craigdarroch Castle Archives collection: *bottom left and bottom right*. Author's collection: *front top right*.

To

Mark Madoff (1949–1990),
whose fearless criticism helped get
the writing back on track.

And to Jim Munro,
whose enthusiasm for the story
never wavered.

Robert m. Joan White
1825–1889

— Elizabeth Hamilton m. John Bryden
  1847–1901

— Agnes Crooks m. James Harvey
  1849–1889

— **James** m. Laura Surles
  1851–1920

— Alexander m. Josephine Wallace
  1853–1900

— Marion m. Charles Houghton
  1855–1892

— Mary Jean m. Henry Croft
  1862–1928

— Emily Ellen m. 1. Northing P. Snowden
  1864–1944 2. Harry Burroughes

— Jessie Sophia m. Sir Richard Musgrave
  1866–1946

— Annie Euphemia m. S. A. Gough-Calthorpe
  1868–1952

— Henrietta Maude m. Reginald Chaplin
  1872–1950

— Robert William (Robin) m. 1. Maude Shoobert
  1877–1929 2. Florence Swindon

— Sarah Byrd (Byrdie) m. Guy Audain
  1878–1925

— Joan Olive White
  1880–1884

— Elizabeth Maud (Bessie) m. 1. John Hope
  1882–1962 2. Robert Droste

— Laura Mary (Maye) m. Arthur Bromley
  1884–1959

— Alexander Lee
  1886–1887

— Emily Elinor (Elk)
  1887–1938

— Joan Marion m. Percy Stevenson
  1888–1952

— Jessie Muriel (Moulie) m. 1. Edward Molyneux
  1890–1959 2. Maurice Wingfield
  3. G. St. Clair Keith

— Kathleen Euphemia (Kat) m. Selden Humphreys
  1891–1941

— James (Boy)
  1894–1915

— Dola Frances m. Henry Francis Cavendish
  1903–1966

Contents

Preface

In their day, Robert and James Dunsmuir were the largest employers of labour in the province of British Columbia. And both men, father and son, entered the provincial legislature to protect their interests. Their business and political careers merit further study, if only because the topics raised—sour labour relations, government largesse, unblushing conflict of interest—seem remarkably contemporary. However, critical analysis seemed out of place within the framework of a family history, so I chose to concentrate on the social and personal side, which is what had attracted me to the Dunsmuirs in the first place.

Their wealth propelled the Dunsmuirs from coal mines to the Court of St. James, from a lonely Hudson's Bay Company fort on Vancouver Island to San Francisco and New York, to Dublin, Hollywood, Aurangabad, Paris and Monte Carlo. Tracing them through the years and around the world proved to be a long, often frustrating, task. Perhaps it was only researcher paranoia, but at times it seemed as if the Dunsmuirs had carefully covered their tracks. Documents that should ordinarily be available were either missing or disappointingly uninformative. For example, documents listed as "deposited" at the Land Titles Office could not be found; and Joan Dunsmuir's probate papers contained little information given the complexity of her estate.

I could not have completed this book without the assistance and advice of many people. I owe a particular debt of thanks to the members of the Dunsmuir family: Kat McCann, who allowed me access to Kathleen Humphreys's papers and photographs; Shane Jameson, who wrote long letters recalling his grandmother, Jessie Musgrave, and her sisters; Gerry Bryden, who provided his recollections of Mary Croft, and Robert Harvey, who shared what he knew and encouraged me to dig deeper.

I am also grateful to the late Humphrey Toms for his recollections of Dola and Robin; to Craig Campbell, who provided information about Kathleen; to Madge Wolfenden for talking about the family and also introducing me to Beth Harris, who gave her impressions of Harry

ix

Croft; to Trevor Green, who shared his recollections and took me on a tour of the Dunsmuirs' Cowichan properties; to Mr. and Mrs. Goldwin Terry for their recollections of Laura and Robin; to John Croft for information on the Croft family and copies of Mary's letters; to Betty Jenkins, whose parents worked at Hatley; to Phyllis Rochfort for her memories of theatre in Victoria, and to Pep Groos for her memories and photographs.

Fellow researchers provided invaluable assistance. Lynne Bowen gave her opinion of the Dunsmuirs, based on her studies of Vancouver Island coalminers, and also took me on a tour of the mine sites. Bill Murphy of North Carolina was generous with his research into the Surles family. Sherry Irvine provided the expertise that led to the information in the Scottish Records Office. Richard Mackie shared his Nanaimo research. Patrick Dunae drew my attention to the correspondence regarding Dunsmuir's knighthood. Terry Herdin shared his Molyneux research and introduced me to Vera Poncin, who modelled for Molyneux during the 1920s. My thanks are also due to the members of the Craigdarroch Castle Society—in particular to Peter Scott, Alan Hurst, Paul Ferguson, Joy Deeks, Jeffrey Cousens, Phil Simpson, and to the castle's director, Bruce Davies. And to Jennifer Nell Barr for all her work in the HBC Archives.

The staff of the B.C. Archives and Records Service went out of their way to be helpful. And at the Land Titles Office I was made to feel welcome during the weeks I spent working in the vault and getting in everyone's way. Carolyn Smyly, Michael Halleran, Charlene Rees, Stuart Stark and Bill Murphy helped in a variety of ways. And I would also like to thank Tess Morgan who took the "author photo."

Writing a family history that covers more than a hundred years and includes dozens of characters has been a complicated business. Bob Halliday, Pam Madoff and Brian Tobin each read the manuscript at some stage and made insightful comments and helpful suggestions. Candy Wyatt deserves special thanks for having the fortitude to read *every* version. Thanks too to David Hill for his welcome enthusiasm and spirited support. Working with my editor, Saeko Usukawa, has been pure pleasure. Her careful attention to detail has been most reassuring and the changes she suggested, including those that I resisted the most, have, I think, improved the book. And it was with great relief that I handed the task of compiling the index over to Tamas V. Dobozy.

My family has been forced to live with the Dunsmuir story for much too long. But even so, Jane and Norah were always prepared to listen to theories and help with the research. I know my husband, Don, will be only too happy to read something without having to have a red pencil in his hand. And my aunt, Margaret Hartt, will be glad that now, finally, I will be able make that trip to Ireland.

The Dunsmuir Saga

PART ONE

Robert Dunsmuir

Robert Dunsmuir.

One

———

Diminutive and fine-boned, a quick-to-anger bantam cock of a man, Robert Dunsmuir possessed a relentless capacity for hard work, an eye firmly fixed on the main chance and several very good reasons for leaving Scotland—just the qualities that boded well for success in a new country. He would parlay an eleventh-hour opportunity to sail for the coalfields of Vancouver Island into a fortune.

He would rise from the position of an indentured miner to become "one of Canada's millionaires," the richest and most powerful man in British Columbia. A coal baron and railway tycoon, he would be seen by some as a capitalist icon, a paragon whose success was due to pluck and plod, an altruist who chose to risk his hard-earned dollars to increase the wealth of the province rather than to line his own pockets. To others he was "King Grab," a rapacious robber baron whose fortune was based on the niggardly wages he paid his employees and on the open-handed assistance he received from the government he was said to "carry in his breeches pocket." A man around whom controversy swirled, his career would strike chords that are still reverberating through the province more than a century later.

———

Later it would be suggested that Dunsmuir's was a true rags-to-riches story. But that was not quite the case. The first child of twenty-year-old James Dunsmuir and his wife, Elizabeth, Robert Dunsmuir was born in Scotland in 1825 into a family that had already moved out of the working class and was poised on the brink of even greater prosperity.

In 1816 his grandfather, Robert Dunsmuir, "a practical miner of good business habits," acquired a coal lease near the village of Old Hurlford a few miles from the Ayrshire market town of Kilmarnock. The valleys of Riccarton and Kilmarnock parishes were dotted with small coal mines, each serving only those customers who were a mile or two from the pit. Where their potential markets overlapped, coalmasters competed for sales by dropping their prices. Dunsmuir moved to correct that unhappy state of affairs by buying out his nearest competitor. And having won control of the local trade, he immediately raised his prices. Next, he turned his attention to Kilmarnock. In 1820 he leased land on the town's main street and opened a coalyard. And as Kilmarnock grew and the number of householders increased and new coal-hungry industries were introduced, Dunsmuir's coal was waiting, stockpiled in his Portland Street depot, ready to meet the demand.

Dunsmuir, his neighbours observed, was "gradually becoming rich." By the summer of 1832, he was fifty-three years old, a man of property and prospects. He had moved his family into a fine new house, and he could note with pride that the gold watch nestled in his pocket was worth £25. The first man to demonstrate that mining Hurlford coal could be "a very lucrative speculation," he had acquired additional coal leases and trained his two sons to manage his mines.

During the 1840s the railway would arrive. Hurlford coal would come within reach of the voracious Glasgow market, and the railway would encourage the exploitation of local iron deposits and lead to the establishment of flourishing ironworks with furnaces fuelled by Hurlford coal. The Dunsmuir family was well positioned to make the most of the great changes that were about to reshape the area. But then, in August 1832, disaster struck.

No letters exist; no diaries record the events of that summer. Providing the only witness are two tombstones standing side by side in an old churchyard near Hurlford. One belongs to young Robert's parents, James Dunsmuir and Elizabeth Hamilton; the other to his grandparents, Robert Dunsmuir and Jean Kirkland.

The first to die, on 13 August, was Robert's mother, Elizabeth. Five days later his father, James, died. His grandmother, Jean Kirkland Dunsmuir, died on 21 August. And the deaths did not end there. By the end of the month, two of his sisters had joined their parents in the grave. Of James and Elizabeth's family, only seven-year-old Robert and his four-year-old sister, Jean, survived.

That five members of one family succumbed within days of each other suggests a local epidemic, and perhaps it was cholera, the "dreadful scourge" of Kilmarnock, Hurlford and other towns and villages of Riccarton parish. Or perhaps they died as the result of typhoid, an outbreak stimulated by August heat and unsanitary drains. Whatever the cause, whether it was typhoid or cholera or whether the deaths were coincidental, the effect on the Dunsmuir family, and particularly on the orphaned children, must have been devastating. And three years later their lives underwent another upheaval when their grandfather died in his fifty-seventh year.

He died a relatively wealthy man. In addition to his coal leases and the property he held in Hurlford and Kilmarnock, he left an estate of £1,294, of which a third had been set aside for the care and education of his orphaned grandchildren. Jean remained in Hurlford with her maternal grandmother. Robert was sent away to school— first to Kilmarnock Academy, the rather grandly named parish school that stood on Portland Street just a few steps away from his grandfather's coal depot, and then to Paisley, where the Mercantile and Mechanical School provided the technical knowledge helpful to boys who hoped to become coalmasters. His education complete, he was sent into the mines to learn the practical aspects of the trade under the tutelage of Boyd Gilmour, a young coalmaster who, a few years earlier, had married Robert's aunt, Jean Dunsmuir.

Robert Dunsmuir seldom spoke about his life in Scotland. Biographical sketches published during his lifetime dismiss his Ayrshire years with a single sentence. And for good reason. A whiff of scandal clings to those early Scottish years. Even after he had risen to a position of power and prominence, vague rumours would continue to suggest that he had left Scotland to escape something shameful in his past. And those whispered stories contained more than a grain of truth.

On 11 September 1847, shortly after his twenty-second birthday, Robert Dunsmuir married nineteen-year-old Joan White, the daughter of a Kilmarnock spademaker. She was a suitable match, a pretty girl with hazel eyes and light brown hair, whose square-jawed, thin-lipped little face suggested a character of iron will and steely determination. But the Dunsmuirs, it seems, were a rather lusty lot. Two months earlier his sister, Jean, had been called before the church elders at the Riccarton Kirk Session to plead guilty to "fornication" with one Hugh Ferguson, who had admitted to having fathered her child but who had apparently shown no inclination to marry her. Now, as Joan White stood before the minister to be married, she was hugely pregnant with Robert's child. She was delivered of a daughter on 19 September—only eight days after they exchanged their vows.

They named the baby Elizabeth Hamilton after Robert's mother, but they were banned from the kirk—forbidden to attend services and barred from having their child baptized—until after they had confessed to their sin and performed appropriate penance. On 10 February 1848 they appeared at the Session of the Kilmarnock Laigh Kirk and admitted to "having been guilty of antenuptial fornication together." And only after being rebuked for their sin were they "absolved of the scandal thereof" and readmitted to the kirk.

Almost three years had passed, and a second daughter had been born, when chance, in the form of Boyd Gilmour's desperation, presented the Dunsmuirs with the opportunity to escape from any lingering scandal.

—

On 5 December 1850 Boyd Gilmour heard a piece of news that convinced him he had just made the worst decision of his life. A few days earlier he had signed a contract with the Hudson's Bay Company, agreeing to take his wife, Jean, and their five children on a 10,000-mile voyage to the end of the earth—to Vancouver's Island off the northwest coast of North America—where he would work the Company's coal mines for three years before returning home to Scotland. Now he learned that the Muir party, a group of colliers who two years earlier had signed a contract similar to his own, had met with some kind of calamity. With shaky spelling and an unsteady hand, he confided his misgivings in a letter to David Landale, the Hudson's Bay Company's recruitment officer.

"We have recevied a deal of bad news from Vancouvers," Gilmour wrote. "Muirs party are all left the Island . . . The present party are very much dishartened. The[y] think it would be much better to lay in jail in Scotland than lay in irons in Vancouvers . . . I do not see how we can proceed in the face of rebelon."

Landale acted promptly. "I disbelieve every word of the story and am surprised that your minds could take in such a monstrous absurdity," he scolded. The Hudson's Bay Company was the "most respectable Company in the kingdom," he wrote. Surely Gilmour should find that guarantee enough that he would be treated fairly.

The most respectable Company in the kingdom has been founded in England in 1670 as the Company of Adventurers Trading into Hudson's Bay. By the beginning of the nineteenth century, it had expanded its field of operations to the Pacific coast, and while its most significant profits continued to come from the fur trade, the Company had begun to dabble in other commodities. On Vancouver Island the most promising source of profit was coal.

Coal had been discovered on a beach on the island's northeast coast, and a brisk trade had developed with Indians encamped at the site who were selling the coal that they gathered on the surface for two shillings a ton. James Douglas, the HBC's principal officer in the west, was convinced that they were harvesting the trailing edge of rich underground deposits. Encouraged by Douglas's reports, the HBC embarked on the construction of Fort Rupert and recruited experienced Scottish colliers to work the mine. John Muir, an Ayrshire collier and the head of "a good, kind, patriarchal Scotch family," had contracted his services together with those of his four sons and two other young colliers.

Problems had arisen almost immediately. Fort Rupert was not what the colliers had been led to expect. They found the proximity of a large Indian village decidedly unsettling. "The Indians has come down and threatened to shoot us," a miner confided to his diary.

Adding to their discontent was the fact that they were earning less money than they had been promised. Their wages were fixed at £50 a year, but they would receive a bonus of two shillings and sixpence for every ton of coal they raised above the 30 tons per month covered by their contracts. They had expected to find a working colliery, or at least a workable seam. At Fort Rupert, they found neither. And until there was coal to mine, there was no hope of earning their bonus. They began by sinking a pit near the palisade. After discovering that it persistently filled with water, they tried a second pit almost a mile from the fort. They reached a depth of 41 feet, and while they had passed through five seams of coal, the largest was only four and a half inches thick.

"We came out here to work for coal not to look for it and do all manner of work," the colliers complained. And they decided to take their grievances to Capt. William McNeill, the HBC officer in charge of Fort Rupert. McNeill had commanded a trader sailing out of Boston before he joined the Company. A square, fierce-faced man, accustomed to viewing problems of discipline from the perspective of a ship's bridge, McNeill regarded the miners' threat to strike as mutiny. He flew into a rage and, snatching up his pistol, levelled it at the men. "You'll return to work or I'll shoot you like crows," he roared. Taken by surprise, they returned to work, but a few weeks later when they were told to dig a drainage ditch, they refused. They were experienced miners, they said, and such a menial task was beneath their dignity. McNeill responded by throwing them into the fort's bastion where they remained for over a week.

By July 1850, they had had enough. All the colliers, with the exception of the oversman, John Muir, seized an opportunity to desert. Borrowing an Indian canoe, they slipped away from the fort, and after having been picked up by an American ship outbound from Fort Rupert, they made their way to San Francisco.

In Scotland six months later, when Boyd Gilmour heard an account of the Fort Rupert affair, he had not known which way to turn. Time was fleeting; his ship, the *Pekin*, was due to sail within the week; his decision could not be delayed. By 7 December he had made up his mind. Better to court disaster on Vancouver Island than be seen as timid and indecisive by the influential David Landale.

"I am fully determined to go through the undertaken or die in the attempt," he informed Landale. But he could not say the same for David Miller, John Holland and Hugh Goldie, all of whom had "fully fixed on not going."

"What can I do?" Gilmour scrawled. "You are not here . . . I do not know properly how to act . . . more hands must be engaged . . . the undertaking can't go on with so few as we are."

Robert Dunsmuir was given only twenty-four hours to decided whether or not he would join Gilmour's party. But perhaps that was more than enough. His aunt, Jean, was the only member of his family with whom he had retained close ties. And he had served his apprenticeship in the mines under her husband. Between family loyalty and the opportunity to make a fresh start, the hurried decision forced on Robert and Joan Dunsmuir may have been an easy one.

By 8 December, Gilmour was relieved to be able to report that he had succeeded in finding replacements for his party. Arthur Queegly had agreed to take Miller's place; Archibald French had decided to join his brother, Adam, the only member of the original party who remained determined to proceed. And Hugh Goldie's place would be taken by Robert Dunsmuir.

—

It took a particular kind of grit for Joan Dunsmuir and Jean Gilmour to face the voyage that lay ahead. Between them they had seven children; Jean's five, ranging in age from fourteen to two; and Joan's two little girls, Elizabeth and Agnes. Hard enough to contemplate months and months of caring for children in cramped shipboard quarters. But worse, both women were pregnant—and their ship, the *Pekin*, was expected to be at sea for six months.

The *Pekin* sailed on 19 December. By March, the passengers were on short rations; by May, most of the children were suffering from scurvy. To Joan and Jean, both by now heavily pregnant, it must have seemed as if the voyage would never end. And then, at the mouth of the Columbia River, with their destination almost in sight, the *Pekin*'s captain ran his ship "hard and fast on a sandbar." The delay was too much for Jean. On 20 June, as the *Pekin* edged its way up the river, she gave birth to a son, and so that neither of them would ever forget the circumstances of his birth, she christened the boy Allan Columbia Gilmour. Finally, on the evening of 29 June, 191 days out from London, their ship tied up at Fort Vancouver's wharf.

Compared to other Hudson's Bay Company outposts on the west coast, Fort Vancouver was a veritable metropolis. Located on the Columbia's wide north bank, the fort was the largest the Company built in the west. Wooden pickets, 15 feet high, enclosed an area of five and a half acres. At one corner stood a three-storey bastion armed with a 9-pound cannon. Arranged in a rectangle within the palisade were twenty squared-log buildings. In 1847 Fort Victoria on the southern tip of Vancouver Island had replaced Fort Vancouver as the Company's western headquarters, and since then the buildings within the fort had been allowed to deteriorate. Fort Vancouver was a "dilapidated, dirty place," one visitor exclaimed.

The crewmen were certainly unimpressed by its charms. Grumbling about short provisions and low wages, sickened with scurvy and boiling with gold fever, most of the *Pekin*'s company, together with collier Arthur Queegly, deserted their posts and headed for the goldfields of California.

The Dunsmuirs, the Gilmours and the Frenches were moved into the bachelors' quarters, seventeen one-storey cottages joined under a single roof and built to house Company clerks and other junior officers. The door of each cottage opened onto a single room, walled with rough unpainted boards and furnished with a small table of coarse pine, a few benches and stools, and one or two board-built bunks. A rear door led to one of the outhouses ranged below the eastern palisade.

In one of these cottages, on 8 July, just nine days after she stepped ashore, Joan Dunsmuir gave birth to her third child, a son christened James after Robert's father. And while she may not have guessed it at the time, years would pass before she would see anything more luxurious than the bachelors' quarters of Fort Vancouver.

On 18 July the Gilmour party set sail aboard the Company's vessel *Mary Dare* for Fort Rupert and the mines. The voyage along the coast of Washington Territory and around the northern tip of Vancouver Island lasted three weeks. They reached Fort Rupert on 9 August, and although almost eight months had passed since they had left Scotland, it was only now that the clock finally began to run on the three-year term of their contracts. And how long the prospect of those three years must have seemed as they surveyed the establishment that was intended to be their home until 1854.

Its location dictated only by the outcrops of coal, Fort Rupert had little to recommend it. The fort stood "in a jolly swamp," a Company man grumbled. Dark firs hugged the beach and land was cleared only after months of labour. The resulting fields proved fertile enough, especially after three thousand rotting salmon had been applied for compost, but the acres of grass needed to support a dairy herd were unobtainable. "We have butter now in the Fort that you would not put to your carriage wheels, for if you did the salt would wear out the axle trees," one unhappy occupant complained. Arranged outside the fort's palisade was an encampment of Kwakiutl, a thousand strong. That they were there to work the mines and to trade with the fort's inhabitants did little to calm the nerves of new arrivals. Neither were the colliers soothed by the creature comforts provided by the HBC. The Company's dwelling houses were simple affairs. Usually limited to a single room, they were built of logs, squared to fit together as snugly as possible, but even so chill winds easily fingered through mud-filled chinks. Mats of woven cedar were hung on the walls, but still the cabins remained draughty and damp. "Window glass unknown, some used oiled paper instead. Furniture none, round logs for seats, bunks for bedsteads ... bugs innumerable, fleas without limit."

Gilmour began by making a good impression. Soon after the colliers' arrival, James Douglas was moved to write, "Mr. Gilmour bears a high character for activity and skill in matters connected with Mining." But soon it became apparent that Gilmour was a man seriously over his depth.

The problem for Gilmour, or anyone else who prospected for coal on Vancouver Island, was the peculiar formation of the deposits. Upthrust by forces within the earth and freed for a time from the sea, the coast of the island had once provided a swamplike setting for trees and plants. Then, as the land mass sank relative to the height of the water, these areas were reclaimed by the sea, and the plant life they had supported was overlaid and compacted by waterborne deposits of silt, sand and rock. Over thousands of years, the compacted vegetable matter gradually turned into coal. It has been estimated that the sea rose and retreated in this manner as many as five times, with the result that five layers of coal might be found in any given location. Surface outcrops hinted that additional layers might be found below and locating them should have been a relatively simple matter.

In an area less geologically active than Vancouver Island, a pit could be dug or a bore drilled through the sedimentary rock and samples examined for evidence of coal. But the coal deposits on the island do not lie in predictable horizontal layers. The area is cracked by a series of faults. Rock on one side of a fault may have been thrust upward while that on the other side subsided. Or one side of a fault may have slipped horizontally while the other side remained in place.

If Gilmour located a seam of coal, it would be almost impossible to determine, until the actual work of mining began, the direction in which the seam might lead or if the presence of a fault would result in the seam's apparent disappearance.

Ten days after he began work, Gilmour decided that their efforts should be directed to some Indian diggings nine miles south of the fort. But as weeks slipped into months and no workable seam was found, James Douglas began to experience nagging doubts about Gilmour's competence. The first report Gilmour submitted, poorly written and so untidy as to be almost illegible, lifted Douglas's eyebrows and raised questions in his mind about the abilities of the new oversman.

James Douglas might have spent most of his adult life in the wilderness, but he knew what to expect from a man with a good Scottish education. Born in British Guiana, the illegitimate son of a Scots plantation manager and a creole woman, Douglas had been sent to school in Scotland when he was seven years old. He wrote a clear hand; he had become fluently bilingual, speaking and writing French with an easy grace; and he struggled to keep himself literate and well-informed, hauling along a library of forty English classics wherever he went and carefully scanning six-month-old newspapers in an attempt to stay abreast of current events. He was appalled by Gilmour's efforts. He wrote a stern letter instructing Gilmour to submit all future reports to George Blenkinsop, the Company officer in charge of Fort Rupert, to "get them copied out fair and put into a neater and compacter form . . . I make these remarks in consequence of the trouble we had in deciphering your last report and I am by no means certain that the copy made for England was exactly correct."

Also irritating to Douglas was the whining tone that Gilmour adopted as he attempted to shift the blame away from his own lack of progress by speaking contemptuously of his predecessor. "His own want of success in finding coal has given no proof that he is more conversant with the subject," Douglas grumbled.

Known to be "rigid and particular in maintaining whatever he considers his right," Gilmour began to have trouble controlling his men. The French brothers wanted to "pick their own work" and when Gilmour insisted that they follow his instructions, they responded by staging a brief strike, "lying idle for a day" before returning to work. Only Robert Dunsmuir continued to "behave well," working steadily and keeping his head down and his mouth shut.

In the spring of 1852 while Gilmour struggled on at Fort Rupert, Douglas decided that the time had come act on Indian reports that there was plenty of black stone to be found at Nanymo Bay on the east coast of the island, about halfway between Fort Rupert and Fort Victoria. Two years earlier, Joseph McKay had been sent to poke around the shores of the bay and had found a coal seam, 37 inches thick. Now, Douglas wanted to examine McKay's discovery for himself. "I rejoice to say that our journey has been productive of very satisfactory results," Douglas reported on his return. The "Douglas seam" would prove to be a huge field—enough coal to keep men working for decades.

On 24 August 1852 Douglas composed official instructions for McKay. "You will proceed with all possible diligence to Wentuhuysen Inlet, commonly known as Nanymo Bay, and formally take possession of the Coal beds lately discovered there for and in behalf of the Hudson's Bay Company."

Soon the Nanaimo seam was producing coal "better than any Scotch coal" and "equal to good English coal," and Douglas decided to abandon the Fort Rupert diggings. He ordered Boyd Gilmour and his party to Nanaimo. "He can be employed there to much more advantage than at Fort Rupert, where he appears to be doing little good," Douglas sighed.

———

Sheltered from wind and wave by Newcastle Island to the north and Protection Island to the east, Nanymo Bay provided one of the best anchorages on the coast. Steep tree-covered hills rose from the water's edge. A stubby finger of land, several hundred yards wide, ran parallel to the coast and was separated from it by a narrow body of water optimistically named Commercial Inlet. On this rocky promontory, where labourers had uncovered the Douglas seam, stood a few rough log cabins.

James Douglas hoped that the seam of coal that bore his name would prove a financial bonanza for the Company. The demand for coal was increasing; there was a ready market for every ton they raised. But before he asked the Company to recruit additional colliers, it was essential to determine the extent of the deposit. Were they dealing with a narrow river of coal or were they standing above a huge field that lay under their feet like a wide, deep, black lake? Joseph McKay, now serving as the officer-in-charge at Nanaimo, had discovered coal outcrops on Newcastle Island. Did the Douglas seam extend under the sea to the island or could it be possible that a second seam of coal existed? To answer those questions, Gilmour was set to work assessing the Newcastle outcrops.

"Mr. Gilmour appears to be undecided in his plans and somewhat at a loss as to where to sink a shaft," Douglas noted. Finally Gilmour selected a site and drove a bore 40 feet into Newcastle Island, stopping when he struck a layer of conglomerate rock. Convinced that no coal would be found below conglomerate and that the coal on the surface must be an isolated pocket, he abandoned Newcastle Island in favour of an outcrop that had been discovered on the banks of the Chase River, a few miles south of Nanaimo.

"The results of Mr. Gilmour's operations on Chase River do not appear to be very satisfactory," Douglas wrote with little surprise four weeks later.

Gilmour tried once again, this time exploring an outcrop that had been found amongst the trees on the landward side of Commercial Inlet. Finally his luck changed; he was sure that he had uncovered "Douglas coal" and even more importantly that he had found a workable quantity in a good location. Only now, after two years of fruitless exploration, could he begin the work of establishing a mine.

James Douglas was not won over by Gilmour's assertion that no coal existed below the layer of conglomerate rock. He decided that one miner should be withdrawn from cutting coal to conduct an experiment. Near Gilmour's workings on Commercial Inlet, a bore would be drilled through the Douglas seam and beyond. Directing the bore was a job that required persistence and careful record-keeping; it went to Robert Dunsmuir.

Dunsmuir, with several Indian assistants, began work on 25 August 1853. At a depth of 11 feet, he encountered an 8-foot-thick bed of Douglas coal, then he hit the underlying layer of conglomerate and forced the bore deeper and deeper.

By 21 December, Dunsmuir's work was done. Eighty-four feet below Douglas coal, through layers of conglomerate, sandstone and shale, he struck a second seam. "This will be a great piece of news for home!" Douglas rejoiced.

—

The agreements signed by Robert Dunsmuir, Boyd Gilmour and Adam and Archibald French were due to expire on 8 August 1854. They could then choose to return to Scotland or they could sign new contracts and remain on Vancouver Island. They knew they were tunnelling into "a magnificent field of coal"; given that they earned a bonus for every ton they raised above the 30 tons a month covered by their contracts, they could look forward to earning upwards of £100 a year. But if money provided an incentive to stay on, their living conditions in Nanaimo did not.

Their cottages, standing on the promontory facing the sea, might have been no worse than those they had lived in at Fort Rupert, but they were certainly no better. The bastion had been finished six months after they arrived, but even so they often felt unprotected. With no palisade to keep them at bay, Indians roamed at will around the settlement. Ordinarily their presence created few problems, for the miners worked with Indian assistants and felt they had little to fear from men they knew. But when Haidas arrived in "fifty of those big canoes" and "sat out in the bay and howled all night," nerves could be forgiven if they frayed.

In addition to their annual salary of £50, the miners were provided with food for themselves and their families—a weekly allotment of flour, salt meat, sugar and tea. Supplementing this were "country provisions"—venison and salmon purchased from the Indians, and vegetables raised in the Company's gardens or on the acre of land that was measured off for each family's own use. And, in addition, a miner could always use part of his wages to buy supplies from the Company store. In theory it was a more than adequate diet, but in practice there were often shortages. When raiding parties were thought to be in the vicinity, local Indians refused to fish. On occasion hunting parties, their canoes heavy with venison, became windbound and reached Nanaimo only after their cargo of deer had become a heap of rotting carcasses. It was difficult for a man who was required to work 310 days a year, eight hours underground or ten hours above, to find the time or the energy to coax a crop from a tree-shaded acre. And the Company store often ran out of tea and sugar and, even worse, tobacco.

By August 1854, when James Douglas arrived at Nanaimo to meet with them, all the colliers had decided to stay—but only if the Company made it worth their while.

"I was prepared to hear many absurd proposals but was certainly not prepared for the extravagant demands they actually made," Douglas wrote. "From the idea that their services were indispensibly necessary, they supposed they might command their own terms."

Douglas was pleased to inform them that the barque *Princess Royal* had already sailed from London carrying twenty-four English miners and their families to Nanaimo. "I positively refused all their demands for an advance or anything beyond their former rate of wages," he reported.

Gilmour was indignant. He would not consider working beyond his contract without a raise in pay. That decision caused Douglas little dismay. Aboard the *Princess Royal* was George Robinson, an experienced English colliery operator whom the Company had hired to manage its Nanaimo coal field. And furthermore, Douglas had come to the conclusion that while Gilmour might be "a good honest man," he was also "indolent and deficient in energy," a man who knew "just enough of Physical Geography to confuse himself and everyone about him."

"He has now made up his mind to leave the country and I have not pressed him to remain in the service," Douglas noted dryly.

By November when the English miners led by George Robinson reached Nanaimo, Adam and Archibald French had decided to return to Scotland with the Gilmours. Of the original party, only the Dunsmuirs chose to stay on.

—

Boyd Gilmour had become convinced that the mine on Commercial Inlet was played out; Robert Dunsmuir was convinced he was wrong. He approached Douglas with a novel proposal. He would reopen the mine Gilmour had "abandoned in despair." He would bear all the expenses, hire his own Indian assistants and then sell to the Company all the coal he raised. He would need an advance to cover his start-up costs, but that advance would soon be repaid once his mine began producing coal.

Douglas had no precedent to guide him. Unable to decide how to handle Dunsmuir's proposal, he was still dithering ten months later, when a strike staged by the English miners helped make up his mind.

On 11 September 1855, grumbling about low wages and poor living conditions and unsettled by rumours of gold strikes in Washington Territory, eight men—one-third of the work force—walked off the job. The following day they deserted, leaving their wives and children at the mercy of the Company's good will and their fellow miners contemplating similar action. A week later, the deserters began to straggle back, and by October most of them were working with a will. But the strike, short-lived though it proved to be, persuaded Douglas that it made little sense to have all his eggs in one contractual basket. If he reached an agreement with an independent collier, then, in the event of a future strike, at least one mine would remain in production.

On 12 October 1855 the officer in charge of Nanaimo made a short but significant entry in the post's journal. "Dunsmuir commenced working on his own account." A month later, Douglas was able to report that Dunsmuir had been successful. The mine that Gilmour thought was played out would soon be producing seven tons of coal a day.

Dunsmuir's proposal had been a sound one. That his mine ultimately failed had nothing to do with any lack of judgement or expertise and everything to do with the enmity of George Robinson. A cantankerous man who made little attempt to control his explosive temper, Robinson suffered from a disposition further soured by tragedy. On 3 January 1856 his wife died of childbirth fever. A few weeks later, her grave was opened to receive the body of her infant son. Robinson sent to England for a tombstone and while he waited for it to arrive, he fought his grief by shortening his fuse, on one occasion smashing a hammer into the head of a man who swore at him after Robinson accused him of malingering.

Charged with the overall management of the coal field and with authority over the contract-miners, Robinson had no direct control over Dunsmuir. Plagued by a recalcitrant work force, he was often forced to report that Dunsmuir's was the only mine that continued to operate during labour disputes. Adding to Robinson's irritation was the fact that Dunsmuir's coal was in demand. After receiving reports that his coal was mixed with shale, Dunsmuir had taken pains to improve his screening process, and soon ships' captains were arriving at Nanaimo with specific requests for Dunsmuir coal.

Robinson's resentment of Dunsmuir was displayed in various ways. He informed the Company that it was paying too much for Dunsmuir's coal, and Douglas followed his advice, insisting on a rate of only nine shillings and sixpence a ton, three shillings less than he had originally promised. On another occasion, Robinson loaded Dunsmuir's coal aboard a ship during Dunsmuir's absence. Robinson had deliberately gone behind his back so that he could underestimate the tonnage, Dunsmuir charged.

James Douglas found himself serving as referee, trying to soothe the temper of both combatants. He consoled Robinson. "His rudeness to you admits of no excuse, as whatever may have been the extent of his real or fancied wrongs, they give him no right to be insolent in his language to you," he wrote. But he admitted that, while he felt bound to defend Robinson's position, he was worried about losing the services of "so useful a man" as Dunsmuir.

It irked Robinson to know that Dunsmuir's mine operated at an advantage over the shafts under his control. Because the slope, or tunnel, into Dunsmuir's mine rose at a slight incline, burrowing upwards into the hill, water that collected in the mine flowed freely out of the entrance. The shaft of the mine Robinson controlled angled down, and an expensively operated steam engine was required to pump the water out.

When Robinson decided to open a shaft adjacent to his own, Dunsmuir was aghast. He had discovered that the seam he was working dipped away. Enough accessible coal remained to keep his mine going for another four or five years. After that, a new shaft would have to be dug to intercept the Douglas seam at a different angle. Now that Robinson was opening a competing slope, both mines would be worked out within two or three years.

Dunsmuir had no choice but to continue working his mine until he was satisfied he had removed all the accessible coal. Two years later the Company reluctantly concluded, "There is no doubt that it was a great error to open the slope, Dunsmuir being capable of working the whole. Mr. Robinson was too intelligent to have made such a blunder and is supposed to have been activated by enmity to Dunsmuir, who suffered severely in consequence."

Vindication came too late, but Dunsmuir had learned a valuable lesson. He would never again invest his own money in any mining operation over which he did not have total control.

Two

No one who knew Robert Dunsmuir during those early Nanaimo years could have predicted that he would become a millionaire. Nor did the coal town seem a likely spawning ground of great wealth. By 1857 Nanaimo boasted 132 inhabitants—58 men, 20 women and 54 children. Thirty whitewashed cabins were ranged under the bastion and along Commercial Inlet. There were no roads or streets; only narrow footpaths criss-crossed the town, zigzagging around stumps as they ran between the cottages, and from the cottages to the store and the mines.

Alfred Benson, the Hudson's Bay Company doctor, had become so impatient with bumping into stumps as he picked his way about the townsite after sunset that he had taken to spending his off hours hacking away at one of the worst offenders in an attempt to straighten the pathway near his house. But he had given it up as a bad job, philosophically concluding that he could see his way in the daylight, and it would be "easier work" to carry a lantern after dark.

Benson was Dunsmuir's nearest neighbour and became one of his closest friends. Cheerfully untidy, he made his way about town with the first button on his coat poking through the second buttonhole and with one pant leg outside, the other inside, his boots. As the Company doctor in a Company town, Benson was responsible for the health of everyone in Nanaimo, and what an oddly assorted lot his patients were. There were sober hardworking miners—men like John Bevilockway and Richard Turner. Bevilockway and his wife had arrived aboard the *Princess Royal* and soon became known as a most industrious couple quite renowned for their frugality and prudence. Richard Turner was a typical Staffordshire miner, "hard as a nail," a good worker who would "never lose half a day if he could help it." Not all the miners were quite so stable. In September 1855 when some of them had gone on strike and decamped from the island, John Meakin had been tempted to join them but was dissuaded by his wife. The day his fellows deserted, Meakin drank himself to the point of insensibility and was reeling about his cabin, waving his gun at his wife and threatening to kill her, when he was overpowered and sent to the bastion to calm down and sober up.

But generally, the English miners were models of propriety compared to the free spirits who made up the Company's labouring class. These men were true transients, who were prepared to move wherever the Company sent them, and who now did odd jobs around the mine. They were men like George Honham, "a bibulous, boisterous customer"; Joseph Cluett, "a rollicking, noisy being"; Big Tomo, a huge Iroquois who had lost a finger, bitten off during a fight; Lazaar Oreasta and Leon Lebine who had squared the logs with which Nanaimo was built; and Jim Kimo, a Kanaka who had been recruited at the Company establishment in the Hawaiian Islands and who served as the town's watchman, blasting everyone awake at midnight by firing off a gun and calling out "All's well."

Seasoning this mixture of Scots, Englishmen, French Canadians, Iroquois and Kanakas were the officers of the Royal Navy who wandered the town in search of conviviality while their ships were taking on coal.

There was nothing, except for his independent status, to set Robert Dunsmuir apart from his fellow residents of Nanaimo. As collier John Meakin put it, "He was just as well off as any of the miners; no better and no worse." He was building a house on the hillside above his mine, but it was little grander than the Company cottages. And Joan Dunsmuir would continue to pad barefoot around the new house, with her boots carefully deposited at the doorstep to keep her floors free of Nanaimo mud and with a growing brood of children to occupy her time. By 1857, she had five children—ten-year-old Elizabeth and her eight-year-old sister Agnes, both born in Scotland; James, born at Fort Vancouver in Oregon Territory and now six years old; a second son, Alexander, born during the family's first summer in Nanaimo; and Marion, born earlier that year and for the time being the baby of the family.

More than a decade would pass before the Dunsmuirs took the first step on the ladder that would allow them to climb to a unique position of power and prominence, and for most of those years it seemed as though circumstances and the colonial administration were conspiring to deprive them of even a modest level of success.

—

The HBC's lease, which included the rights to all the coal found on Vancouver Island, expired in 1859. The Company was then obliged to purchase the 6,193 acres that made up its Nanaimo claim. With title to the land secure, the Company decided to sell its holdings. Knowing it would be next to impossible to find a buyer for an operation that could boast of only two all-but-played-out mines, the HBC decided to open a new pit which would angle into the Douglas seam where it dipped away from the level worked by Dunsmuir and Robinson. The Douglas pit, as the new mine was called, was opened in 1860, and the Company, in a sudden burst of corporate enlightenment, offered the position of mine superintendent to Robert Dunsmuir, the one man who knew the Douglas seam like the back of his hand.

With the Douglas pit operational, the Nanaimo mines attracted the interest of the London-based investors of the Vancouver Coal Mining and Land Company. In September 1862 the mines, the wharves, the Company store and all its overpriced stock, the townsite of Nanaimo with its hundred houses and shacks, and the 6,193 acres that made up the Company's coal claim were conveyed to the Vancouver Company for $200,000.

After 1859, when the lease giving the HBC control of Vancouver Island expired, it became possible for any firm to acquire prospecting rights to land outside the Company's claim. But while it might have been possible, it was not easy. The land office was in chaos. In 1849, when the Company had assumed responsibility for managing the Colony of Vancouver Island, land sales had been simple affairs. But then in 1858 gold had been discovered on the Fraser River, and Fort Victoria had become the stopping-off place for thousands of Californians who flooded through the colony on their way to the mainland goldfields. The land office was besieged as speculators snapped up the town lots that had been laid out around the fort. With property changing hands three, four and five times within a few months, the land office became a hopeless muddle. Then in 1859, title to Vancouver Island and responsibility for managing the land office reverted to the crown. Two years of legal wrangling ensued, and when the island was finally reconveyed in 1861, no one was quite sure just who owned what.

With the attention of the colonial government riveted on gold, little thought was given to formulating a rational policy regarding coal. Not that the governor and his advisors were not eager to see coal mines developed, rather that they seemed obsessed with the notion that coal lands would fall into the hands of speculators. To avoid that unhappy outcome, they decided to grant mineral rights only to *bona fide* applicants. However, the criteria developed for assessing those applicants gave every indication of having been formulated by men who knew little about coal mining and nothing about raising private capital.

Dr. Alfred Benson had discovered an outcrop of coal near the Chase River, south of Nanaimo. In September 1863 he applied to lease 3,000 acres and was informed that a lease would be granted only *after* he had formed a company. And as to the terms of that lease, the government was maddeningly vague, blandly assuring Benson that it would be granted "upon such terms as shall permit the favourable development of the mine." Benson was ready to throw up his hands, despairing of raising private capital on so imprecise a promise. But then a man with more money than sense hove obligingly into view.

Lieut.-Comdr. the Honourable Horace Douglas Lascelles was twenty-eight years old. The seventh son of the Earl of Harewood, he had left his family's vast Yorkshire estate to join the navy. By 1863 he was commanding the *Forward*, a gunboat stationed at Esquimalt, the navy's newly established base three miles west of Victoria. A somewhat eccentric young man who kept a tame silver fox and a golden pheasant in his Esquimalt cottage, Lascelles was just what Dr. Benson might have ordered. He was rich; he was a sporting gentleman; and he was quite addicted to strong drink. One autumn evening, the air of Benson's cabin thick with tobacco smoke and redolent with the fumes of HBC rum, Benson told Lascelles about the coal find and invited him to become a partner.

With Lascelles providing most of the start-up capital and the name of the enterprise, the Harewood Coal Company was formed. After "mature consideration" the partners decided to acquire the land by outright purchase, and in December, Benson applied for 9,000 acres of land, south and west of the Vancouver Company's claim. Lascelles paid the going rate of a dollar an acre, but even so, the Harewood Company was given the mineral rights for only eighteen months. If after that time the government was not satisfied with the steps taken to develop the field, the rights to the coal under the Harewood Company's land could be claimed by others. With a deadline facing them, Lascelles and Benson began to beat the bushes for additional investors.

Viscount Milton looked like a promising prospect. Twenty-three years old and a friend of Lascelles, Milton arrived in Victoria in December 1863. A sickly young man given to periodic fits and seizures, he was accompanied by Dr. Cheadle who acted as his companion and his keeper. After several rum-soaked nights in Victoria, Lascelles took them to Nanaimo aboard the *Forward* for a tour of his property.

"Went off with Dr. Benson on an expedition thro' the woods to see an outcropping of coal, the field of which he and Lascelles had engaged from Government under the hope of forming a Company to work," Cheadle recorded in his journal. They wandered through thick bush for an hour, with Dr. Benson bringing up the rear. "Dr. Benson, who had lagged all the time, and kept up a continual halloaing to know where we were, arrived very red in the face and assured us we were going wrong."

That neither of the partners was able to find the outcrop was not a state of affairs calculated to inspire investor confidence. What the Harewood Company needed was a mining expert, and who better fitted that description than Benson's old friend, Robert Dunsmuir. In return for a share of the company's profits, Dunsmuir was persuaded to resign his position as superintendent of the Vancouver Company's Douglas pit. He joined the Harewood Company in April 1864 and within weeks proved his worth by tracing the outcrop to a workable seam of coal.

But now Benson and Lascelles were faced with a new problem. Their acres were landlocked, blocked off from the sea by the Vancouver Coal Company's land. And even if the colonial government could be prevailed upon to force the Vancouver Company to allow an easement through its land, an expensive railway 5 miles long would be required to get the coal to the water's edge. Lascelles had already invested $30,000 to purchase the land, to survey the route of the railway and to construct buildings, bridges and roads, when in the summer of 1865 he travelled to England in an attempt to raise the additional $70,000 he estimated would be required. He was absent for almost a year; he returned discouraged and empty handed.

While Lascelles was away, Benson and Dunsmuir tried to find other investors. In August 1865 Her Majesty's Ship *Clio* arrived on the Esquimalt Station. Aboard was Charlie Beresford, a nineteen-year-old midshipman and the son of the Marquis of Waterford. Charlie took to visiting Dr. Benson when the *Clio* was coaling at Nanaimo and during the course of one happy evening was invited to become a partner.

"I wrote at the time to my father, asking him to let me have a thousand pounds to invest in the coal business," Beresford recalled. "But he replied firmly that, until I ceased to exceed my allowance, he did not think it right that I should embark on a gambling project."

The marquis was quite right; the Harewood mine was a gamble. By 1869, underfinanced and handicapped by the snail's pace the government took in granting access to the sea, the Harewood Company was submerged by debt.

Recognizing the list of a sinking ship, Dunsmuir had returned to the Vancouver Company before Benson and Lascelles were forced to abandon their mine. Unlike the other partners, he could regard the mine's failure with the equanimity of a man whose purse had not been lightened. If anything, he had profited from the experience. Carefully noting the problems encountered by the Harewood mine, he was armed with valuable insights for when his own time came. And that time was fast approaching. Robert Dunsmuir was forty-four years old and he had been on Vancouver Island for eighteen years when he made the discovery that changed his life.

—

One Sunday afternoon in October 1869 Robert Dunsmuir went fishing. At least that is what he said he was doing when he headed off in the direction of Diver Lake, a trout-rich pond in the Wellington District a few miles north and west of Nanaimo. "I was in the bush about three miles from the sea ... not exactly for the purpose of prospecting for coal," he remembered two years later. "I came across a ridge of rock which I knew to be the strata overlying the lowest seam that had as yet been discovered."

"I've found coal!" he told Joan that evening. He had found coal before—but this outcrop was on the ridge of rock that overlaid the Newcastle seam. Either Newcastle coal extended farther than anyone had imagined or he had come across a third, untapped coalfield.

He hired two men and, following his instructions, they soon discovered a seam of coal 3 feet thick and 30 feet below the top of the ridge. That was enough to propel Dunsmuir to Victoria to register a claim, carrying with him a sketch map that outlined a 1,600-acre tract running in a band 1,000 yards wide and 4 miles long, including within its boundaries the northern half of Diver Lake and ending at the water's edge at Departure Bay.

On 8 December 1869 Joseph Trutch, the colony's chief commissioner of lands and works, informed him that he would be given mining rights to the area for two years; he would then have the option of purchasing the land at a dollar an acre. But there were conditions. He must guarantee that during the two-year term of his licence he would keep a minimum of four men employed. In addition, he must arrange to have the land surveyed, and if any land within the claim had been pre-empted, then that land would be excluded from his licence.

Those conditions were at least more definite than those under which the Harewood Company had operated, and on 21 January 1870 Dunsmuir wrote to Trutch to tell him that the arrangement was "perfectly satisfactory." But could he, Dunsmuir asked, delay the survey for a few weeks, until the weather improved.

Short of funds, he was reluctant to invest in an expensive survey. He had already spent almost $400 and he had to husband his resources carefully. Investment capital was hard to come by and, in any case, he was hoping to avoid taking on partners. "That I don't want to do," Dunsmuir said. "I know that I can bring the undertaking out more successfully by not having too many voices in the matter."

In January 1870 he was forced to suspend mining operations while he spent $100 to build cabins—on land for which he did not yet hold a lease—to accommodate a workforce that he would have to pay out of his own pocket. It was risky, but as Dunsmuir put it, he was "not afraid of future success."

The chief commissioner soon became impatient. "The survey is necessary for your own protection as well as for our convenience," he informed Dunsmuir in May. But by then, Dunsmuir had once again suspended mining operations. He had paid a contractor $2,000 to dig into the hillside and open a slope, or roadway, into the seam. He was now ready to mine, but first he had to divert funds to build a wagon road from the mine site to the sea.

Later, it would seem incredible that Dunsmuir had ever been forced to count pennies, but that was the position in which he found himself during the summer of 1870. He knew he was sitting on top of a rich coal seam, but he could develop it only slowly, one step at a time, and the land still had not been surveyed and his mining licence still not officially registered.

—

More than the expense encouraged Dunsmuir to delay the survey. He was buying time to do further prospecting. When he did get around to having the land surveyed, he wanted to be sure that the boundaries drawn around his claim encircled the best possible mining sites. In July 1870, almost a year after his original discovery, he found another outcrop half a mile closer the sea. Tilly Smallbones, who lived with her parents on their 100-acre holding on the shore of Diver Lake, thought she knew just how he had come across that second outcrop.

"Dunsmuir was an awful drinker," Tilly recalled. "There was a saloon not far away in a little town. Dunsmuir used to go down there every night and drink. He had to follow a trail past our house and through our land. He would come back late and always drunk. We often watched him passing. One night he was so drunk he fell down and went to sleep. During the night he got kicking around and in the morning when he woke up sober found he'd kicked all the moss away and there was a coal mine right on our land."

According to Tilly, he had then rearranged the moss to hide the coal and kept quiet about his discovery. "My father was getting discouraged. He wasn't doing very well and thought he would go back to Oregon. He talked to Dunsmuir about it. Dunsmuir said that he was going to stay, but if he wanted to pull out, he would give him seventy-five dollars and take the land. Father signed all the papers and we went back to Oregon. Father found out later that Dunsmuir had opened a mine on our property and made a fortune. Too bad, wasn't it?"

Encouraged by the coal he had found on the Smallbones' land, Dunsmuir drilled another bore even closer to the sea, almost two and a half miles from the original mine site. At 132 feet, he struck an 8-foot-thick seam. Dunsmuir could hardly contain his excitement. Below his feet was a coal deposit that seemed to extend over 1,200 acres. He reckoned that each acre would yield 7,000 tons. He was tottering on the brink of a coal deposit of almost eight-and-a-half million tons; at $6.50 a ton, the amount charged by the Vancouver Company, the value of that coal was almost $55 million. Fifty-five million dollars! And he did not have the money to develop it. Even worse, he had discovered that he did not have legal access to the sea.

He solved his financial embarrassment by going cap in hand to San Francisco moneylenders who, at "an exorbitant rate of interest," provided the loan that enabled him to complete the wagon road and to build a wharf and storage sheds at Departure Bay.

In September 1870 he made his first sale when the Royal Navy ship *Boxer* took on 65 tons. The *Boxer* had agreed to conduct a test of the coal from three Nanaimo area mines—two operated by the

Vancouver Company and Dunsmuir's new mine at Wellington. The chief engineer's report was unequivocal—Wellington coal was superior. By the end of November, Dunsmuir had sold a total of 180 tons for which he had received almost $1,200. It had cost him $5,821 to get it out of the ground, but he was finally on his way. The only problem now facing him was acquiring assured access to the sea.

William Hughes, who lived on his small holding at the northern end of Departure Bay, had watched with some consternation as a road was pushed through his land and a wharf appeared on his waterfront. But he had known Dunsmuir for a long time and presumed that he and his friend would be able to work out some kind of lease arrangement. In the meantime, he was happy to do what he could to see him get established. What he did not know was that Dunsmuir was not interested in leasing his land. He wanted to buy, and he was prepared to do whatever was necessary to force Hughes to sell.

—

Not long after Dunsmuir first applied for a mining licence, a new mineral act had come into effect on Vancouver Island. Dunsmuir had a choice; he could continue to work under the old system or he could reapply and come under the provisions of the new. What Dunsmuir wanted was the best of both worlds. A clause in the new act assured mine operators a path to the sea; no prior claim would be allowed to impede their access. But another clause limited the amount of land the government was prepared to grant to prospectors. A company of ten could apply for as many as 2,500 acres, but an individual applicant would receive no more than 500. Dunsmuir decided to petition the government.

Could he be allowed to come under the new act but still retain the 1,600 acres for which he had applied? No, he could not, the government responded. To receive the benefits of the new act, he would have to relinquish his former claim and then reapply. And, like everyone else, he would be limited to 500 acres. Why, the chief commissioner wondered, didn't he simply form a company?

Dunsmuir was furious. He had already been forced to take on one partner. Wadham Diggle was a young naval lieutenant. As the commander of the *Boxer*, he had been the first to recognize the quality of Wellington coal. When Dunsmuir had been strapped for capital, Diggle had written to his clergyman father and received $8,000 to invest. The lieutenant was malleable enough, accepting without argument the senior partner's decisions, but Dunsmuir continued to resist the idea of working with the nine partners the government required.

In April 1871 Dunsmuir received word that the government remained adamant; no concessions would be made. By then almost $12,000 had been invested in the Wellington mine. Dunsmuir was beside himself. What more proof did the government need to show that he was serious about mining? "I was not thoroughly aware how matters stood . . . or operations would have been stopped before now," he steamed.

He now had two choices. He could continue under the terms of the old system and negotiate with Hughes for his land, or he could form a company, obtain a crown grant and request that the government expropriate a corridor through Hughes's property.

"I have tried to come to arrangements with Hughes in every shape I could possibly put it," Dunsmuir grumbled. "He asks $300 per annum which is out of all question . . . I really don't know what Hughes is up to."

But Hughes thought his old friend knew very well. "I will not sell it as I made this land over to my children," he explained. And Dunsmuir knew all about that; he had witnessed his will. "My occupation of catching fish to make oil is injured by the erection of their wharf. I cannot set no nets by reason of vessels coming for coal would destroy them on me," Hughes said. And Dunsmuir's road separated his house from the bulk of his land. He thought the terms he was suggesting were reasonable.

To Dunsmuir, Hughes was simply being stubborn and opportunistic. If the government insisted that he form a company to get his own way, well, all right then, he would give them a company. He had come to realize that he needed more capital than Diggle could provide. Rear Adm. Arthur Farquhar, Commander in Chief of the Pacific Fleet, had expressed an interest. On 24 November 1871 Farquhar climbed aboard, bringing with him a personal investment of $12,000 and four officers of his flagship, HMS *Zealous*, who agreed to lend their names to the company until the government was satisfied that its requirements had been met.

With its directorship raised to the necessary number by the addition of Dunsmuir's sons, twenty-year-old James and eighteen-year-old Alexander, and James Harvey, who had recently married his daughter Agnes, the enterprise, christened Dunsmuir, Diggle & Company, received the government's blessing. Thirteen days after registering the crown grant that would allow the company to flex its muscle to force a sale on William Hughes, the paper partners, James and Alexander Dunsmuir, James Harvey and the officers of the *Zealous,* obediently relinquished their interest in Dunsmuir, Diggle.

27

After two years of anxious negotiations, Dunsmuir could finally begin to devote all his energies to the Wellington mine. He had the title to the land and its coal; he had working capital, and while he had been forced to take on two partners, both Diggle and Farquhar were prepared to leave all the decisions to him; he was the most experienced mine manager on the island; he had spent years observing the operations of other coal companies, and he had learned from their mistakes.

He saw two principal markets for Vancouver Island coal—the Royal Navy and the booming town of San Francisco. Of the two, the San Francisco market was the more important, but the Vancouver Company had continued to rely on "chance craft" to ship the coal down the coast. Like his grandfather, Robert Dunsmuir recognized that getting his coal to market was the key to success. What was needed was a fleet of coal carriers, owned or chartered by the colliery, to sail between the city and the mine on a regular schedule. A guaranteed supply would lead to growing demand, and the San Francisco market would become increasingly dependent on Nanaimo coal. And a smart mine owner would establish a sales office in the California city.

After serving an apprenticeship of more than twenty years, Dunsmuir now had the opportunity to put his theories into practice. By 1873 the Wellington colliery was producing 16,000 of the 40,000 tons raised from island mines. The following year he secured a stable access to the California market by forming a partnership with Henry Berryman, who agreed to handle the distribution of Wellington coal from his San Francisco sales office and to charter ships for the run from the Golden Gate to Departure Bay.

His partnership with Berryman soon produced spectacular results. In August 1875 Berryman informed Dunsmuir that he had pulled off a sales coup of monumental proportions. The San Francisco agent for the Pacific Mail Steamship Company had signed a contract, binding for five years, in which he had guaranteed to buy 4,000 tons of Wellington coal each month. What was more, he had agreed to a purchase price of $12 a ton, a dollar more than the best quality coal was currently fetching on the California market.

As mine manager, Dunsmuir had to walk a fine line, carefully adjusting supply to match demand. If he had no coal on hand when a customer came calling, his colliery would soon earn a reputation as an unreliable supplier. But if he hired more men and maximized the output of his mine, he might be faced with the expense of "binning" thousands of tons of unsold coal. So finely had he balanced the scales of supply and demand that at the end of 1874, a year during which the output of his mine had risen to almost 30,000 tons, he had been left with as few as 2,400 tons unsold, only 45 more than he had had on hand at the beginning of the year.

With the Pacific Mail line agreeing to an annual purchase of 48,000 tons, he could feel easy about increasing production; in fact, he would be forced into a period of rapid expansion to keep his side of the bargain. He increased his workforce from 145 to 242, and to lure men away from the Vancouver Company, he offered to pay miners $1.20 for every ton of coal they raised—a particularly good wage since Wellington coal was relatively heavy, a cubic yard weighing "considerably more" than a ton. At Departure Bay he built a new wharf, 350 feet long and providing a depth at low tide of 25 feet, enough to accommodate the largest of the Pacific Mail Company's steamers. Overlooking the wharves, he built a new company office, "a neat and tasty building" with dark walnut fittings "in excellent taste." He had relied on a horse railway to carry the coal from the mine to Departure Bay. Now he laid new track and ordered the latest thing in steam locomotives, a 16-ton model that had been exhibited at the Philadelphia Exhibition, to speed the coal on its way.

By the end of 1875 Dunsmuir was able to report that he had increased production to 50,000 tons. The value of his plant and rolling stock had reached $110,000, and his miners were earning as much as $5 a day.

—

Once his mine became fully operational, Dunsmuir's rise was meteoric. By the time he entered his fifties, he was one of Nanaimo's wealthiest and most highly regarded citizens.

As his fortune expanded, his family had continued to grow. One baby, a little boy, had lived for only a few hours, but from 1857 to 1875 Joan had successfully delivered five other children and provided Jim and Alex with more sisters than any boys could possibly need. In addition to Elizabeth and Agnes and Marion, there was now Mary, born in 1862; Emily Ellen born two years later; Jessie Sophia born in 1866; Annie Euphemia born two years after Jessie; and Henrietta Maude, Joan's last child, born in 1872 when her mother was forty-five.

By 1876 only two of the girls, Elizabeth and Agnes, had found husbands, and when Robert Dunsmuir decided to loosen his purse strings to build a new house, he was guided by the practical necessity of providing his family with elbow room as much as by the desire to demonstrate his growing bank account. Still, "Ardoon" was a handsome house, one of the finest in Nanaimo, two storeys tall with a deep verandah and with delicate gingerbread clinging to its steeply pitched eaves. And Joan became quite the *grand dame* with a Swedish gardener to tend her roses, a Chinese cook in charge of her kitchen and an English parlourmaid to keep Ardoon free of Nanaimo's gritty black dust.

Nanaimoites took pride in Robert Dunsmuir as a home-grown success, his achievements all the more praiseworthy because they were the result of "pluck and plod." A correspondent to the *Nanaimo Free Press* feared no contradiction in writing, "When you see a spirited man have the grit to go into an enterprise, run chances and when he succeeds that man deserves credit. The people of Nanaimo can look Mr. Dunsmuir in the face and say they feel proud of him. He started on a small capital and through his industry and sagacity, he is today a credit to himself and an honour to Nanaimo."

Dunsmuir's rising status led to a wide variety of civic appointments. He served as a member of the school board; he agreed to put in time as a member of the court of revisions; and he accepted appointment as a justice of the peace. His was one of the first names suggested when a chairman was required for public meetings, whether those meetings were held to honour a visiting dignitary or to celebrate the anniversary of Robbie Burns's birth.

But if Dunsmuir was becoming a power to be reckoned with in Nanaimo, he ruled as the veritable laird of Wellington. By 1876 Wellington had begun to take on the appearance of a proper town— the most prosperous in the province, some people said.

"Six years ago it was a wilderness and is now a flourishing village with a church, school and considerable population, all thriving, busy and contented," one happy resident proclaimed.

On the ridge above the mine, on Jingle Pot road, the rough track that led through the bush to Nanaimo, stood the mine manager's house, a bulky, no-nonsense two-storey frame building designed to double as a home and office. Dunsmuir, Diggle & Co. had offered five hundred "town lots" for sale at $5 and $10 each, but most married miners preferred the company-owned houses, the little two-roomed cottages that clustered around the pit head and rented for $6 a month. Single men could find a home away from home at the company's boarding house, run by Walter Akenhead, a Nanaimo saloon-keeper, or they could take a room at Chantrell's Wellington Hotel on the shore of Diver Lake which lured residents by providing the best of everything, including meals at all hours, "the usual brands of wines, liquors and cigars" and a first-class billiard table. Wellington boasted a brass band, a library and a lake so filled with trout that they could be "caught by the bucket either from boat or shore."

Some described the town as "a Little Arcadia," but Wellington was hardly that. Rather than being an ideal rustic paradise, it was dusty, dirty and isolated. There were four dogs to every man, some people said, and there was no doctor—the nearest one was in Nanaimo, 6 miles away. And more than anything else, it was a company town. In one way or another, the company controlled every aspect of life in Wellington and, as everyone knew, the company was Robert Dunsmuir.

Coal miners were not renowned for their contentment. That Dunsmuir was not regarded as an oppressor, resented because of his power and his profits, was due to a personal management style that could not help but find favour with his men. He had spent most of his life working for other men and felt an empathy with the men who raised his coal. He treated them fairly and took a benevolent interest in their welfare, whether that benevolence was demonstrated by making sure that the boarding house had a licence to dispense liquor or by small acts of impulsive charity, which moved one man to remark, "Much credit is due to this gentleman for the generous manner in which he has treated his workmen."

George Vipond could personally testify to his employer's generosity. In 1874, a few weeks after signing on at the Wellington Colliery, he asked for a loan so that he could send for his family in the United States. And Dunsmuir had handed him the money and had been content to have it trickle back in small payments stretching over two years.

A year later, Vipond was working underground when a section of the roof gave way, breaking his leg above the knee. Although Dunsmuir felt the accident had been due to Vipond's own carelessness and laziness, he agreed to help him, allowing him to work as a subcontractor, hiring a team of men to run the coal out of the mine. "Before the end of the first month, he came to me and said that he was unable to pay his men," Dunsmuir remembered. "I threw the contract aside, and not only made up the deficiency to his men, but paid him wages for every day he worked."

The miners referred to Dunsmuir as "the old man" and regarded him with a mixture of familiarity and respect. Hard-working and plain-talking, the old man was everywhere. No facet of the operation escaped his attention; every decision was his alone to make; he was on hand to deal directly with any complaints; and, as the men agreed amongst themselves, there was no one who could say that the old man was not fair. But then in 1876, when he was fifty-one, he tinkered with the formula that had kept the men at work and his mine producing an ever-increasing supply of coal. He decided to pass the responsibility for the day-to-day operation of the mine to his son Jim, and within six months, Wellington was shut down by the longest and most serious strike any of the Vancouver Island mines had yet experienced.

Three

—

From the moment of his birth, the course of James Dunsmuir's life had been set. He would follow his father, grandfather and great-grandfather into the mines. An unimaginative young man, he seems to have regarded his father's expectations as immutable plans. By the time he was sixteen, he was working underground, chipping away at the pit face of one of the Vancouver Company's mines. And there he might have remained, obediently preparing for the career his father had planned and with little ambition to aim higher, if Robert had not discovered the Wellington seam.

To a man as reluctant to share decision-making as Robert Dunsmuir, a son, especially a stolidly obedient son, made an ideal lieutenant, and he saw to it that James was carefully trained to assume that role. After serving his underground apprenticeship, he was dispatched to the Willamette Ironworks in Portland, Oregon, and in 1874, after leaving the ironworks as a trained machinist, he was sent to the Virginia Agricultural and Mechanical College in Blacksburg, Virginia, to study mining engineering. In August 1876 his father appointed him superintendent of the Wellington mine. James had no management experience and was assuming his new responsibilities at a most inopportune time.

—

The trouble had begun in July 1876, a month before James arrived home, when the Pacific Mail Steamship Company decided to renege on its contract. Freighters outbound from England to load grain in San Francisco had taken to carrying coal as ballast. They could easily afford to sell the ballast, which might otherwise have been tipped into San Francisco Bay, at less than market value. Coal from Vancouver Island, which had been bringing from $10 to $11 the previous year, plummeted to $8.75 a ton and threatened to go even lower. Eager to wiggle out of a contract that bound them to $12 a ton, the directors of the Pacific Mail line argued that the agreement of 1875 had not been ratified by their New York office; no legal obligation bound them to Dunsmuir, Diggle & Company.

For Dunsmuir, their decision was a severe blow. The Pacific Mail line had accounted for almost all of his offshore sales. In San Francisco, Henry Berryman launched a legal action against the steamship company, claiming that the colliery was owed $109,000 for breach of contract. Meanwhile, Robert was faced with the problem of overproduction.

He called the men together and explained the situation. Coal prices had fallen; he had lost the mail line contract; he would be forced to "bin" thousands of tons of unsold coal. He could no longer afford to pay them $1.20 a ton. However, he was prepared to keep them all at work if they agreed to reduce their rate by twenty cents to a dollar a ton.

"God knows, $1.20 is little enough to dig that coal," he exclaimed, and he promised to return them to the old rate as soon as the market improved. "I will pay you that sum when you are least aware of it," he vowed. "By heavens, I'll take you by surprise!"

Faced with a similar marketing crisis, a more cautious man might have shut down most of the mine, increasing production slowly as he found new markets and negotiated new contracts. But Dunsmuir chose the more audacious course, keeping the mine in full production and stockpiling coal against future sales. The wage reduction he was suggesting would help to cover the cost of "binning" and would at least begin to make up for the decreased profits he expected to experience in the dull San Francisco market.

He thought he was being exceptionally fair. He felt that his men had been well paid—so well paid that he had insisted that he would welcome the formation of a miners' union, for then his rates would be driven down to come into line with those paid by other collieries.

When the men rejected his offer, he was indignant. All right, he said, he would close down part of the mine. Seventy miners would be thrown out of work; the remaining thirty-six would be paid at the old rate. "I told them they would give me as much coal as I wanted," Dunsmuir said. "They could go to work at $1.20 and the rest could play."

While the fortunate few returned to work, Dunsmuir settled himself comfortably in the mine manager's house, where he waited for the delegations that he knew would soon begin to call. Over the next week, he met with small groups of men at all hours of the day and evening and into the night. His response was always the same. He would reopen the mine only if they accepted his terms.

By the beginning of August, the men had given in. With no union to insist on solidarity, their efforts had been badly fragmented. They had no choice but to accept Dunsmuir's terms, but they returned to work determined to protect their rights.

—

When James Dunsmuir took over the management of the mine shortly after the strike ended, he was faced with men who were grumbling about their pay cut and determined to get every penny they felt they had earned. He did not handle the situation well. Just past his twenty-fifth birthday, he was younger than most of the men in his employ. He lacked his father's easy confidence and he commanded none of the respect his father accepted as his due. And he knew that his father was hovering in the background, ready to question every decision and quite prepared to push him aside and assume control if he faltered. Young, inexperienced and unsure of himself, he became stiff and suspicious, interpreting any complaint as a personal affront and a challenge to the company's reputation for honesty.

During November and December, the men began to suspect that the scales were giving incorrect weights. A collier's pay depended on the amount of coal he raised. When he went to work in a Dunsmuir colliery, he was assigned a specific area of the mine as his own. He paid for the powder that he used to blast large hunks of coal from the face, and he paid the men who worked as his assistants, the haulers and draggers who moved his coal from the face to the mine entrance. As the coal he had hewed was removed from the mine, it was weighed on a massive scale, and he was then paid based on the precise amount of coal he had raised. The accuracy of those scales now became a matter of great importance.

From experience, colliers knew that a fully loaded coal cart should weigh 1,100 pounds. Now, no matter how high they piled the coal, the scales would register no higher than 900 pounds. The first to take his concerns to James was a miner named Haggerty. He suggested that they check the scales' accuracy by weighing three or four coal carts at the mine, and then haul them down to Departure Bay to compare the first results with those produced by the scales on the wharf.

"No, that's too much trouble," Jim said.

The men would take them down themselves, Haggerty argued. The company would be put to no expense.

"No!" Jim said with finality. And when Haggerty persisted, he wheeled on him. "Do you think the company is cheating you?" he demanded.

"Yes, I do," Haggerty said. "All the men in the mine think so too."

"Then pick up your tools and get off the property," James stormed, and Haggerty was out of a job.

By the beginning of January, the scales were still not right. "The coal is getting lighter every day," John Bolton complained.

"You're always grumbling about weights and scales," Jim growled. But after the weighman suggested that something did indeed seem to be wrong, he finally agreed to conduct a test. He placed two 28-pound weights on the scales, and the result was a precise 56 pounds. Then he weighed himself and declared that the scales showed exactly what he had weighed in town the day before.

But the complaints continued. By the middle of January, Jim decided that perhaps he had better take the problem seriously. He called George Vipond and several other men together. After they weighed all manner of objects, including each other, it became clear that the scales made no sense at all on amounts over 400 pounds. Vipond discovered that the upper and lower plates were almost touching. When amounts in excess of 400 pounds were placed on the upper plate, it began to rest on the lower, dispersing the weight. "James, this is where the trouble is," he exclaimed.

"It was hard to make James Dunsmuir believe it," Vipond recalled.

"The more coal the less pay, you bet!" Bolton exclaimed. "On January 30, I lost about 600 pounds of coal, but I knew that it was no good to complain to Dunsmuir." But it might do some good to talk to his father.

On 1 February, Robert Dunsmuir arrived at Wellington to find a group of about sixty men gathered around the scales. Told that they were showing incorrect weights, Robert promptly swung himself into an empty cart, and as scales hovered at 150 pounds, he declared them to be accurate. But, he said, if the men still felt that they had been cheated, then they should go down to the company office and make a claim for the amount they felt was due them.

The old man couldn't be fairer than that, some of the men agreed. But others argued that Dunsmuir's solution smacked of charity. "It was beneath my dignity to go and get my coal made up," one of them said. Only two or three men took him up on his offer. The others decided to hold a meeting.

A deputation waited on Robert Dunsmuir later that evening to list the miners' demands. Haggerty must be reinstated; the scales must be fixed; and the rate must return to $1.20—otherwise they would go on strike. They had agreed to give him two days to think it over.

"I don't need two days," Robert retorted. "The market won't bear an extra twenty cents a ton."

On 5 February, one hundred miners struck. As an unfamiliar quiet settled over Wellington, the men prepared to wait Dunsmuir out. Meanwhile Robert Dunsmuir made plans of his own.

—

He published in the *Nanaimo Free Press* a notice that ran for the duration of the strike.

> There is an impression in the community that we are obliged to
> accede to the miners demands but for the benefit of those whom it
> may concern we wish to state publicly that we have no intention to
> ask any of them to work for us again at any price
>
> SIGNED DUNSMUIR, DIGGLE & COMPANY

Then he sent a telegram to Berryman, instructing him to recruit strikebreakers in San Francisco. And while he waited for them to arrive, he made life for his men as difficult as possible. He shut the gate across the road that led into the town. "Mr. Mayer, who was supplying us with groceries at a much cheaper rate than the store at Wellington, could not fetch the goods to Wellington," Vipond charged.

"Is it any business of his?" Dunsmuir demanded. "Suppose we build a stone wall 18 feet high around every inch of it?"

"He told the butcher not to kill any more beef, the baker not to fetch any bread and the Doctor not to visit us," the men complained. He had simply warned the doctor that the miners would be unable to pay him, Dunsmuir sniffed.

On 23 February, two and a half weeks after the strike had begun, the first replacement miners arrived. There were thirty-three of them and they were a rough lot. The Wellington men regarded them as the outscourings of the saloons of San Francisco, and even Robert Dunsmuir felt a stab of remorse when he met them at Departure Bay to welcome them to his coal mines.

"That's a fine example of wharf rats you have here," a Wellington man commented, and Dunsmuir nodded his head in agreement. "Yes," he said. "And I'm sorry for it."

The new men spent the evening at Departure Bay settling into the wharf-side shanties that were to be their homes. The following day, Robert led them up the hill to Wellington to introduce them to the mine. When they reached the town, they found waiting for them a crowd of strikers who called out to them, urging them not to go to work.

When the miners began to follow the new men down the slope that led into the mine, Dunsmuir shooed the San Franciscans on ahead and then stood, his arms outstretched, a small but determined man, barring their way and defying them to pass. And a hundred angry men stopped in their tracks. They hung about for over an hour until the new men emerged. "Come for a drink," they called. But the San Franciscans were loaded into wagons and carried away to Departure Bay.

Sometime later about half their number decided to make the trek back to Wellington. They collected in the barroom of the Wellington Hotel, where the miners stood them to drinks and detailed their grievances.

"We shouldn't go to work for a man that is wrong in weights and wages," one of the new men exclaimed. That was exactly the reaction the Wellington men were hoping for, but as the whiskey continued to flow, things began to get out of hand.

"If I was in your position, I'd shoot any son-of-a-bitch who would go to work for him," a would-be strikebreaker bellowed as he accepted another drink.

"Give me ten dollars and passage out of the country and I'll blow the old son-of-a-bitch Dunsmuir's brains out," another man vowed.

"No, no. We want the old man to live a little longer," the Wellington men cautioned. They had agreed amongst themselves that no company property was to be damaged. The last thing they wanted was violence. For the present, they would be content if the strikebreakers returned to San Francisco, and they urged them to do just that, promising to cover all their expenses while they waited in Victoria for a steamer and to pay their passage home.

The evacuation began the next morning when the miners arrived at Departure Bay, entered the strikebreakers' cabins, hauled their luggage down to a canoe and then, pushing and shoving the few men who were reluctant to leave, began to escort them along the hilly road to Nanaimo.

James Dunsmuir met them on the way. "Where are you going?" he demanded.

"We're taking them to Nanaimo," one of the miners yelled as they shouldered him aside. "We're going to tell them the truth, that you've told us lies."

John Bolton, the man who had had a *contretemps* with James two months earlier, was part of the crowd. "He stopped one or two of the new men and wanted them to go back with him, but they would not do so," Bolton remembered. "He then told them if they wouldn't go back they were liable to be put in prison. He got excited when the men wouldn't turn back."

"You've taken the law into your own hands," Jim spluttered as the men pushed past him.

In Nanaimo that Sunday afternoon an interesting meeting was taking place in the house on the hill above the little harbour at the south end of Commercial Inlet. Gathered together with Robert Dunsmuir in the parlour of Ardoon were Wadham Diggle, John Bryden and Capt. Warner Spalding.

The attendance of John Bryden, manager of the Vancouver Company's mines, was not surprising. Born in Scotland in 1831, he had served a successful apprenticeship in the Ayrshire mines before being recruited by the Vancouver Company to take over the management of its island mines. A handsome man, well over six feet tall and "straight as an arrow," Bryden had married Dunsmuir's eldest daughter, Elizabeth, in 1867, and Robert had acquired a son-in-law whom he respected and admired, a man he regarded as a great friend and a man whose counsel he valued.

But Bryden was there to do more than offer advice. Change was in the air in all the island mines. In the legislative hopper in Victoria was a new Mines Regulation Act. Owners and managers of small and large collieries had been meeting together, preparing to head off any proposed legislation that might impinge on the profitable operation of their mines. At the same time, miners had been gathering to discuss and propose changes to the new act. At those meetings, the scent of unionism hung heavy in the air. And so it behooved Bryden, as manager of the Vancouver Company's mines, to share in planning the strategies that would bring the strike to an end.

The presence of the fourth member of the group was more significant. Capt. Warner Spalding was the city's stipendiary magistrate, charged with the responsibility for maintaining the rule of law in the Nanaimo district. In theory he should have remained neutral, siding with neither the mine owners nor the strikers. But in addition to his official duties, he served as the legal representative of Admiral Farquhar and, as subsequent events made clear, he was at least as interested in protecting the admiral's investment in the Wellington mine as in preserving the peace.

Dunsmuir, Diggle, Bryden and Spalding prepared a series of letters that were meant to appear to have been independently written but were in fact a co-operative effort.

The first, signed by Dunsmuir, Diggle & Co., was addressed to Stipendiary Magistrate Warner Spalding. "On account of a strike of our miners at Wellington for an advance per ton, which we refused to grant, we discharged them, and procured thirty-three men from San Francisco. These men agreed to work, and it was intended that they should have commenced tomorrow morning; but to-day the miners formerly employed came down in a body to Departure Bay, where we had provided accommodation for the new hands, and, by threats and violence, compelled them to leave and come to Nanaimo; we therefore, beg that you, as Magistrate, will grant protection to those men whom we have employed and who are willing to work if protected."

That letter having been pushed across the table to him, Spalding wrote one of his own. Addressed to the lieutenant-governor of the province, it was nothing less than a call to arms. "It appears to me that the miners hitherto employed by the Wellington Colliery are determined to proceed to extremities, and have already committed such acts of violence as will necessitate the employment of an armed force to reduce them to order and compel them to respect the law."

Spalding's was a most extraordinary letter. There had been some pushing and shoving, a great deal of swearing and more than a few angry words, but there had been no violence, and the only authority the miners had defied was the company's. But his was not the only letter Diggle carried to Victoria which claimed that Nanaimo and Wellington were on the brink of some kind of insurrection. Also in his pocket was an excited missive from Robert Dunsmuir addressed to the provincial attorney-general. "For goodness sake, act promptly in this matter, I am afraid that there will be blood-shed among us at this time; I know the miners as well I think, as any one, and I can see that we have all a hard battle to fight. Diggle will, of course, tell you all."

Dunsmuir knew that since most of the strikebreakers were preparing to leave Nanaimo that night, the possibility of bloodshed was virtually nonexistent. But he also knew that real trouble could be expected when he began to evict the miners from their cottages. On 8 February, three days after the miners struck, Robert had given them one month's notice to quit the company houses. To overcome the resistance that he was sure he would meet, he would need the help of the government.

The tide seemed to turn in the miners' favour when, on 26 February, the Wellington strike became the subject of a meeting attended by men from all the island mines. James Harold, a miner who had made it his business to become familiar with mining legislation in Britain and Australia, had dragged himself out of his sick bed to deliver himself of a speech framed in language calculated to make a mine owner's blood run cold.

"Dunsmuir has carried on a species of autocratic tyranny," he declaimed. "He thinks that miners should be slaves to a person who happens to own a small piece of coal land ... If any man dared to insinuate that the company robbed these men they were told to leave the place! What do you think of such a man? The men were fully justified in striking. What right had Dunsmuir to put a gate on a public road so that people could not buy of whom they wished; or to refuse to allow the Doctor to visit the sick? He tried to starve the people out and leave them to rot, so that he could ride in his carriage."

"Will the men stand it?" Harold asked in tones of a man who knows he has his audience in the palm of his hand. "No! While there is breath in me I will fight for our rights!"

Charged by the passion of Harold's remarks, the meeting voted to resolve itself into a mutual protective society and made its first item of business a resolution to collect money to help defray the costs the Wellington men had incurred in sending the strikebreakers back to San Francisco.

Its second item of business would be appearing in court, for as soon as Robert Dunsmuir read the *Nanaimo Free Press*'s verbatim account of Harold's remarks, he decided to sue, charging the newspaper's editor, George Norris, with publishing a libel. Eventually he would drop the lawsuit, and the charges of obstruction and intimidation that he would bring against eight of the miners would be dismissed. But the ease with which Dunsmuir, with Spalding's cooperation, gained access to the courts was in itself a form of intimidation.

On 27 February, Dunsmuir wrote a second letter to the attorney-general. "Such a lot of men I never had to deal with before, and there will be no peace with them until they get a proper lesson."

Dunsmuir had a few lessons of his own in mind. He laid a charge, readily accepted by Spalding, of obstructing with violence against four of the Wellington men who had defied his son on the road from Departure Bay. In Victoria, one of the new men was persuaded to press charges against the miners who had accompanied him from Nanaimo. And in case that failed to bring them to their senses, Dunsmuir kept up the pressure on the attorney-general with dire warnings.

"We are going to have trouble if not bloodshed, when we commence to evict the miners from their houses," he wrote. "I am tired of all this trouble we are having, and I see no other way out of it but that we shall have to shut down the works altogether for some months."

As well as preparing the ground for government intervention, Dunsmuir did his best to undermine the support the Wellington men were receiving from the miners who worked for the Vancouver Company and the recently reopened Harewood mine. He bought space in the newspaper to publish "A Card" in which he listed the amounts the strikers had earned during their last month at work.

"I would have published a list of the wages made by the late miners of Wellington earlier in this strike," Dunsmuir said, "but knowing that men elsewhere were making less money on an average, I did not think it right to cause any feeling of dissatisfaction amongst them, and I have only been induced to now from a knowledge that begging Committees have been sent throughout the Island for the purpose of collecting funds from those who are not earning as much money as they themselves were doing when willing to work." And when miners from other collieries studied the figures, they could not help but agree that the daily average of $3.52 compared favourably with the rates they were receiving.

On 12 March, a second group of strikebreakers arrived. The Americans were met not by the angry mob they had been warned to expect but by women with babies in their arms and children clinging to their skirts. "Have you come to take the bread and butter out of our mouths?" the women asked. And the strikebreakers melted away.

Dunsmuir now applied to Spalding for eviction notices for two dozen company houses. The eviction of striking miners was a common practice in England and Scotland and on Vancouver Island. From the earliest days of the island mines, the HBC had used the technique, threatening the wives of deserting miners with eviction and refusing to contribute to their support. The eviction notices came as no surprise to the Wellington men; their resistance came as no surprise to Dunsmuir.

When the deputy sheriff arrived to carry out the eviction orders, the miners stood firm, defying his authority and forcing him to leave without accomplishing his mission. Dunsmuir was becoming impatient. "We are in a fix—cannot get possession of our property and the law set at naught," he wrote to the attorney-general. The sheriff should come in person and he must bring force.

Thomas Harris was the sheriff of Vancouver Island and a more unlikely officer of the law would have been hard to imagine. Sixty years old, a 300-pound mountain of a man who made no attempt to hide his fondness for strong drink, he operated a butcher shop in Victoria. That he had served a term as that city's mayor had not elevated his status one whit. Victoria's gentlefolk regarded him as uncouth, uneducated and boorish. Even Madame Bendixen, a hotel proprietor with an obscure if not shady past, felt herself superior to *le gros boucher*. He was a ridiculous figure whom no one took seriously, least of all the miners he had come to evict.

They looked on with amusement when the wheezing sheriff arrived in Wellington. "Now gentlemen, let's proceed to business," Harris said as he caught his breath and led the bailiffs toward the first cottage. The miners followed Harris and his men, treating them to a volley of good-natured jibes, but after Harris emptied two cottages and moved toward the little house occupied by Alexander Hoggan, their mood quickly changed.

Three Hoggan brothers worked for Dunsmuir, Diggle & Co., and the company's record-keeper found it hard to keep them straight. The eviction notice Harris carried was issued in the name of David Hoggan, and his brother Alexander counted on that technicality to render his own tenure secure. In addition one of his children was very ill and had been judged by a doctor to be too sick to be moved.

Harris marched up to the cottage. "David Hoggan. In the name of the Queen, open the door," he bellowed importantly, repeating his command three times.

"I'm David Hoggan and that's my brother's house," the man standing beside him said.

"That don't make any difference. I've got to clean it out any how," Harris responded, and he directed his men to break in the door.

When he burst into the room, he found Hoggan's wife, a doctor's certificate in her hand. They had been up most of the night, she said. Their child had a raging fever; the doctor thought he might die. "Madam, I can't help that," Harris intoned.

The bailiffs picked up a table and were about to carry it out of the house when Alexander threw open the bedroom door and launched himself at the sheriff. "Let go of my table you son-of-a-bitch," he shrieked as he grabbed hold of Harris's coat and tried to wrestle him out of the house.

The miners collected outside Hoggan's house and shouted encouragement. "Go at it Hoggan!" "Let them have it!" "Give it to the sons-of-bitches!" And then they stormed into the room, manhandled Harris and his men out of the house, and set them on the road to Nanaimo.

Robert Dunsmuir wrote yet another letter to the attorney-general. "If the law cannot be carried out, I shall have to shut down the works for twelve months, and if there is not something done next week, I shall do so," he threatened. "I have been put to too much expense for want of a proper force."

On 30 April when the sheriff returned to resume his evictions, he was escorted by 107 officers and men of the volunteer militia, a mounted lieutenant-colonel who carried orders to prevent any disturbance of the peace and to suppress the "anticipated riot," and a "war correspondent" from the *Daily Colonist*, a Victoria newspaper with an editorial policy guided by the principle that a capitalist could do no wrong.

Confidently expecting trouble, the militia found instead a community numbed by the death of four-year-old Jimmy Craig who had drowned in a well and whose funeral had concluded only an hour earlier. "Some few women came on the scene and wept and raved and abused the Dunsmuirs, but no one talked of using violence," the war correspondent noted with some disappointment. Only William Baker lost control. He had been coaxed out of his house by four of his fellow miners and he stood, his anger simmering under the hot sun, as the bailiffs began to remove his furniture. When he saw a man with an axe who seemed about to break up his bed, his temper snapped. He hurled himself back into his cottage and threw himself upon the bailiff. Handcuffed and led away to a shady spot to cool off, Baker later excused himself by explaining that his wife had died on that bed and he had been overcome by the thought of it being broken apart.

Recognizing that the strike was virtually over, Dunsmuir instructed the sheriff to use some discretion in effecting the evictions. When old Mrs. Haggerty pleaded that her son was away and she did not know where to go, she was allowed to remain in her cottage. Harry Ross was left alone after he told the bailiffs that his daughter was ill. A man and his wife who were both recovering from a severe illness were allowed to retain possession of their cottage as were several other families who pleaded special circumstances.

The Wellington men hung on for twenty-four more days. But then on 24 May the steamer *Maude* arrived at Departure Bay with forty fresh strikebreakers aboard. The following day, thirty Wellington men broke ranks to inform Dunsmuir, Diggle that they would return to work for a dollar a ton. Two days later, the remaining strikers straggled into the company's offices to apply for work.

Robert Dunsmuir would have known that the time to appear magnanimous had arrived, but he was away from the office that day and his son Alexander could not resist the opportunity to rub a little salt into the wounds. He selected twenty-five men, whom he characterized as being the least obnoxious, and told the others that he would have to talk to his father before deciding whether or not they should be rehired. But even as they stood in line, patiently waiting to add their names to the list, Alexander readily accepted applications from "strangers" and sent them straight to work.

"The sudden collapse of the strike proves that the remuneration was ample, and as good, if not better, than the men could have made elsewhere," the *Colonist* opined. "For years to come the result of the Wellington strike will be quoted as an instance when Labor, when clearly in the wrong, had to succumb to Capital."

Four

—

"The Coal Mines of Vancouver Island have, during the year 1878, passed through a period of unprecedented discouragement," the provincial mines inspector, Edward Gawlor Prior, concluded in his annual report. So bad had the market become that two smaller coal companies ceased operation entirely and the Vancouver Coal Company shut down for several weeks to reduce production, but even so it had ended the year with tons of unsold coal.

But while other collieries were struggling to survive, Dunsmuir's business was booming. In 1878 he mined 88,000 tons, almost doubling the output of the previous year. More significantly he succeeded in selling it, reaching year-end with a stockpile of only 935 tons. The following year his output increased once again, topping 113,000 tons and leaving the Wellington Colliery unchallenged as the largest producer of coal on Vancouver Island.

Dunsmuir's success resulted from his aggressive approach to sales. To lure ships' captains to Departure Bay, he often agreed to cut his rates, and by constantly upgrading his facilities, he guaranteed them a fast turn-around time. The merit of that approach was clearly demonstrated after he took over a competing coal company.

In 1878, on land he owned between Wellington and Nanaimo, San Franciscan Richard Chandler had opened the South Wellington Colliery and tapped into the Wellington seam. He had drawn out 20,000 tons, most of which still loomed unsold in his bins, when in November 1879 he sold his holdings to Dunsmuir, Diggle & Co. It took the new proprietors only six weeks to dispose of all of Chandler's stockpiled coal.

Even though he was selling his coal for far less than the dizzying heights it had reached during 1875, Dunsmuir was amassing huge profits. But if it ever flitted across his mind that perhaps he should share those profits with his workers, he refused to allow the thought to linger. His men had defied him by going on strike; they were making wages comparable to those paid by the Vancouver Company, and besides, he needed the money for expansion.

Dunsmuir was now in the business of acquiring land. Sometimes he did it by resurrecting his mythical partners to acquire crown grants, sometimes by outright purchase, and sometimes through third parties who had no apparent connection with the company but who signed over the land to Dunsmuir, Diggle & Co. within days of registering the title.

Mark Bate, manager of the Vancouver Company's sales and shipping office, found Dunsmuir's ability to select land that later proved to contain valuable coal seams almost uncanny. But if the story of a miner named Richardson was to be believed, there was nothing mysterious about it at all.

One September day in 1880, Richardson called at Bate's office with an interesting tale. A year or two earlier, when Richardson was working at Wellington, Dunsmuir had asked him to take a small party of men who could be counted on to keep their mouths shut and work a bore on land adjacent to Dunsmuir's at the south end of Diver Lake. They were to take samples of any coal they found to Ardoon—but only after dark, when they would not be seen. They were to be well paid for saying nothing—"bribed to keep quiet," Richardson said.

Was Dunsmuir conducting secret bores on another man's land? Bate certainly thought so. Richardson said that he had found four seams of coal, two of which were of particularly good quality. And Bate remembered that about the time Richardson said he had completed the bore, Dunsmuir had shown a "manifest desire" to get Chantrell's Diver Lake property. And now Chantrell's land was contributing to the colliery's profits.

When Dunsmuir became interested in the coal leases of the Union mine 70 miles north of Nanaimo, Bate was delighted to discover that he had been able to acquire only one of the eleven shares. What Bate did not know was that the lawyer who had purchased the other ten shares would soon be transferring them to Dunsmuir, Diggle & Co.

—

Thanks to its quality and to the efforts of Henry Berryman, coal from the Wellington Colliery enjoyed an enviable reputation in San Francisco. But by 1877 Dunsmuir had begun to suspect Berryman of sharp practices, of using his position as sales representative of Wellington coal to his own financial advantage. And perhaps most importantly, Robert no longer needed Berryman, and it irritated him to have to share his profits with the San Franciscan. It was time to negotiate a fresh arrangement. A new man would be added to Berryman's office, a man who would serve as an assistant but who would function as a watchdog, keeping an eye on Berryman's activities and, if possible, discovering a legal means by which Dunsmuir's partnership with Berryman might be abrogated. And he had a particular man in mind—his twenty-four-year-old son Alexander.

In many ways the two Dunsmuir boys, Jim and Alex, were alike. Separated by only two years, they were friends as much as brothers. Having reached their twenties before their father began to spend money on luxuries, they were simple men, uncultured and unsophisticated, devoid of social grace and with a brusqueness of speech that many interpreted as rudeness. But there was an important difference between them. Alex was quick where Jim was slow. Even though he was the older brother, Jim deferred to Alex, seeking his advice whenever he could and reversing decisions that did not meet with his brother's approval.

Robert Dunsmuir recognized Alex as having the greater potential, and while Jim might be trusted with the management of the mine, he planned a more demanding role for his younger son. In 1874, after attending college in Ontario, Alex returned to Nanaimo and went to work for his father. Described as a clerk at Departure Bay, he was always more than that. He became his father's right-hand man, ready to accept any job Robert sent his way.

By January 1878 Alex was on his way to San Francisco. Six months later, he had accomplished his mission. Dunsmuir, Diggle & Co. filed an injunction against Berryman, alleging that "the defendant has been guilty of serious misconduct, in that he represented, when the partnership was formed, that he had on hand and within his control 2,210 tons of coal. Plaintiffs were accordingly charged with 1/2 the full value of the coal but about 837 tons of it was at the time pledged by the defendant as a security for an indebtedness." Given the huge amount of coal that had been sold through Berryman's office, it seemed a rather flimsy excuse for ending the partnership, but soon Robert Dunsmuir was able to announce that he had "successfully adjusted partnership affairs" by taking over Berryman's business.

Dunsmuir, Diggle & Co. now controlled Wellington coal from the moment it was removed from the ground to its sale in California. Wadham Diggle resigned from the navy and moved to San Francisco, where he took over the company's marine operations. While Diggle dealt with ships' captains, negotiating the lowest possible rate for the charter of their vessels, Alex made himself known to the city's business community. He became a member of the Merchants Exchange, where he met with other coal dealers to discuss prices and supply, and he joined a variety of gentlemen's clubs where he formed friendships with the ships' owners and railway men who were potential customers of his father's coal.

As he looked at the sales figures for 1879, which showed that Alex and Diggle had arranged for the sale of more than 100,000 tons of coal, Robert Dunsmuir was encouraged that his first experiment with company reorganization had turned out well. So well, in fact, that he did not hesitate when the opportunity to further fine tune his operation presented itself a year later.

———

John Bryden envied his father-in-law's ability to deal directly with his men without having to filter decisions through a board of directors far removed from the scene. He admired the way Robert Dunsmuir had handled the strike of 1877, and three years later when his own miners went out on strike, he attempted to apply the lessons he had learned. But the Vancouver Company's directors ignored Bryden's suggestion that they bring in strikebreakers. Nor did they follow his advice about the importance of standing firm. Five weeks into the strike, Bryden was instructed to "resume work immediately, on best terms."

Bryden felt he had lost face. "My influence with our Men will be very much lessened," he worried. "I do not think that I would be doing justice either to the Company or myself by remaining in my present position. I therefore beg to place my resignation in your hands."

The ink had scarcely dried on Bryden's resignation when Robert Dunsmuir offered him a job. There were those who suspected that Bryden had been working for his father-in-law all along. Had he shared his knowledge about the Vancouver Company with his father-in-law? And could that account for Wellington's progress while the Vancouver Company struggled to stay in second place? Those were the questions in Mark Bate's mind as he recorded in his diary the number of times Robert popped his head in the office looking for

49

Bryden. But now it was official. John Bryden would join Dunsmuir, Diggle & Co., replacing James Dunsmuir as manager of the Wellington mine.

———

Jim's tenure as mine manager had come close to being a disaster. Under his management Wellington had become the most dangerous of all the island mines. He had directed the opening of the mine's tenth and deepest level. And his lack of expertise, his unwillingness to accept advice or consider the warnings of the mines inspector, had cost the colliers dear.

At three o'clock on the morning of 16 April 1879, a messenger reached Ardoon with the alarming news that the Wellington Colliery was on fire. The mine's tenth level was choked with thick black smoke.

"My father and I went out to the mine together," Jim recalled. "We went down the mine immediately . . . then my father took management of the mine."

While Jim melted into the background, his father began shouting orders. A stream of water was directed at the flaming coal face and a "curtain" was placed across the entrance to the burning stall. Robert remained underground for almost twelve hours, his only respite the twenty minutes he allowed himself for breakfast. By three o'clock in the afternoon, he decided that the danger had passed; the water directed at the coal face was still raising steam but the flames had abated. Leaving James in charge, he returned to Nanaimo. "I considered everything safe when I left the mine, or I would not have gone home," Robert said.

At half-past six the following morning, James was asleep in the manager's house on Jingle Pot road when he was jolted awake by the sound of an explosion. He hurried to the mine and scrambled down the slope. At the eighth level, he found the body of William Rennie—killed less than an hour after reporting for work on the morning of his sixty-first birthday.

After brattices, heavier wood-framed curtains, were set in place on the upper levels so that the full force of the air rushing down the slope could be directed to levels nine and ten, rescue parties began to search for survivors.

George Norris of the *Nanaimo Free Press* arrived on the scene. "The sight at the mine's mouth . . . would melt to tears the hardest heart," he wrote, "wives wailing for their husbands, and parents for their children."

At the entrance to level ten, the rescuers found fourteen-year-old Reuben Gough, dead but "without a mark about him," a victim of the gas rather than the explosion. Andrew Scott was alive when he was found gasping for air and with a gash in his forehead "clear to the brain." Scott was the only man who had been on or near the tenth level to be brought out alive.

Twelve hours after the explosion, they found the body of a Chinese, known only by his nickname "Fatty." During the evening the death toll continued to mount, until eleven bodies had been removed from the mine. Appolis Damey "severely injured and burned about the lower part of his body"; John Hoskins "instantly killed by the explosion" and "badly burned about the head and face"; Edward Campbell asphyxiated by gas. At midnight, they found Louis Prelee and then, early the next morning, they found John Dixon and two Chinese, "burned to a cinder."

"The fact that Dixon and the Chinamen being so badly burned shows that the gas must have been fired in their immediate proximity," the *Nanaimo Free Press* concluded. For some inexplicable reason, John Dixon, the father of six children and "a miner of great experience" whose job it was to regulate air flow in the mine, had ventured behind the curtain into the smouldering stall with his two Chinese assistants. One of them, and some evidence suggested that it might have been Dixon himself, had been carrying a lamp with a naked flame.

At the inquest, conducted by the ever-present Warner Spalding in his role as coroner, Edward Prior, the inspector of mines, testified that he had many times warned James Dunsmuir that there was "a good deal of explosive gas being given off in the tenth level." But Jim had refused to listen.

"Mr. Prior several times drew my attention to the gas in that level," he admitted. "He used to be telling me of accidents and cautioned me." He had seen gas explode on that level when they first began working it, James agreed. And later, several men had been burned, but the accidents had been "slight" and the explosions "trifling."

Described by the inspector of mines as the "heaviest calamity that has ever overtaken the mining community of this Province," the accident at Wellington convinced Robert Dunsmuir to take the problem of explosive gas more seriously. Air circulation in most island mines was achieved by positioning a large furnace at the deepest level of the mine at the bottom of a chimneylike shaft. As the furnace burned, the air it sucked in from the outside was directed by a system of brattices to the working levels of the mine. With the notable exception of the tenth level, the furnace at Wellington had worked well. But in 1880 when Robert began to develop the South Wellington Colliery, he ordered the installation of a 30-foot-wide fan. "This is the first ventilating fan, on a large scale, in the Province," the inspector of mines rhapsodized. "Great praise is due the managing partner for expending so much in the erection of such a machine."

—

Meanwhile, at the Wellington Colliery, two more men lost their lives. On 8 July 1880 Rees Evans was working on the seventh level when Jim Dolan, who had served on the coroner's jury investigating the Wellington explosion the year before, asked for his help in putting up a stringer to support the roof of the area in which he was working.

"I went as soon as I finished filling my box," Evans said. "Thomas Corbet was there before me, and they had one end of the stringer up waiting for me to come." Rees and Dolan and Dolan's Chinese assistant, Ah Bow, held up the beam while Corbet fixed it into position. "Thank you boys! I can get along now," Dolan called out.

Evans and Corbet, heading back to their own stalls, had travelled fewer than 10 yards when they heard the sound of a cave-in. They rushed back. "I could see the hand of the Chinaman, Ah Bow, sticking out from under the fallen timber and stone," Tom Corbet shuddered. He was quite dead, as was Jim Dolan, crushed to a pulpy mass by the fallen roof.

—

In 1879 and 1880 fifteen men lost their lives in Vancouver Island mines. All but one of them died in the mine managed by James Dunsmuir. But neither the coroner nor the miners held him responsible. The explosion was blamed on the man who had used a naked flame; and Dolan had brought about his own demise by removing the prop that supported the stringer.

On the question of safety, the miners were their own worst enemies. Although they worked in mines owned by other men and although those men set the rates they received for their coal, miners took pride in their status as independent contractors. Recognizing this, the Coal Mines Regulation Act, passed in 1877, placed the onus for safety on the miners rather than the managers. As the mines inspector asserted, it was up to the men "to do their best to make their place secure." But building the wooden framework that supported the roof took time, and when a miner was not cutting coal, he was not earning money. Compounding the problem was the miners' cavalier attitude to safety. Their refusal to recognize danger lay behind their rejection of safety lamps in favour of the naked flame that provided better light.

It behooved a mine manager to concern himself with safety, if only to keep the mines open and in production. But he knew that if he became too fussy, he would be accused by the men of interfering with their ability to earn a living. For this reason, the Mines Regulation Act made specific provision that allowed a manager to insist that a man leave his place if it was found to be unsafe.

But it took a confident, strong-minded manager to assert his authority. Jim, or an assistant, tried to inspect each stall once a day, and he counted on the "fire-man" to check each level for accumulated gas, but other than that he left the miners to their own devices.

—

For Robert Dunsmuir, the chance of replacing his son with a man of Bryden's experience was an opportunity not to be missed. While Bryden made plans to move into the manager's house, James was shuffled off to Departure Bay where he was given the less demanding job of directing the loading of coal carriers at the company wharves.

With John Bryden at Wellington, Alexander in San Francisco and James out of harm's way, Robert Dunsmuir was left with one last item of business to complete his corporate adjustments. He wanted to buy out his last remaining partner, Wadham Diggle.

In 1879 he and Diggle had purchased Admiral Farquhar's share and likewise, Captain Egerton, who had joined the partnership in 1873, had been induced to sell. Only Diggle now stood between Dunsmuir and his ultimate goal of total control. But at least Diggle had never interfered in his running of the company and his naval experience allowed him to mix easily with ships' captains whether he was negotiating the use of their vessels or wooing them into buying Wellington coal.

But however good a salesman Diggle might be, he possessed a singular liability as far as Dunsmuir was concerned. As an equal partner, he was entitled to half the colliery's profits. And worse, he showed no inclination to sell. At least he had demonstrated no such inclination until chance once again played into Dunsmuir's hands.

Diggle had settled contentedly into his life in California. Thirty-two years old, he decided that the time was right for him to marry. In 1880 he flitted back to England, scooped up a bride, one Emma Donna Cookson of Worksop Manor in Nottinghamshire, and brought her back to San Francisco. They had been married just over a year, when tragedy struck. One day Emma was out riding with her husband; the next day she was dead, the victim of acute pneumonia. Beside himself with grief, Wadham had Emma's body embalmed and accompanied her coffin home to England. And there he remained, his enthusiasm for California and the coal business buried with his wife. Two years later he was ready to let Dunsmuir buy him out.

On 12 May 1883 Diggle signed a dissolution of partnership. He received $600,000—a tidy profit on his $8,000 investment. Dunsmuir, Diggle & Co. was renamed R. Dunsmuir & Sons, and Robert Dunsmuir became sole owner of a colliery that was producing profits of $500,000 a year.

Five

—

In 1881 Robert Dunsmuir began to toy with the idea of building a railroad. When British Columbia entered Confederation in 1871, the province had been particularly insistent about one of the provisions of the Terms of Union—within two years construction was to begin on a transcontinental rail line, linking the west coast with the Canadian provinces in the east. The proposed route lay through central British Columbia. After meeting the sea at Bute Inlet, the tracks would cross Quadra Island and bridge Seymour Narrows to reach Vancouver Island at a point 85 miles north of Nanaimo and 160 miles distant from the proposed terminus of Esquimalt.

When construction began almost ten years later, Victoria businessmen, who had been delighted by the prospect of their city becoming the western terminus of a great transcontinental railroad, were appalled to discover that the contract signed by the syndicate constructing the Canadian Pacific Railway made no mention of the Vancouver Island section of the line.

As agitated islanders began to talk about separation, it occurred to Robert Dunsmuir that he might undertake to build the island line. He knew a little something about railway building—by 1880 his colliery operation boasted five locomotives and 10 miles of track. And furthermore a railway that ran along the island's east coast could easily be extended to Wellington to connect his colliery with its best local customers, the Royal Navy at Esquimalt, and Victoria, the province's largest city. It was public knowledge that a large tract of land had been reserved by the government as a subsidy for potential railway builders, and it was Dunsmuir's belief that much of that land was underlaid with coal.

There was no question that an island line would be built. The Canadian prime minister, Sir John A. Macdonald, knew that if he reneged on his promise to extend the tracks to Esquimalt, none of his government's Vancouver Island members would survive the next election. That he was one of those members only added to his interest in the issue. But just who would build the line was a question that remained unanswered during the summer of 1881 when Sir Charles Tupper, the minister of railways, arrived to visit the unhappy voters of Vancouver Island. When he and Lady Tupper paid a call on Nanaimo, Dunsmuir invited them to stay at Ardoon, and Tupper, alerted to the fact that his host was a man with considerable capital at his disposal who had already expressed some interest in the railway, took the opportunity to broach the subject. The government was still clinging to the hope that the CPR might be induced to build the island section, Tupper warned. But failing that, he and the prime minister would welcome proposals from local men.

As Tupper left to continue his tour, Dunsmuir hurriedly drafted a rough contract. Five pages long, handwritten, with words and phrases scratched out to allow for second thoughts, it committed Dunsmuir, Diggle & Co. to undertake the construction of a narrow-gauge railway from Seymour Narrows to Esquimalt in return for a 20-mile-wide swath of land along the entire route.

When Dunsmuir presented the document to Tupper a week later, he assured the minister that it was "merely a general basis of agreement" and that he was prepared to fill in the details later, after a full discussion with the government. Early in 1882 when the CPR finally and definitely stated that it had no interest in building the island line, he was prepared to make a definite proposal and he had the financing in place.

That proposal was significantly different from the first one he had presented to Tupper. Given that the CPR had selected Burrard Inlet rather than Bute Inlet as its western terminus, it seemed folly to extend the line all the way to Seymour Narrows. Instead, Dunsmuir proposed a line a scant 75 miles long, running between Esquimalt and Nanaimo. And, he informed the government, he would require a subsidy of $10,000 a mile.

Dunsmuir estimated that the line would cost $ 1.5 million to build. The government subsidy would cover half the cost. The remainder could have come from the profits of the Wellington Colliery, but he was thinking ahead. The value of the line would be greatly increased if it became part of a transcontinental system. While federal politicians continued to promote the island line as an extension of the CPR, Dunsmuir visualized it as part of an American railroad system. And so he had turned his attention south, to the three surviving members of San Francisco's "Big Four."

The four richest men in California had begun as small-time Sacramento shopkeepers. Charles Crocker ran a drygoods store; Leland Stanford was a grocer; Mark Hopkins and Collis P. Huntington were partners in a hardware business. In 1861, they had been persuaded to invest $800 to form a corporation that would raise funds for the construction of a railroad running from Sacramento across the Sierras to the silver mines of Nevada. The partners had envisioned the Central Pacific as nothing more than an efficient way of getting their goods to waiting customers in Nevada's booming silver towns. But in 1862 the government in Washington decided that the time had come to build the long-delayed transcontinental railroad. The Central Pacific won the contract for building the western section of the line, from Sacramento through Nevada to Promontory Point in Utah, and became the beneficiary of federal subsidies running as high as $48,000 a mile. By 1870 their estimated worth was $20 million.

Mark Hopkins died in 1878, leaving a wife quickly branded by the press "America's Richest Widow" and three partners who had achieved their goal of controlling almost all transportation to, from and within California.

Dunsmuir knew that Crocker, Huntington and Stanford were canny enough to recognize the importance of the coal lands lying within the railway belt. The Northern Pacific Railroad had expressed an interest in those lands and the San Franciscans might be persuaded to invest, if only to keep the coal out of a competitor's hands. And once the Californians had put money into the island line, surely they would soon see the value of linking it with the railroads they were planning to extend into the Oregon and Washington territories.

He had no concern about doing business with men who were rumoured to be ruthless, unscrupulous and particularly adept at taking over other companies. "I have never allowed any man to get the better of me if I could help it," Dunsmuir boasted, "and I never go into any undertaking unless I can control it!" And the deal he had struck with Crocker, Huntington and Stanford left him firmly in control—he was the president of the company and he owned half the shares.

—

Dunsmuir decided to take advantage of a planned European trip to

57

present his railway proposal to the prime minister in person. But first he took the precaution of stopping off at Victoria to collect the letters of introduction that would guarantee him entrée to the prime minister's office.

The first was from John Hamilton Gray. A Father of Confederation, Gray was responsible for bringing New Brunswick into the Canadian union, and a grateful Macdonald had appointed him to a federal judgeship in Victoria. "He is not only the wealthiest but undoubtedly one of the most respected men in this province," Gray enthused.

The second letter was written by Joseph Trutch. Trutch had served on the three-member committee that had negotiated the terms of British Columbia's entry into Confederation. In 1871 Macdonald had rewarded his efforts by appointing him the province's first lieutenant-governor, and when his term expired in 1876, he became the Ottawa government's official B.C. agent, and, perhaps more importantly, Macdonald's confidential advisor.

Trutch had been particularly insistent about including a transcontinental railway in the Terms of Union, and he had been stung by the criticism of islanders when it became evident that the agreement he had negotiated did not oblige the government to extend the tracks to Esquimalt. His enthusiasm for Dunsmuir's offer was only heightened by the fact that he had been given the chance to invest in Dunsmuir-controlled companies, the profits of which depended on the construction of the railroad.

On 18 February 1882 he penned two letters to the prime minister. The first was a bland introduction. The second, marked "Confidential," was more to the point. Dunsmuir would, Trutch said, make a formal tender for the construction of the island railway. "I can see no prospect of any one coming forward to take up the work more likely to carry it to a successful result than Mr. Dunsmuir ... He is altogether by far the most substantial man financially in BC ... In fact there is no one else in BC who can be said to have *any capital* in *comparison with him* ... Mr. Dunsmuir is a thoroughly practical— in fact self-made man— and he has an undoubted reputation for integrity and trustworthiness."

The *Toronto Globe* put a sinister interpretation on the acceptance Dunsmuir found in Ottawa. "Mr. Dunsmuir came to Ottawa from British Columbia a total stranger. He knew nobody and it happened that one of the first men he consulted concerning the object of his mission was a promoter of the Langevin testimonial. 'We are getting up a testimonial for Sir Hector Langevin and you must give us a subscription. It will help you immensely in your business.' 'Who is Sir Hector Langevin?' he asked. 'Oh, he's the Minister of Public Works and leader of the Quebec Conservatives.' Mr. Dunsmuir's cheque for $1000 was forthwith handed over."

Having splashed money around Ottawa and demonstrated that he was a man of substance to whom $1,000 was a mere trifle, he left the capital confident that the contract would soon be his. "I went on to Europe," Dunsmuir said, "never dreaming for one moment but that the company I was in could get incorporated by the legislature." He was in for an unwelcome surprise.

Dunsmuir was in Glasgow when he received word that the bill incorporating his company had not been passed. Already on the floor of the British Columbia legislature, while his bill was still being debated in committee, was a proposal from a San Francisco syndicate headed by Lewis Clements. And Sir John A. Macdonald, a wily politician on the eve of an election, had decided it would be prudent to allow the provincial legislature to make a choice between the two bids. Some members favoured passage of both bills. But others were opposed. A bird in the hand was worth two in the bush, they argued, and they preferred to reject Dunsmuir's bill for fear it would jeopardize Clements's proposal. When the house dissolved in April, only the Clements bill had received legislative approval.

Dunsmuir was astounded to learn that the Clements syndicate had undertaken to build the line all the way to Seymour Narrows without asking for a cash subsidy and that Clements had launched the scheme without having secured financial backing. When he was told that the syndicate could not come up with a performance bond and was in danger of losing the contract, he was frankly delighted. "Sitting at my breakfast table in Paris I got a telegram," Dunsmuir chortled. "It said, 'Do you want to buy our charter for $50,000?' "

Two weeks later he was in London when he received a telegram from his son Alexander telling him that Clements would now accept $30,000. "Don't waste the sole leather off your shoes going to the telegraph office to tell me anything more about the bill," he wired back. He would let the Clements contract collapse and see how matters stood when he returned home in September.

—

The Wellington brass band struck up "Home Sweet Home" as his steamer neared the Nanaimo wharf. When he stepped onto the gangplank, a resounding "Three Cheers" broke forth from the large dockside crowd. The *Colonist* noted with pleasure that Dunsmuir seemed "much benefitted and invigorated" by his European sojourn. Ready to take up the question of the railway once again, he was in fine fettle when the Marquis of Lorne arrived.

On 20 October 1882 the marquis was treated to a tumultuous Nanaimo reception. Not only was he Canada's governor general but also, as the husband of Queen Victoria's daughter, the Princess Louise, he was the closest thing to royalty the city had ever seen. While his entourage settled itself into the Provincial Hotel, Lorne made himself at home at Ardoon, the guest of Robert Dunsmuir.

Nanaimoites may have thought that Lorne was simply sightseeing when he and his party were piled into carriages and carried off to Wellington. And the governor general was prepared to play the role of tourist, peering appreciatively at the "beautiful section of coal," 10 feet thick and surmounted by a Union Jack, which had been placed in front of the company offices. But Lorne and Dunsmuir both knew that his visit had more serious implications. With the prime minister's approval, the governor general had come to talk about the railroad.

On 24 October he sent a confidential letter to Macdonald. "I saw a good deal of Mr. Dunsmuir," Lorne wrote. "I think he desires to make the Esquimalt & Nanaimo Railroad, but his terms are at present the acquisition of all the 'Railway Belt' from Esquimalt to Seymour Narrows . . . and dealing with the Dominion and not the Provincial government . . . His coal is doing very well and he is making a large fortune and has undertaken a foundry business at Victoria."

Dunsmuir, who would later find it to his political advantage to portray himself as having been coaxed and cajoled into building the railroad, had a slightly different version of events.

> By the bye the Marquis of Lorne came out here, and a few days after he arrived I got a telegram that he wanted to see me. I went to Government House and walked with him in the garden for three hours, when he insisted that I should build the Island railway, adding that he wanted to see it settled before his commission was out.
>
> I told him that I did not want to touch it, that I was getting old now, and that it would only worry me, but he said that he did not see any other person who would build it as well as I could, and he wanted me to undertake it.

But Dunsmuir was being coy. He would hardly have undertaken the foundry business Lorne had mentioned if he had not intended to pursue and win the railway contract. A few weeks before Lorne's visit, he had convinced Joseph Spratt to sell the Albion Iron Works. The largest foundry north of San Francisco, the ironworks was valued at $125,000—an amount Dunsmuir could easily have found in his private purse, leaving change to spare for the $50,000 expansion he was planning. But why do that, when he could form a joint stock company and provide prominent Victorians, including Joseph Trutch, with the opportunity to invest, and thereby guarantee their support for the railway that promised to become the foundry's best customer?

As Dunsmuir had insisted, all negotiations were conducted with the dominion government, but the provincial legislature would have its say when the time came for the province to transfer the land in the railway belt to the dominion so that it could, in turn, convey the land to Dunsmuir. When the Settlement Act, so called because it was intended to settle the railway question, was introduced in the provincial house, revealing the details of the contract signed on 20 August 1883 between Dunsmuir and the minister of railways, voters of all political stripes were aghast. Dunsmuir and his colleagues would receive a subsidy of $750,000—and a land grant of almost 2 million acres, including all the coal that lay under that land and all the timber that grew upon it. For all this, he would be required to build a railroad only 75 miles long, less than half the length of the line the railway belt lands were intended to encourage.

In Ottawa, members of Macdonald's own party recoiled in horror at the munificence of the government's gift. "You cannot imagine the value of the property that is being given over to this alien," one member declaimed. "In the district of Comox, the productive coal measures amount to 300 square miles, containing about 600,000,000 tons of coal." Another Conservative member of the House charged, "The Province will be deprived of lands, timber, coal and other minerals to the value of $20,000,000 for which she is to receive a railway involving a cost of about $2,500,000."

Macdonald was prepared to shrug off criticism, and as for Dunsmuir, it was "water off a duck's back," according to the *Colonist*. He was sure that his opponents were outnumbered by his supporters—men who agreed with the correspondent to the *Colonist* who signed his letter "Progress": "We want more Dunsmuirs, more men of action, less men of straw and cheek, and more men of brains and energy to complete our provincial destiny."

There seemed not the slightest chance that the legislature would not pass the Settlement Act. Political parties did not then exist in the

B.C. legislature. Instead, like-minded men who described themselves as "friends" of one of the two national parties formed loose alliances whose membership shifted and changed. The larger group formed the government; the other the opposition. Dunsmuir had had the foresight to get himself elected to the provincial house, where he sat as the senior member for Nanaimo. The alliance to which he belonged held a majority of the seats; and the premier, William Smithe, who represented Cowichan, a country district south of Nanaimo, was a great supporter of the railroad.

The Settlement Act breezed through the house on 28 March 1884. Encouraged by the fact that their jobs were thus guaranteed, the employees of the Albion Iron Works marched to "Fairview," Dunsmuir's new Victoria home, to offer their congratulations. When news of the act's passage reached Wellington, residents of the town likewise found cause to celebrate. Led by the brass band, a torch-light procession marched to the manager's house where they serenaded John Bryden and gave three cheers for Dunsmuir, for his mine manager and for the Settlement Act.

Opponents of the bill were dismayed by the display of support. The Wellingtonians had assembled "to show how servile men can become, to prove the meanness human nature is capable of, and to insult the intelligence of the district." An anonymous correspondent to the *Nanaimo Free Press* claimed that all the more intelligent residents of the town had held themselves aloof, jeering the procession as it passed, and scorning the "idiots" who composed it, "the meanest, most degraded 'black-legs and nobsticks.'"

Amid charges that 99 per cent of the population of the Nanaimo district considered the bill a disaster and Dunsmuir a grasping monopolist, calls went out for his resignation. But his opponents would have to bide their time, for the senior member for Nanaimo had no intention of resigning.

———

Robert Dunsmuir had first won election to the provincial house in 1882—while he was half a world away and without going through the bother of a campaign. Before leaving for his European holiday, he had let it be known that he would not much mind if, while he was away, he received a telegram telling him he had been elected to the legislature.

There were only three other candidates for the two-member Nanaimo riding, and none of them posed a serious threat. Edward Quennell was a butcher; William Raybould had worked for the Vancouver Company before retiring to help his wife run her Nanaimo dress shop; and William Hinksman worked for Dunsmuir as a coal miner at Wellington. The most pressing issue of the campaign was the island railway and the terms the government was prepared to accept for its construction. Given that the Clements proposal had failed, it was expected that Dunsmuir's bill would be reintroduced at the first sitting of the new legislature. Before the campaign began, a rumour began to circulate in Nanaimo. If Dunsmuir won the railway contract, he intended to evict squatters from the land within the railway belt. Informed of the charges, Dunsmuir sent a telegram to the *Nanaimo Free Press*. "Never intended to lock land from squatters."

William Hinksman was incensed. His opponent thought that he could win election without lifting a finger. "He has only condescended to send one laconic telegram from Glasgow," he stormed.

When Hinksman revealed details of the subsidies believed to be included in Dunsmuir's proposal, John Bryden was on hand to charge him with telling deliberate lies. Bryden was joined by another Dunsmuir son-in-law, James Harvey, who heckled Hinksman with calls that he was so ignorant a man that his speech must have been written by someone else.

On polling day, 24 July, a total of 424 ballots were cast. Dunsmuir received 226 and emerged with a clear majority. But Hinksman, who had won the support of 152 electors, had touched a nerve. And as the first man to take to a public platform to attack Dunsmuir as the recipient of government largesse and to define him as the symbol of a corrupt system, he was setting a precedent that many others would soon follow.

——

When the Settlement Act passed and the terms of the bill became both indisputable and widely known, some of Dunsmuir's Nanaimo constituents, particularly those with old scores to settle, became his severest critics. Among the electors who signed a petition requesting Dunsmuir's attendance at a public meeting to discuss "the gigantic monopoly that will be created" were George Vipond, one of the leaders of the strike of 1877; David Hoggan, whose brother Alexander had been arrested after tangling with the sheriff in his Wellington cottage; and Rees Evans, who had narrowly missed death in the Wellington cave-in of 1880.

Robert Dunsmuir found that "important business matters" prevented him from attending the meeting. Instead, he sent a letter, which was dutifully read to the packed hall.

"The 'Island Railway' is no new thing. It has, in one form or another, been before the country for many years, and during the past four or five years it has been going begging among capitalists."

In 1881 the land and the subsidy had been offered to the CPR, Dunsmuir argued. In 1882 the Clements company had attempted to undertake the project on the basis of the land grant alone, but that had proved to be a "wild speculation" taken up by men who had no money of their own. "Capitalists wouldn't touch it!" Dunsmuir exclaimed. Furthermore, his plans were far superior to those which had been approved in 1882 with nary a whimper of protest. "The Clements' scheme permitted a 'cheap and nasty' road, with any class of iron rails, and such gradients, curvatures and structures as the company pleased, whereas the present contract is governed by the strictest specifications ... In a word, under the Clements scheme the cheapest and most worthless class of railway could have been built, whereas the present requires the best class of road to be built on the continent."

He ended with a veiled threat, a hint that the railway might pass Nanaimo by. "Let me say in conclusion, and in all sincerity, that any opposition to the Settlement Bill comes rather late. The opposition of Nanaimo cannot stop the railway, but it may inflict injury on herself, and that in more ways than one."

No amount of opposition would prevent him from building the line. "Having put my hands to the plow, I am not the man to turn back. I have the contract and I am going to build the roadway and telegraph, and operate them too, in spite of any opposition emanating from jealous individuals who act the part of the fabled dog in the manger; and in faithfully and vigorously carrying out the contract I have the satisfaction of knowing that I shall be acting in the true interests of the province in general, and my own constituents in particular, no matter what may be thought now by misguided individuals."

The misguided individuals who packed the meeting hall reacted to Dunsmuir's letter with "very uncomplimentary remarks." It was "an impudent, outrageous and untruthful document," Dr. Walkem roared. Joshua Martell, a miner with the Vancouver Company, got to his feet to deliver himself of the opinion that the government had become the master of the people rather than their servant. "The voice of the people is overpowered by capitalists," he declaimed. "Freedom is giving way to monopoly and fraud."

Called on by the crowd to give his views, Dr. Robert O'Brian mounted the platform to announce that the people were not being represented by men of honesty and integrity. "I do not know of so venal a legislature and one so utterly devoid of principle as the one now at Victoria," he cried.

The meeting concluded by unanimously adopting a resolution. "That inasmuch as Mr. Dunsmuir, the Senior Member for this district, has acted and still acts in direct antagonism to the interests and wishes of his constituents, that he no longer enjoys their confidence, and that he is hereby called upon to resign his seat."

—

The voters would have to wait until the summer of 1886 before they were presented with the opportunity to express their opinions about Robert Dunsmuir, his railway and the government. He claimed that he had not intended to run again. "I thought that you might consider my time was so thoroughly occupied with my own business affairs that your interests could be better entrusted to other hands than my own," he confessed. However, when he was presented with a petition signed by more than three hundred electors, he changed his mind.

"I cannot disregard the requisition you have so kindly sent me." And no wonder. If only the petitioners voted for him, he would top the polls. But while his victory was virtually assured, he was not unopposed. His most potentially effective challenger was Dr. Robert O'Brian, a Nanaimo physician who could count on the support of at least one newspaper—the *Westward Ho!*, an erratically published Nanaimo paper which the doctor owned and edited.

Westward Ho! was O'Brian's attempt to counteract the sycophancy of the *Victoria Daily Colonist*, which applauded Dunsmuir's every move. "What the *Colonist* doesn't know about dishonest journalism, isn't worth learning," he grumbled. O'Brian had proposed that the people of Nanaimo "charter a steamer, proceed en masse to Victoria and 'clean out' the Legislature a la Cromwell if they attempted to pass the Settlement Act." Now he was brought to the point of apoplexy every time he thought about the land subsidy Dunsmuir's railway had received. It was evil, O'Brian said, for one man to control so large a tract of land.

According to a provision of the Settlement Act, the railway lands were to remain open to actual settlers for a period of four years. During that time, pre-emptors could claim up to 160 acres at the rate of a dollar an acre. Once the line was completed and the land was transferred to the railway, applicants would be forced to deal directly with the company, and the company would be free to set any price it wished. Settlers who hoped to beat the four-year deadline found their applications bouncing back and forth between the federal and provincial governments. Suspicions grew that Dunsmuir was behind the delays.

"Things are coming to a fine pass if Crocker's gold can corrupt the Minister of the Interior, the Minister of Justice and the Smithe Government," would-be settlers complained.

O'Brian echoed the charge, labelling Dunsmuir "the greatest tyrant in the country." To which Dunsmuir responded by accusing O'Brian of being "an agitator, a communist, an internationalist, an anarchist, a nihilist, a monopolist," and worst of all, "no Scotchman."

The 610 voters who went to the polls on 9 July 1886 had a plethora of candidates from which to choose—Dunsmuir and William Raybould representing the government; two opposition candidates who supported former premier Robert Beaven; coal miners Jim Lewis and Sam Myers, who had won nomination as the Workingman's Candidates; and, of course, Robert O'Brian. Given that the province had instituted the secret ballot, all the men of the Nanaimo district, and in particular the miners of Wellington, had the chance to show their opposition to "old Dunsmuir" without fear of retribution. But once again, Dunsmuir topped the polls, and once again he received a clear majority, winning 366 votes. His running mate, William Raybould, took the second seat with 267 votes.

O'Brian, who had convinced himself that victory was within his grasp, found some consolation in his third-place finish. "We look upon the 200 votes given us as a distinct protest against the prevailing low tone of politics in this country," he avowed.

The most surprising result was the poor showing of Lewis and Myers. Lewis won only 78 votes; Myers only 30. Miners apparently preferred to elect a "grasping monopolist" rather than one of their own.

O'Brian thought he could account for Dunsmuir's success. It was bought and paid for. "We cannot be held responsible for the ignorance, the prejudice, and the mercenary motives of about half our population," he wrote. "In the recent election some novel transactions took place in voting."

—

O'Brian had built up quite a head of steam during the election campaign. In the days that followed, he released the pressure by launching even more vituperative attacks on Dunsmuir. "Dunsmuir is said to be in debt to Crocker and Stanford to the extent of $750,000 and to the Bank of British Columbia for $230,000," he reported. The Wellington Colliery was played out; Dunsmuir was facing bankruptcy; he had been saved from insolvency by his San Francisco partners. "Perhaps one of the good results of what has been going on for some years is that Dunsmuir himself has been brought to the verge of ruin. Crocker and Stanford fished for him with a glittering bait and, like a greedy pike, he swallowed the hook."

That was too much for Dunsmuir. He could tolerate almost anything except being called a poor businessman. He decided to sue for libel, but before launching an action, he had his son-in-law, James Harvey, go about town encouraging other men who had felt the sting of O'Brian's barbs to begin similar actions.

Faced with charges brought by eight Nanaimo businessmen, including Dunsmuir and Harvey, O'Brian cried foul. He sent a "telegraphic despatch" to the federal minister of justice. ROBERT DUNSMUIR WHOM I OPPOSED AT LATE ELECTION IS ENDEAVORING TO THRUST ME INTO JAIL ON ACCOUNT OF AN ALLEGED LIBEL. AT HIS INSTIGATION 9 OR 10 SUITS HAVE BEEN BROUGHT AGAINST ME AND BEFORE A MAGISTRATE OF HIS APPOINTING. IN THE INTERESTS OF DOZENS OF POOR PEOPLE WHO HAVE NOT THE MEANS TO DEFEND THEMSELVES FROM HIS TYRANNY, I DEMAND AN ENQUIRY INTO THIS ADMINISTRATION OF JUSTICE IN B.C.

O'Brian was wasting his time. His telegram was forwarded to British Columbia's lieutenant-governor, who sent it on to the recently re-elected members of his government's Executive Council who, one can safely presume, found good reasons for allowing it to gather dust.

———

Dunsmuir's opponents had an unexpected chance to register their disapproval six months later when William Raybould, the second member for Nanaimo, died in a freakish accident. Raybould had been in bed in the little house on Commercial Street that stood beside his wife's dress shop. Like all buildings on the water side of Commercial Street, the back of the Rayb014's shop was built on pilings and extended well over the water—a most convenient location for Raybould, who kept his boat moored directly below. Hearing a noise and thinking that someone was tampering with his boat, he heaved himself out of bed, raced to the rear of the building and tumbled off the end of the wharf. The tide was out. He fell 30 feet and was found on the beach in a spreading pool of blood.

Raybould had worked at the pit head of one of the Vancouver Company's mines for almost twenty years. Although he supported the government, he was seen as being sympathetic to miners' causes. There was a feeling that he had attracted votes that might have gone to the Workingman's candidates. The same could never be said of George Thompson, the government candidate who offered himself in the by-election necessitated by Raybould's death. After arriving in Nanaimo in 1873, Thompson had gone to work in James Harvey's store. He was an avowed supporter of the Smithe government and the railway.

"During a residence of nearly a quarter of a century in this province, we never saw so little interest taken in a Provincial Election," George Norris of the *Nanaimo Free Press* mourned, apparently missing the fiery partisanship of the *Westward Ho!*.

Of the 511 votes cast, Thompson received 335. Jim Lewis, running once again as the Workingman's Candidate, managed to win the favour of only 52 supporters. The results were "a strong verdict for the Smithe government," the *Nanaimo Free Press*, which had campaigned mightily against the Settlement Act, reluctantly concluded.

More than that, it was yet another mandate for Dunsmuir, a mandate that some found all the more remarkable because he no longer lived in the district. For the past three years he had been living in Victoria—the Vancouver Island town that was seen as reaping the most benefit from the construction of the railway.

Six

―

For a man acknowledged to be British Columbia's wealthiest citizen, Victoria was the *only* place to live. The oldest permanent settlement on Vancouver Island, Victoria had been founded by the Hudson's Bay Company in 1843 as a fur trade fort. For fifteen years, Fort Victoria had dozed on, a quiet backwater with fewer than four hundred people settled on nearby farms or living in the scattering of small houses that had appeared on the streets laid out around the fort's perimeter. But then, in 1858, the discovery of gold on the Fraser River had shaken it rudely awake.

Twenty thousand prospectors flooded through Fort Victoria during that gold-mad summer. Overnight the palisade became an impediment to progress, and down it came as entrepreneurs scrambled to build hotels, flop houses, bath houses, saloons, brothels and billiard parlours. When Victoria was incorporated as a city in 1862, it was very much an American town. Its first architects had come from San Francisco and had used San Francisco–produced bricks and boards and cast-iron to build a town that could have settled happily anywhere along California's gold rush "Trail of '49"—a hodgepodge of shacks, stables and false-fronted hotels and saloons, its narrow streets clogged by winter mud and choked by summer dust and with raw sewage running in its gutters.

In 1868, after the gold had run out and many of the city's American residents had returned home, Victoria escaped the fate of other western boom towns when it was selected as the capital of the Colony of British Columbia. Three years later, when it became the provincial capital, its future seemed secured.

By 1883 when Robert Dunsmuir moved to the city, Victoria had shaken off most of its gold rush rudeness. Two-storey brick buildings were adding an impression of permanence to its business district, and exuberantly decorated houses were turning farmers' fields into pleasant residential neighbourhoods. And the city, at least to American observers, had taken on a distinctly English air.

"The people of the town seem to live for the sake of enjoying their journey through this world instead of rushing through existence like a rocket," one San Franciscan reported. But that impression belied Victoria's importance. As well as being the capital of the province and home of the provincial legislature, it was British Columbia's largest city, the centre of trade and industry, with several breweries, a soap factory, an iron foundry and a graving dock, and with regular steamship service connecting it to Tacoma, Seattle and San Francisco. To be in Victoria was to be at the centre of things in British Columbia. That alone would have been enough to encourage Dunsmuir to take up residence in the city. But Victoria had an added appeal. It was here, in the city already becoming known for its grace and charm, that the leaders of provincial society made their homes, and while elbowing his way into their midst might have been irrelevant to Robert Dunsmuir, the same could not be said for his daughters.

Dunsmuir had decided to move to the city as early as 1881, but it was not until 1883 that a house that suited him became available. One of the most expensive residences in the city, it featured a double-height bay window and a two-storey demi-tower topped with an odd coronetlike decoration. The house, christened "Fairview," provided just that.

It stood at the corner of Quebec and Menzies streets, only a block from the shores of James Bay and immediately across the street from the legislative buildings. From the parlour windows of Fairview, Dunsmuir could look north to the wharves of the Inner Harbour where the ships of the Canadian Pacific Navigation Company disembarked passengers from Puget Sound. And then he could allow his gaze to wander up towards the Gorge, the tidal inlet that meandered more than three miles inland and provided, along its lower reaches, a protected waterfront location for industry. There he could catch sight of the smoke rising from the Albion Iron Works, which would soon be working overtime to fill orders from the E & N Railway. That he was the major shareholder in both the ironworks and the steamship company improved the view no end.

Soon after moving to Fairview, the Dunsmuirs began to entertain with a vengeance, and Victorians who counted themselves members of the city's upper classes pondered the problem of just how to deal with a family whose claim to status was based on wealth alone. Victoria's society was led by the lieutenant-governor who as the queen's representative produced the most important guest list. The Admiral of the Fleet and the officers of the Royal Navy enjoyed pride of place at any Government House function. Also included were the mixed-blood children of the fur traders who had become the city's largest landholders and were recognized as being its founding families. Forming the third layer of Victoria's upper crust were families of men who, had they remained in England or Scotland or Ireland, would have spent their lives as members of the middle class. Well schooled and often with professional training, they were the engineers, surveyors, lawyers, policemen, accountants and clerks who had been recruited in London to serve as the colony's first administrators and who became attorneys-general, magistrates, gold commissioners, chief justices and land commissioners.

Peter O'Reilly was fresh from the Irish Revenue Police when he had presented himself on Governor Douglas's doorstep in 1859. Short of qualified men to fill important official positions, Douglas had immediately appointed him as magistrate and assistant gold commissioner in the Cariboo. Within a few years of his arrival, O'Reilly further improved his position when he married Caroline Trutch, whose brother Joe would become the province's first lieutenant-governor.

Invited to attend the Dunsmuirs' first party at Fairview, Peter O'Reilly was intrigued. He had heard that it was to be "a party, a grand affair," he confided to his daughter Kathleen.

"I suppose some of us will go," his wife Caroline sniffed. Like the other members of her set, she had to admit that while the Dunsmuirs might not be worth knowing, they were now too rich to ignore. They were, quite simply, in a class by themselves. O'Reilly's net worth hovered at the $100,000 mark; Dunsmuir counted his fortune in the millions. And so, for a time, Victoria's society ladies treated the Dunsmuir girls with an odd mixture of deferential awe based on their wealth and vague contempt for their humble beginnings and their tendency to overspend and overdress.

No mixed feelings were experienced by the male members of society. Prepared to pursue potential profit with quite ungentlemanly eagerness, they were already nestled in the palm of Dunsmuir's hand. He carried with him the aura of success. If he became involved in a business, then that business was bound to succeed. Any enterprise backed by Dunsmuir capital ran little risk of failing. That notion had lured many prominent men into purchasing shares in the Albion Iron Works and the Canadian Pacific Navigation company, and that notion must have been uppermost in the minds of Senator Hugh Nelson and Victoria's mayor Robert Rithet when, during the summer of 1884, they invited Dunsmuir to attend a meeting of influential men at the Driard Hotel to discuss a matter of great civic importance.

In 1882 the Theatre Royal, an odd building cobbled together out of two old salmon warehouses, had been demolished. Since then the theatrical touring companies that ventured from London and New York to bring culture to the west coast had been unable to include Victoria on their circuits. What was needed was a new theatre, an opera house, elegant and up to date and more appropriate to the city's increasingly dignified image.

The location of the new theatre had been easy enough to determine. There was an empty lot at the corner of Douglas and View streets immediately beside the Driard, the city's best hotel. Coming up with the money to finance construction presented a thornier problem. It had been estimated the theatre might cost as much as $50,000 to build. That was where Dunsmuir came in. Nelson, Rithet and the three other men who made up the directorship of the newly formed Victoria Theatre Company proposed to raise the money by selling one hundred $500 shares. After agreeing to purchase ten shares apiece, they shifted their gaze to Dunsmuir. Would he come up with the remaining $25,000? Well, yes, he would, but not by buying the outstanding shares. Instead, he would advance the company the required amount in the form of a mortgage—with an interest rate of 7 per cent. That was not exactly what the directors had in mind, but at least it would get the theatre built; with a sigh of relief they accepted Dunsmuir's terms and elected him president of the company.

To Robert Dunsmuir went the honour of wielding the silver trowel to lay the theatre's foundation, and when "The Victoria" opened on 16 October 1885, he was the man of the hour. A thousand Victorians, dressed in their best, filled the theatre with expectant murmurings and delighted exclamations as they surveyed the gilt and lilac grandeur and the massive central chandelier, bright with fifty gas jets and heavy with encircling prisms and chains of glass beads. At precisely eight o'clock the lights dimmed, silence descended and the plush crimson curtain parted to reveal Robert Dunsmuir seated centre stage, bathed in the glow of 110 gas-fired footlights.

Dunsmuir had made a good investment. He might have considered $25,000 well spent, if only for the acclaim he received that evening. But he had done rather better than that. If the theatre company defaulted on its mortgage, he would become the proud possessor of a key piece of Victoria real estate and an 880-seat theatre with its attached hotel rooms and shops. In the meantime it would provide him with a magnificent stage on which to strut as he accepted civic honours or defied his political opponents. And it would serve as a splendid setting for Sir John A. Macdonald to greet his grateful constituents when he arrived in Victoria on his way to the ceremonies marking the completion of the Esquimalt & Nanaimo Railway.

—

Sir John A. Macdonald had not been present when the CPR's last spike was driven on 7 November 1885. Now, in the summer of 1886, he had the pleasure of riding the train all the way across Canada to Burrard Inlet. Then, he sailed for Vancouver Island, where on 13 August on a stretch of track near Shawnigan Lake, he hammered home a silver spike and declared the lonely 75 miles of track to be "an extension of the Canadian Pacific."

"Let me congratulate you, Mr. President, on the completion of this work," he beamed at Dunsmuir and then, turning to address the crowd, he continued. "Everyone must admit the pluck and energy of Mr. Dunsmuir which has brought this important work to a successful conclusion."

Sir John A. Macdonald and Robert Dunsmuir enjoyed a convivial relationship that went beyond their shared political views. In 1882 when they had first met, they found good reason to establish an instant rapport. Both men were Scots, born only ten years and fewer than a hundred miles apart. Both shared a liking for good whiskey and both were possessed of wives who disapproved of their drinking.

Once, when Robert had been about to leave for San Francisco, Joan, who knew enough of the city to be aware that its bibulous reputation was well deserved, decided to change his plans. With Robert standing conveniently close to the stove, she had "accidentally" upset the teakettle. His foot badly scalded by the well-aimed cascade of boiling water, Robert had been forced to cancel his trip and postpone the pleasures of unrestricted imbibing in the barrooms of the Merchants Exchange and the Palace Hotel.

As host to the prime minister and the bevy of dignitaries who had joined them for the first ride over the line, Dunsmuir had made sure that his private "palace" car, the *Maude,* was well-stocked with creature comforts. "The weather was warm, but as there was a plentiful supply of *ice* on board, every one managed to 'keep cool,'" one appreciative passenger reported.

After a multicourse luncheon at Nanaimo's Royal Hotel, Dunsmuir conducted the official party to Wellington, and once there, he expansively invited the entourage to descend with him to the lowest level of the colliery's deepest pit. Lady Macdonald found it easy to decline that dubious pleasure, and when the prime minister was safely subterranean, Dunsmuir produced two glasses and a bottle of Scotland's finest, and together he and Sir John toasted the completion of the railway in masculine peace.

—

The *Colonist,* an unabashed supporter of both Dunsmuir and Sir John and quite overcome by the celebrity of the occasion, launched a trial balloon. "If her Majesty were to bestow upon him the dignity of a knighthood, few would be found to begrudge this progressive man the honor."

A knighthood for Dunsmuir was a suggestion that his friends in the provincial government decided to take very seriously. In 1887 Queen Victoria would be celebrating her Golden Jubilee and she was expected to mark her fiftieth year as monarch by showering honours upon her loyal subjects. Recognizing the importance of timing, the Executive Council delayed passing a formal motion until 21 June 1887, the precise anniversary of the date Queen Victoria had ascended to the throne. Signed by the president of the council, Alex Davie, the recommendation was forwarded to the lieutenant-governor. That office was now occupied by Hugh Nelson, one of Dunsmuir's partners in the Victoria Theatre. Nelson added his imprimatur to the recommendation the same day he received it, and by 28 June the council's missive had arrived in Ottawa, accompanied by a private letter from Davie to the prime minister.

> We all should be glad that our province should in some way be recognized by Her Majesty in this the Jubilee year and can suggest no more fitting manner than bestowing knighthood on one who without doubt is the leading citizen of B.C. and well able to support the position. He has been amongst us from the earliest history of the province, is philanthropic and commands the respect of all classes. Besides taking an active part in public affairs, he is always to the fore in private enterprise.

The honor has not been sought by Mr. Dunsmuir though it is right to say he has been spoken to on the subject and will accept it.

I presume that financial standing as well as social status is taken into consideration in these matters and in this respect Mr. Dunsmuir is well qualified for he is one of Canada's millionaires.

If wealth were the only criterion for knighthood, the former Ayrshire coal miner would no doubt have become Sir Robert Dunsmuir. For despite his somewhat humble beginnings, he, more than any other British Columbian, had the wherewithal to appear as if to the manor born.

Was it the thought of an impending knighthood that encouraged him to build "Craigdarroch"? Since 1882, he had been acquiring land on a rocky hill above Victoria. Steadily, he had added to his acres until, by 1885, he was possessed of the single most spectacular residential building site in Victoria, a wonderland of wildflowers and oak glades and rocky outcrops softened with a cloak of springy green moss. A ten-minute walk from the city's business district, Dunsmuir's 28 acres offered a view that stretched for 20 miles in all directions—the city and the Sooke Hills to the west, Mount Douglas to the north, sea glimpses to the east and to the south, the Strait of Juan de Fuca and the snow-shrouded heights of the Olympics.

But to Dunsmuir the view was of only secondary importance. A house built on those acres, the highest land Victoria had to offer, would become a landmark, visible from all the city's neighbourhoods. And there can be little doubt that Dunsmuir had come to see the planned house as a monument—a sandstone palace that would dominate the city's skyline as he had come to dominate the business and political life of the province.

Having settled on an imposing site, Dunsmuir hired an architect who could be counted on to produce an extraordinary house. San Francisco-trained, Warren Williams had moved his business to Portland where he designed elegant houses for that city's business aristocracy. He was adept at producing variations on the style most favoured by newly rich clients on America's west coast—overdecorated Italianate houses with two-storey-tall double bay windows. But his new Victoria client had something different in mind.

Robert Dunsmuir was nothing if not a proud Scot. A founding member of the Caledonian Society, he never missed an opportunity to point out that Robert Burns's first book of poetry had been published in Kilmarnock, the Ayrshire city in which his wife, Joan, had been born and where he had attended school. Like other men of his generation, he cherished a particularly romantic view of his homeland. He was nostalgic not for the Scotland of sooty colliery towns but for the land that lived in the works of Sir Walter Scott, a romantic medieval paradise of stags and crags, of gothic castles and noble knights, of pageantry and chivalry.

And so Warren Williams knew what would appeal to Dunsmuir. Something medieval—a richly panelled hall with a huge stone fireplace; a touch of the gothic—a delicate spirelike tower; and certainly a house to be named "Craigdarroch" after Annie Laurie's Ayrshire home should be built of stone.

By the summer of 1887 Williams's plans were complete and work on Dunsmuir's dream castle had begun. No one outside the family would ever know just how much he spent on his monument. Estimates of its cost ranged from $185,000 to a high of $500,000. And even if the lowest guess was the closest to the truth, Craigdarroch would still rank as the most expensive residence British Columbia had ever seen. During the eighties and nineties, a workingman's frame cottage could be built for $500 and a substantial, not to say lavish, three-storey brick house was to be had for $25,000. But Craigdarroch, with its exquisitely crafted stained-glass windows, its seventeen fireplaces, its grand entrance hall adorned with mounted stags' heads, its fourth-floor ballroom and its observation tower a giddy 60 feet above the garden below, was being built for the province's richest man.

However, if Dunsmuir looked forward to the day that he would take up residence in his castle as Sir Robert Dunsmuir, he was to be sorely disappointed. It was important that when the Queen's Honours List was announced, it contained names that could be received by the public with pleasure and approval. It might have been supposed that, after the railway became a *fait accompli*, criticism of Dunsmuir would begin to wane. But instead, within days of the line's completion, his opponents found fresh fuel to stoke the fires of outraged indignation. And worse, before the jubilee year was out, Dunsmuir would be charged with treason, and his loyalty to the queen would become the subject of noisy debate.

Seven

—

In December 1887 Dunsmuir travelled to Portland, invited by Charles Crocker and his son, Fred, to celebrate the driving of the last spike of their California & Oregon Railroad. But Dunsmuir had a lot more than the railroad celebrations on his mind when he made his way south. Now that the Crockers' newest railroad was complete, they would be free to shift their interest to the E & N.

Despite Sir John A. Macdonald's assertions, it required boosterism bordering on temporary insanity to take seriously the claim that the E & N was a true extension of the CPR. Rather than seeking ways to link the mainland and Vancouver Island railways, the CPR's vice-president, Cornelius Van Horne, seemed determined to suck the commercial lifeblood from the island to transfuse the railway's mainland towns and, in particular, its new terminal city of Vancouver. The little settlement clustered around "Gassy" Jack Deighton's saloon had happily shaken off its official name of Granville and its quaint sobriquet of Gastown to adopt Van Horne's chosen designation of Vancouver. That action had brought islanders to their feet in howls of protest. Van Horne had "snatched from the Island of Vancouver the name it had attained as a shipping point"; he was determined "to wipe Victoria off the face of the map."

Dunsmuir had been quick to recognize the implications of Van Horne's choice. In 1886 when the provincial house had met to pass the city's incorporation, he had argued against the use of the name Vancouver. But by April 1887 he had become resigned to it. And while he voted against the adoption of a special charter for the city, arguing that all municipalities should be treated equally, he spoke against an amendment that would have reinstituted the name of Granville.

Unlike other Victoria businessmen, Dunsmuir would not allow himself to become jealous of Vancouver's success. "The Canadian Pacific Railway have a perfect right to build at the end of their line. It is their duty to do so, and they would be wrong if they did not. But it is our duty down here to counteract that, I think," he argued. And after hedging his bets by purchasing land in the CPR's new city, he continued to make plans to link the E & N with a more willing transcontinental rail line.

The Crockers owned 3,750 of the E & N's 15,000 shares. Unlike Van Horne, they had a vested interest in improving the island line's profit-making potential. For several years Dunsmuir had been corresponding with the Crockers, urging them to extend the Southern Pacific into Washington Territory—to Port Angeles, a town on the American side of the Strait of Juan de Fuca. If the Crockers agreed, then he would apply to the dominion government for a charter to run a fleet of huge ferries, large enough to accommodate railcars, across the 20-mile stretch of water that separated Victoria from the American mainland. Once E & N cars began to roll off those ferries and onto the Southern Pacific's track, the island railway could truly claim to be part of a transcontinental network.

"This is the way you counteract jealousy," Dunsmuir said. "You must act for yourself."

Finalizing those plans became the main topic of discussion when Dunsmuir joined the Crockers in Portland. His conviction that Vancouver Island's future prosperity lay in establishing firm economic links with the south rather than looking east to Canada was uppermost in his mind when he agreed to an interview with a reporter from the *Portland News*. "The only regret we have heard him express respecting his situation is that Vancouver Island is not part of the United States. It would be to his pecuniary advantage if that were the case, for during the first eleven months of this year he paid $210,000 in duties on his coal in San Francisco. But, apart from this private consideration, he is rightly of the opinion that it would be better for British Columbia if it belonged to the United States, since all its natural commercial interests are with this country."

Dunsmuir was not the only businessman or politician who would look longingly at a map of North America and wish that political divisions had followed geographical boundaries. But even though the established trade routes ran north and south, and even though the CPR, the government's supposed agent of national unity, had been permitted to thumb its nose at British Columbia's capital city, to fantasize about British Columbia's union with California, Oregon and Washington Territory was regarded as treachery. His remarks, gleefully repeated by opposition newspapers in Victoria and Vancouver, caused a sensation.

He returned to Victoria on Christmas Eve to find himself at the centre of a storm. Was this the sort of behaviour the people should expect from "a cabinet minister abroad," the *Victoria Times* asked its readers. "Bobbie the Boodler" had proven himself to be one of the queen's most disloyal subjects, the *Vancouver News Advertiser* opined.

For a man whose knighthood might be hanging in the balance, the charge of being disloyal to the crown could not have come at a more inopportune time, and Dunsmuir moved quickly to repair the damage. He silenced the *News Advertiser* by launching a $25,000 libel action and threatened a similar lawsuit to force the *Victoria Times* to grovel in apology. The article they had copied from the *Portland News* had done Dunsmuir a "grave injustice," the editor intoned. Dunsmuir was not arguing for an "unrestricted commercial treaty"; instead, he favoured free trade of natural resources. "It is well known these are Mr. Dunsmuir's views, and that he has often so expressed himself. He is a thorough loyalist in every respect."

—

Tom Humphreys could not have agreed less. At least he was not prepared to accept the *Times*'s explanation and, adding Dunsmuir's off-the-cuff remarks to his quiver, he prepared to take aim.

A one-time gold prospector and self-described "needy adventurer," Thomas Basil Humphreys had chosen to boost a sagging political career by becoming a fearless critic of Dunsmuir and everything he stood for. After being repudiated by the electors in various other districts, he had decided to toss his hat in the ring in the Comox by-election that December. Despite the fact that the *Colonist* branded him a "carpetbagger" and a "political castaway" and stated that he had referred to the "sturdy yeomanry" of Comox as "chaw-bacons," he had emerged triumphant. By the beginning of January he was girding his loins to do battle with Dunsmuir when the legislature resumed sitting at the end of the month.

An opportunity to take on his opponent came sooner than he had expected. On 3 January, Edward Prior resigned his seat to seek election to the federal house. Polling to choose his replacement would take place three weeks later; and Robert Dunsmuir decided to become intimately involved in the by-election campaign, apparently prepared to move heaven and earth to see that the government candidate, Simeon Duck, was elected.

With seventeen members compared to the opposition's seven, the government had no fear of losing the confidence of the House. But Dunsmuir saw the election as a personal popularity poll. If he campaigned for Duck, and Duck emerged victorious, then Dunsmuir could claim that the electorate had dismissed as ridiculous any questions about his loyalty. And, in addition, he was beginning to enjoy his role as the power behind the fledgling provincial Conservative party.

British Columbia politicians were beginning to move away from the old system of loose associations toward official alignment with one of the two national parties. Staunch Tories, such as Joe Trutch, regarded Dunsmuir as the only man likely to succeed in forging a provincial Conservative party. As Trutch wrote in a confidential letter to Macdonald: "Being the only considerable capitalist and the most extensive employer of labour in various branches of enterprise, Mr. Dunsmuir can influence political results to a greater degree than any other person in the Province. His political affinities are entirely Conservative and have always been so—in the old country and here ... Indeed I consider that Mr. Dunsmuir is the man who should take the lead in a Conservative organization in this Province ... and I am depending on his taking this position being fully assured that no one else here would be likely to exercise so much influence throughout B.C. generally."

The opposition drew the first blood of the campaign when they staged a public meeting in the dingy confines of the Philharmonic Hall. Sharing the stage were the candidate, Robert Williams; the leader of the opposition, Robert Beaven, and the member for Comox, "Windy Tom." Known as "a ready speaker, never at a loss for a word," Humphreys was suffering from a severe cold and not at his oratorical best. But nothing, he said, could stop him from condemning the government.

"The present government is the most corrupt that ever existed on the face of the earth. There is no part of Canada or Great Britain where unprincipled scoundrels have secured by corrupt means so great an amount of land," Humphreys declaimed to loud applause. "I will not go into details as to what corrupt means were used by Mr. Dunsmuir to secure fully one-third of the lands of Vancouver Island. Suffice to say that the settlement bill was the most iniquitous that ever passed in any legislature ... The venom of that man has followed me for five years in an effort to banish me and my family from the province ... I care no more for Mr. Dunsmuir than I do for a beggar . . . I will allow no millionaire or aristocrat to tread anywhere near my toes." And urging the voters to teach the "monopolist" a lesson, he resumed his chair satisfied with his performance and blissfully unmindful of the devastating counterattack that would soon be launched.

Every seat in the sumptuous Victoria Theatre was occupied on the evening of 21 January when the government held its own public meeting. Robert Dunsmuir, who had learned a thing or two about stage-managed performances, made his entrance by striding down the centre aisle and bounding onto the stage to take his place beside Simeon Duck and a clutch of government supporters.

Duck, a carriage-maker who augmented his income with the rentals he received from some of Victoria's more notorious whore houses, was given an appropriately enthusiastic response, but most people had come to hear Dunsmuir. The senior member for Nanaimo did not disappoint them. Giving the appearance of a man who was thoroughly enjoying himself and relishing every moment, Dunsmuir began by disarming the audience. "I am not very big," he said, "but I am big enough to stand a good deal of abuse anyhow." And then, after detailing his side of the railway negotiations, he gave the crowd what it had come to hear.

"Mr. Humphreys must be my target a little tonight because I was his the other night and tit for tat is fair play," he announced to the cheering crowd. Humphreys had blamed him for his electoral defeats, he reminded the audience. "Mr. Humphreys told you that I had opposed him in Comox. I told some of my friends that I had nothing to do with it. Neither did I; but what I do know is that if I had held up my little finger, Tom Humphreys would never have had his seat in the house."

He might have paused to consider that this was a rather rash admission of naked political power, but flushed by cheers, and now really hitting his stride, he continued. "Gentlemen, it was through using my name that he got into the house and I will prove it to you." And to accompanying laughter, he pulled a letter from his pocket and read it. "Please let me know if it is true what T. B. Humphreys says. Are you anxious to see him elected for the Comox district? Please answer at once."

After the gales of partisan laughter subsided into titters, Dunsmuir assumed a sober face. "Now gentlemen, I come to the most painful thing, but I have to do it in self-defence. It is to me, I think, the most painful thing I ever encountered." And having brought the members of the audience to the edges of their seats, he continued. "You will remember the other night that Tom Humphreys said, not once, but twice, that my venom had been following him for five years. He said I had been trying to drive his wife, himself and his children from the country. Remember that!" And he paused to allow his words to take effect.

"Gentlemen, that is one of the greatest falsehoods that ever came out of a man's mouth!" And again he paused to let the cheers subside.

"Gentlemen, less than two years ago he came into my office and said to me, 'I am in serious trouble and if you don't lend me $400 I shall have to go to jail.' I was sorry for him. I said, 'Tom, you can have it.'" He had written out a cheque and received Humphreys's note in return.

"And here, gentlemen, here it is!" he exclaimed, holding proof of Humphreys's indebtedness aloft.

"I said to myself, well, there is $400 gone; it is far away, like the wind that blew through my shirt, gone never to return."

"Now, gentlemen, is there any venom in that?" he demanded as the theatre rocked with applause.

Tom Humphreys had met his match. It had never occurred to him that Dunsmuir would ignore the gentlemanly code that shrank from public disclosure of private indebtedness. He scrambled to reclaim his reputation. In an "Open Letter to the Hon. R. Dunsmuir" published in the *Times*, he wrote, "Twice I have offered to repay you the note of $400 you have against me, and twice you have refused to take the money." If Dunsmuir cared to appear at the opposition meeting scheduled for 24 January, then he would receive payment in full. "You can't own me, either direct or indirect, for $400—nor $4,000,000."

Dunsmuir responded in kind, in an open letter of his own, published in the *Colonist* and addressed "To the Citizens of Victoria." If Humphreys wished to clear his debt, then he should contact Dunsmuir's solicitor who, on receiving Humphreys's cheque, had been instructed to hand $200 to St. Ann's Convent and the remainder to the Protestant Orphans' Home.

The *Colonist* was stirred to its partisan best. "Which would you believe from what you know of both men, Robert Dunsmuir or Thomas Humphreys?" the editor asked. "You see in the former an honest, truthful, sincere and unassuming man, while you know the latter to be a dishonest, untruthful, faithless and swaggering braggart."

Victorians, who perhaps appreciated that they were being treated to some of the best theatre their city had ever seen, were waiting in anticipation for the two rallies scheduled for election eve. But on the morning of 24 January, the happy anticipation with which they were contemplating the no-holds-barred battle turned to shock and horror when news of the most appalling kind reached the city from Wellington.

—

Sixty-three-year-old William Morgan was an experienced miner and an exceptionally lucky man. He had survived eight mine explosions, the first in his native Wales when he was only nine years old. On the morning of 24 January 1888 he and his Chinese helper were working on the west slope of Wellington's No. 5 pit, 150 feet below the shores of Diver Lake, when suddenly their ears were filled with a heavy reverberating buzz that grew and grew until they felt as if their heads had been pierced by a knife from ear to ear. "What's the matter?" the Chinese cried. "I think there's been an explosion," Morgan replied as the other man slapped his hands over his ears in an attempt to block the painful hum. Morgan walked to the next stall, where John Matthews was working. Yes, Matthews said, he had felt something too, but he didn't think it was serious.

Unable to shake the feeling that something was terribly wrong, Morgan decided to investigate. At the head of the incline, he found a mule standing unattended. He called out several times and, getting no response, was about to return to his stall when he heard a low moan. Following the sound, he found a Chinese crawling along the passageway. Morgan hurled himself back to his stall, pulled on his jacket and ran to Matthews's stall. "Come out as quick as God will let you!" he cried.

Above ground it was immediately obvious that there had been an explosion. A loud noise, sharp and then rumbling like the discharge of a cannon, split the air. Sooty black smoke shot up from the air shaft that ventilated No. 5 pit. And then everything became ominously quiet, the "inky blackness" of the snow around the air shaft the only sign that a catastrophe had occurred.

In Victoria, fifteen minutes later, Robert Dunsmuir received a telegram. There had been an explosion; 150 men had been working below ground; no one had yet been brought out alive. "He was very much affected by the painful news," the *Colonist* reported.

Morgan made his way to the cage that hoisted miners to the surface only to discover the lower 30 feet of the shaft blocked by debris; the cage was inoperable. Soon fifty or sixty scantily clad survivors had collected around him. And there they waited, huddled together at the bottom of the shaft where they shivered in the dark, chilled by the rush of cold winter air being directed down the shaft by the ventilating fan, while work parties struggled to unblock the shaft. Brought to the surface two hours later, Morgan collapsed in the murky slush. "Saved again," he breathed. He had survived his ninth explosion.

Dunsmuir commandeered a train and made haste for Wellington. Drenched by the heavy rain that continued to fall throughout the day and into the night, he remained at the pit mouth until five the next morning, directing rescue operations and counselling and encouraging the sobbing wives, parents and children gathered at the mine entrance.

By the next afternoon only bodies were being taken from the mine. Fifteen blanket-wrapped corpses "mangled and blackened beyond recognition" had been laid out in the railway's carpenter and blacksmith shops where relatives and friends examined the remains for the shreds of clothing that in many cases provided the only clue to a victim's identity. Meanwhile, rescuers pressing farther into the mine were being faced with truly terrible scenes.

A Chinese was found, stripped of all his clothing and with the soles of his boots blown off. John McNeill, the father of six children, was found dead, standing on his head where he had been thrown against the timbers of his stall. Nearby, they came across the body of Elisha Davis. "His leg was torn out of its socket and blown forty yards from where, at last, his mangled trunk was discovered. A portion of his head was blown off, and his body was crushed into a shapeless mass." By now the rescue party had come to an inescapable conclusion—no one working on the east slope had survived. Seventy-seven men had died in a mine believed to be the safest and best-ventilated on the island.

—

In Victoria, the government supporters, shaken by the tragedy, aware of its political implications and deprived of the services of their chief spokesman, chose to cancel their election-eve rally. The opposition party decided to go ahead, and after offering his sympathies to the new widows and orphans of Wellington, the meeting's chairman asked if the deaths might have been prevented if amendments to the Mines Regulation Act, introduced by William Raybould, had not been defeated by Dunsmuir and his supporters. "Is there proper inspection of the mines?" he asked. "Is the govern-

Robert Dunsmuir spent almost thirty years working in other men's mines before he discovered the Wellington Seam. When he died in 1889, he was British Columbia's wealthiest man.

PRIVATE COLLECTION

An indomitable woman, regarded as the backbone of the family, Robert's wife, Joan, was the only real business partner he ever had.

B.C. ARCHIVES AND RECORDS SERVICE/
HP2698

As his fortunes grew, Dunsmuir's accommodations improved. The mine manager's house at Wellington, while modest compared with other Dunsmuir residences, was a mansion beside the miners' cottages.

With its imposing fence, manicured grounds and well-kept stables, Fairview, Robert Dunsmuir's first Victoria home, was one of the finest in the city.

Robert Dunsmuir died a year before Craigdarroch, designed as a monument to his success, was completed. Today it is open to the public and attracts over 100,000 visitors annually.

*When the first E & N train pulled into Victoria, Robert
Dunsmuir was the man of the hour. The attitude of
most Victorians is typified by the banner on the station
house—"Dunsmuir and More of 'Em."*

The oldest Dunsmuir daughter, Elizabeth, married Scottish-born John Bryden, a man who shared her father's background in mining.

Of the eight Dunsmuir sons-in-law, John Bryden was the only one Robert Dunsmuir trusted with a job.

Agnes married coalminer turned shopkeeper James Harvey before her father became a wealthy man.

B.C. ARCHIVES AND RECORDS SERVICE/
HP44983

Devilishly handsome and well liked in Nanaimo, James Harvey was regarded as a man of little consequence by his Dunsmuir relations.

B.C. ARCHIVES AND RECORDS SERVICE/
HP44988

When Marion became engaged to Charles Houghton, she may not have known that he had left a wife and two children on his Okanagan ranch.

During the 1877 strike, Lieut.-Col. Charles Frederick Houghton led the militia into Wellington. Two years later he married Dunsmuir's third daughter, Marion.

While capable of appearing sweet and demure, Mary had an imperious nature. To her nieces and nephews, she was known as "Aunt Mary God Almighty."

B.C. ARCHIVES AND RECORDS SERVICE/ 63651

A quiet and gentle man, Harry Croft struggled mightily to prove himself worthy of his wife, Mary, and the Dunsmuir family. He died without even a dollar he could call his own.

B.C. ARCHIVES AND RECORDS SERVICE/ 5349

Jessie's spectacularly excessive 1891 wedding to Sir Richard Musgrave was the social event of the year. Her new-found status improve her sisters' chances of landing aristocrats.

Dunsmuir weddings set standards few Victoria women could hope to emulate. When Emily married Northing Pinckney Snowden in 1886, her dress of embroidered satin and imported lace was the height of fashion. B.C. ARCHIVES AND RECORDS SERVICE/HP77982

In 1898, when Maude became the bride of Reggie Chaplin, a polo-playing young officer in the 10th Hussars, her wistful beauty and the easy grace with which she wore her jewel-encrusted gown set a new standard of elegance.

B.C. ARCHIVES AND RECORDS SERVICE
HP63652

Effie became the second Dunsmuir daughter to win a place in Debrett's Peerage *when she married Somerset Arthur Gough-Calthorpe in 1901. A fragile beauty, she spent much of her long life in an insane asylum.*

CRAIGDARROCH CASTLE COLLECTION

While the Dunsmuir brothers, James and Alexander, laboured to increase the family fortune, their sisters lived in luxury. Ashnola, Emily's imposing waterfront home, cost $25,000 when it was built in 1891.

Mary's home, Mount Adelaide, was built on 16 waterfront acres in Esquimalt and was deemed one of the handsomest in the city. Few Victorians knew that Joan Dunsmuir held the title to it.

Sent to California to run the San Francisco sales office, Alex spent twenty years trying to keep his mistress, Josephine Wallace, a secret from his family.

CRAIGDARROCH CASTLE COLLECTION

Josephine's daughter, popular New York actress Edna Wallace Hopper, expected to inherit a fortune. When she discovered that was not the case, she took James Dunsmuir to court.

PRIVATE COLLECTION

San Leandro, built by Alexander for Josephine, is now called "Dunsmuir House" and is open to the public. It has served as a location for several films, including a Bette Davis horror flick and a James Bond thriller.

PRIVATE COLLECTION

The Dunsmuirs' steamer Thistle, *where Alex spent his last sober hours. When the* Thistle *burned to the waterline in 1907, James Dunsmuir replaced it with a much grander yacht.*

ment doing its duty?" Robert Beaven, too, brought up the subject of Raybould's bill. "If the bill would have protected the life of one human being, even if it were the life of a Chinaman or an Indian, it was the duty of the legislature to pass the measure."

Given the overheated political atmosphere, the criticism seemed as mild as it was valid. But not to the *Colonist*, which accused Beaven of making political hay and which chose to see Dunsmuir as one of the disaster's principal victims.

> Sympathy for Mr. Dunsmuir was very general, since it was felt that his sensitive heart would feel keenly the untimely cutting off of so many of his employees.
>
> After pitying the anguish of the bereaved widows and orphans, and picturing in the imagination the homes from which the dear ones have gone forever, after feeling heartfelt emotions of pain and grieving for them and theirs, one's thoughts next turned to the honored owner of the colliery, who hastened by special train the moment the news reached him to do his sad duty at the appalling scene. Can you believe, humane hearted reader, can you realize right feeling men and women, that advantage was taken by Mr. Beaven last night of the explosion to use it for political purposes?

On 25 January the humane-hearted, right-feeling voters of Victoria went to the polls to elect Simeon Duck.

But could responsibility for the accident be laid at Dunsmuir's doorstep? Was he a "greedy capitalist" who put profits before safety? Or was he a fair-minded employer who recognized that safety and profits went hand in hand?

There was a certain logic behind the opinion of the man who identified himself as a coal miner and who pointed out that accidents actually cost the colliery money. "I have worked for Dunsmuir off and on for more than seven years and I know my friends will back me up when I say that there never was a man who *tries* harder to keep the pits in a safe condition as the 'old man.' Money is never wanting for any such purpose, and he is always willing to listen to anything a man working in the pit may suggest. Is it likely he would begrudge a few dollars a day if by spending them he could save having an explosion?" Every explosion cost the mine from $10,000 to $50,000, he argued, and besides, "All who know him at all know him to be one of the tenderest hearted men alive when there is any affliction."

But why then had Dunsmuir voted against amendments to the

Mines Regulation Act introduced by William Raybould? Hardly a radical measure, Raybould's bill would have required firemen to hold certificates of competency and inspection of the mines every month rather than every three months. But Dunsmuir had regarded Raybould's bill as unnecessary interference. He objected to any legislation that forced him to do what he was prepared to do willingly.

The provincial inspector of mines often found much to praise about the safety standards in Dunsmuir's mines, but no matter how much care Dunsmuir and his managers took, accidents continued. In 1884 the inspector had visited Wellington's No. 3 pit and declared, "I never saw a mine in better order, and it did not appear in want of anything that was necessary." But a few weeks later, an explosion had taken twenty-three lives. The coroner's inquest that followed the disaster absolved Dunsmuir of blame. When miner John Frear had reported for work that morning, the fireman had handed him a safety lamp and told him that he had discovered an accumulation of gas near his stall. But Frear had ignored the warning. He had marched into his stall with a naked flame and blown himself and twenty-two others to kingdom come.

Dunsmuir's was not the only colliery in which men died. In 1887 an explosion in the Vancouver Company's mine had taken 148 lives. Struggling to explain the calamities, the mines inspector, Archibald Dick, concluded that the fault lay with the miners rather than the managers.

In 1888 the coroner's inquest investigating the cause of the explosion in Wellington's No. 5 pit reached a similar conclusion. Archibald Dick reported that "nothing seemed lacking" in the way of safety measures. Robert Dunsmuir had asked the miners to appoint a committee to conduct independent safety inspections, and a few days before the accident they had visited every section of No. 5 pit and pronounced it to be in excellent order. After hearing from miners and managers, and after sifting all the evidence, the coroner's jury concluded that Launcelot Robson had used too much powder in the charge he had used to blast the coal from the face and had accidentally ignited additional powder stored in cans in his stall.

But it seemed unsatisfactory, in the face of so many deaths, to blame careless miners. At miners' meetings held throughout the district, men debated amongst themselves the possibility that coal dust itself might have explosive properties, but no one could cite an expert who was prepared to state that such was the case. They complained about the competency of the firemen, but no one could show that a fireman's negligence ever had caused an explosion. In the end, with no obvious culprit in view, they decided to blame the Chinese and to accuse Dunsmuir of jeopardizing their safety by employing them in his mines.

As John Hough put it, "I am an old miner, and not afraid of dust at all, but I am afraid of Chinese far more than anything else in a mine."

With that point of view, other miners readily concurred. "We have three great dangers in the mine we know of—they are gas, dust and Chinese. The company promise all they can to keep away the gas; they will adopt means to keep the dust watered well. Now will they, for fear of a few dollars, refuse to keep out the Chinese?"

—

The first Chinese had arrived on the coast in 1858, lured north from San Francisco by the promise of gold. They had panned along the Fraser's bars, worked their way to Barkerville, the gold rush town in the northern interior, and then, when the gold ran out, they had trickled back to Victoria. They established a Chinatown on the northern edge of the city and made themselves useful by opening groceries and laundries and by hiring themselves out as domestics, serving as cooks and gardeners and houseboys to the city's elite. A few drifted north to Nanaimo where they were employed by the Vancouver Company to load coal at the pit mouth and the wharves. Characterized by the press as "Celestials" or "Johns" and often made objects of fun, they were regarded by their employers as childlike but trainable and hard-working. So long as their numbers were small and the demand for labourers was high, they were not regarded as a threat by their fellow workingmen. By 1871 thirty-six Chinese were working in the mines, and the *Colonist* was able to report, "their presence, though naturally distasteful to the white miners, has not caused any ill-feeling."

Dunsmuir had no reservations about employing Chinese, and by 1877 ninety men were making their home in Wellington's Chinatown. But as the Chinese population steadily grew, so too did demands for Oriental exclusion. The Workingman's Protective Association, formed in Victoria in 1878, had as its objectives "the mutual protection of the working classes of British Columbia against the influx of Chinese, and the use of legitimate means for the suppression of immigration."

By 1884 Dunsmuir had become the largest employer of Chinese labour in the province, with Chinese crews laying tracks for the E & N and with seven hundred working as miners at Wellington.

Publicly he claimed that he did not like to employ Chinese, that he only did so out of economic necessity. Amend the Mines Regulation Act, he said. Allow him to employ boys as young as fourteen who would accept the same low wages he now paid the Chinese; then he could afford to operate without them. Privately, he admitted that he found them excellent workers—peaceable, industrious, temperate and frugal, and particularly desirable because they expected only half the pay of white miners and labourers.

Those same qualities made them equally appealing to the miners. A miner's semi-independent status allowed him freedom to hire assistants to load his coal into carts and haul it to the pit mouth, and by the 1880s many white miners found it to their advantage to employ Chinese helpers. It soon occurred to some men that they could train their Chinese assistants and then leave them to do most of the work. As Dunsmuir pointed out, half the men at Wellington could not make a living without a Chinese helper. "One miner went on holidays and left his Chinaman to do the mining and still managed to clear almost three dollars a day."

But after every accident or explosion, the grumbling grew. Miners claimed the Chinese could not read warning signs and did not understand instructions; working underground, they represented an ever-present danger.

Of the seventy-seven men who met their deaths on 24 January 1888, forty-six had been Chinese. None of the evidence submitted at the inquest so much as hinted that any one of them had been responsible for the explosion. But that did not trouble the Knights of Labor.

A secret society patterned after the Masons and given to elaborate rituals and "mysteries," the Noble and Holy Order of the Knights of Labor had been founded in Philadelphia in 1869. The Knights had soon begun to think in terms of establishing one big union, "a union of all trades and callings," a labour monopoly to counteract the power of business monopolies. By 1885 their membership had risen to over 100,000, and they had begun to recruit members in Canada.

Among the Knights' stated objectives was the setting aside of all public lands for genuine settlers. "Not another acre for railroads or speculators," they cried. With that goal, more than a few men in Nanaimo and Wellington found they could agree. The first assembly of the Knights was held in Nanaimo in December 1883. A few months later a Wellington branch, boasting forty-one charter members, was formed.

Philosophically opposed to Dunsmuir because of the land grants his railway had received, the Knights had made their presence felt in 1886 when they threw their support behind the Workingman's Party, nominating one of their members, Sam Myers, in an unsuccessful attempt to defeat Dunsmuir in the provincial election.

Confounded by the stubborn independence of many of their fellow miners, the Knights chose to rally support by arguing that Dunsmuir was endangering their lives by employing cheap Chinese labour. "If Dunsmuir had to work for four dollars a day, would he have his millions now? Not he! And yet he would run men down to death to make a few more dollars."

It was an undeniable fact that miners too benefited from the willingness of Chinese to work for less. But as the cause of calamity, the Chinese would have to do. In an unusual demonstration of solidarity for which the Knights could take full credit, men from Wellington and Nanaimo voted to refuse to work until the managers agreed to banish Chinese from the mines. And as Victorians began to shiver through a coal famine, and ships, their holds empty and their San Francisco customers becoming impatient, began to crowd the wharves at Nanaimo and Departure Bay, both Dunsmuir and the Vancouver Company gave in, promising to remove Chinese from underground employment and agreeing to phase them out altogether as replacement labour became available.

Mine safety, Chinese exclusion and the growing influence of workers' associations like the Knights of Labor were problems with which Dunsmuir would grapple for the rest of his life, and they were problems his sons would inherit after his death. But, as important as those issues might be, they temporarily paled into insignificance when he learned of the surprise Tom Humphreys had been preparing for him.

—

The lieutenant-governor had just finished reading the Speech from the Throne outlining the government's legislative agenda, when Tom Humphreys rose from his seat to file a Notice of Motion charging Dunsmuir with treason. The preamble to his motion was damning enough.

Whereas the Hon. Robert Dunsmuir, President of the Executive
Council and member of the Legislative Assembly, commonly called
Robert Dunsmuir, owner of coal mines, steamships, and President of
the Esquimalt and Nanaimo Railway Company, did at divers times
and places, in the presence of credible witnesses, who are prepared to

aver on oath that the said Robert Dunsmuir did openly express his desire to annex Vancouver Island to the United States of America. And further, that the said Robert Dunsmuir did utter his determination to exert his power and influence to promote such annexation; and the said Robert Dunsmuir did allege that such annexation would make him the richest man on the Pacific Coast, and that he would save the American customs duty on his coal by the operation.

But Humphreys went farther. Reading the "offensive article" in the *Portland News* into the record, Humphreys alleged that Dunsmuir was determined to use his power and influence to bring about annexation. His "open and advised" enthusiasm for an American union was "disloyal to the Queen" and "a violation of allegiance and oath of office."

Few members of the legislature, least of all Robert Dunsmuir, took Humphreys seriously, and Humphreys himself knew that his motion stood no chance of winning the approval of a House so firmly in the grip of the large government majority. As he cast his gaze to the government side of the legislature, he saw men whose support of Dunsmuir was based on more than political like-mindedness. The speaker of the house, lawyer Charles Pooley, had represented R. Dunsmuir & Sons at the Wellington inquest; the attorney general, Theodore Davie, was acting for Dunsmuir in his action against the *News Advertiser*; the premier, John Robson, was father-in-law to Joseph Hunter, who had surveyed the route of the E & N and was now its chief engineer; the member for Chemainus was Henry Croft, the husband of Dunsmuir's fourth daughter, Mary. But Humphreys knew that while his motion might not be approved, the fact that it had been introduced and debated would sting the man he saw as his principal opponent.

Humphreys may have been rather rash in claiming to have credible witnesses to Dunsmuir's disloyal statements. On 10 February, when the debate on the Speech from the Throne concluded and the time came to bring his motion forward, he demurred. Premier John Robson was not amused. "There is a charge of high treason against one of the members of the government and I do not intend to allow such an accusation to hang over the head of one of its members." And to loud applause, Dunsmuir rose to state that if Humphreys had made the charges outside the House he would have been jailed. "I would place him where I saved him from two years ago."

After stalling as long as his pride and the Speaker of the House would allow, Humphreys introduced his motion on 20 February. It included two resolutions. The first requested the governor general to appoint a royal commission of inquiry to investigate the remarks attributed to Dunsmuir; the second called upon the lieutenant-governor to remove Dunsmuir from his position in the cabinet until such an inquiry was concluded.

Much as they might have wanted to, the members of the government realized that to defeat Humphreys's motion would be politically inexpedient. Such an action would be branded a triumph of party over principle, and the question of Dunsmuir's loyalty would remain unanswered. And so they decided on a face-saving compromise. Instead of a federal royal commission, they voted in favour of appointing a Select Committee of the Legislature to call witnesses and examine Humphreys's evidence.

Dunsmuir would pay witnesses to stay away, Humphreys stormed. To which Dunsmuir replied, "I'd be more likely to pay them to come." With opposition members refusing to serve on the committee and Humphreys refusing to appear before it, the select committee conducted but one session at which Dunsmuir appeared as the sole witness to state that the charges were untrue and that he was in a position to prove it. Not too surprisingly, the committee's report cleared Dunsmuir's name. But the damage had been done.

Newspapers outside the province had been fascinated by the spectacle of a cabinet minister charged with treason. The *Toronto Globe* gleefully repeated Humphreys's charges. The *St James Gazette*, a leading London journal, described Dunsmuir as a minister of the queen who was "Looking-to-Washington." And the *Ottawa Free Press*, in an article headlined "Disloyal Dunsmuir," reported, quite incorrectly, that Humphreys's motion had been defeated by only one vote.

Perhaps without realizing it, Humphreys had driven a last spike of his own. He had finally nailed shut any further discussion about a knighthood for Robert Dunsmuir.

Eight

THROUGH TO VICTORIA! The *Colonist* trumpeted the news.
Thursday, 29 March 1888—a red-letter day in Victoria. The peak of
Robert Dunsmuir's career and perhaps the single most satisfying day
of his life. The long-promised railroad had arrived at last.

For seventeen years Victoria had waited for the railroad and now
that it had finally arrived, it was not the promised extension of the
CPR. It was better! And for that they could thank one man—Robert
Dunsmuir. He had agreed to extend the tracks of the E & N from
Esquimalt to Victoria. He had announced his intention of establishing a link with the Southern Pacific. He was already working on the
extension of the line to his new mines at Comox. And after Comox,
what then? The northernmost tip of the island and a ferry link to
Alaska?

Quite giddy at the prospect of Vancouver Island becoming the
bridge between Alaska and Washington Territory and envisioning
their city as the real terminus of a great transcontinental system,
Victorians in their thousands turned out to celebrate.

"Never before in the history of Victoria was such a crowd gathered in so small a compass," a reporter for the *Times* exclaimed as
he surveyed the throng collected around the Store Street depot.
"Every available space is literally alive with people." They lined the
railway bridge, packed the platform, perched on the roof of the station house, clung to the top of the fence surrounding the station yard
and crowded around the bleachers where five hundred school children waited for the signal to jump to their feet to sing "God Save
the Queen."

Everywhere there were banners: "Victoria-New York" and "Wel-

92

come Dunsmuir" and "The Right Man in the Right Place" and "Dunsmuir, and more of 'em." Flags, bunting, and red, white and blue streamers fluttered brightly in the breeze, and every eye turned to the west as a distant rumble and a faraway whistle announced the train's approach.

As Robert Dunsmuir, with his son Alexander by his side, stepped onto the platform, the band struck up "See the Conquering Hero Comes," and amid deafening cheers the mayor came forward to welcome him to Victoria and to conduct him to a waiting carriage for a parade through the city. Just as the procession was about to start, the men of the Albion Iron Works—one hundred strong and "a better looking body of men than have ever been seen on the streets of Victoria"—unhitched the horses from Dunsmuir's carriage and took their places to drag him through the streets. Led by a military band, they marched through town, past buildings bedecked with flags and below banners reading "Success to R. Dunsmuir, Victoria's best friend" and "Long looked for, Come at last." Hanging from the New England bakery was a banner that seemed to sum up the warm feelings of the day—"In honor of the Grand Old Man."

Later that evening the grand old man was the guest of honour at a civic banquet held in the plush surrounds of the Driard Hotel. One hundred and twenty-five men, the movers and shakers of British Columbia society, gathered to drink his health and toast his success. His friend, Lieutenant-Governor Hugh Nelson, came closest to expressing the feelings that animated the evening when he said, "This gentleman, like many of us, came to this country a comparatively poor man. By industry and indomitable perseverance, he has risen to the first place in the country in honor and wealth ... I see many around this festive board who I consider to be budding millionaires who no doubt will imitate the example of their townsman in developing the revenues of the country."

It had been Dunsmuir's day. Now it was his night, and as he rose to speak, he was aware that never again was he likely to have a better opportunity to express his personal philosophy.

"I witnessed a sight today I will never forget," he began when the rounds of applause subsided. "To-night I am amongst friends, many of whom have taken a warm interest in this demonstration." And to his friends he explained that he had seen the construction of the railway as a duty. "I had decided to make British Columbia my home, and having made a considerable amount of money on Vancouver Island, I thought if I could do British Columbia, my adopted home any good it was my duty to do so. I was possessed of a certain feeling of pride in this, a strong desire and ambition to go ahead. This, as you possibly may know, is my nature."

And while he was on the topic of capitalist sainthood, he said a few things about labour. "It is a great pity there is so much 'striking' in the world ... all over the world there is so much strife between capital and labor. Now, if there were no capital, there would be no wages. I think no individuals in our community should rejoice more in the abundance of capital in our province than workingmen." He was interrupted by applause from the budding millionaires. "Workingmen should not regard capitalists as their enemies. Workingmen should take the view that it is the miser, he who hoards his gold in an old stocking, those who do not display energy, pluck and enterprise to invest their capital—those are the men who should be despised by the workingmen.

"In this country, with the wages paid, the workingman by denying himself of what he would otherwise spend, can become a capitalist himself, the same as I did. But if he goes on spending everything he makes, he never shall become a capitalist."

And he drew a deep breath before delivering his definitive statement. "A capitalist is a man who lives on *less* than he earns."

No one could have said it better. He was a self-made man. He had become rich by following the course he was now recommending. For more than twenty years he had worked for other men; his family had lived humbly while he had set aside his earnings; and then, when the opportunity came, he had risked his savings, gone into debt and triumphed. With pluck and perseverance, anyone could make a fortune; investing one's money was a noble preoccupation; his employees should be grateful.

—

He was not a mean-spirited or grasping man. In fact some found him to be genial, kind-hearted and generous. But he had no sense of proportion. When he made the proud boast, "A capitalist is a man who lives on less than he earns," he did not stop to think that even as he spoke there was rising on his hill above the city a house that was a symbol of uncounted wealth, of profit and power rather than perseverance and pluck. Craigdarroch would take three years to build. According to the most modest estimate, the cost of his sandstone palace was around $185,000, while his Wellington Colliery was paying its miners from $3.50 to $4.50 a day.

The glow of the evening had hardly begun to fade when on 4 April the *Times* responded with a nasty piece of doggerel, meant to be sung to the tune of "God Save the Queen," which the editor suggested might do well for a new provincial anthem and which contained the interesting opinion that Dunsmuir was destined to spend eternity in some place other than heaven.

I am King Grab, you see
I own this country
I am King Grab
Now my bridge is complete
Mayor, Councilors en fete
Come, grovel at my feet
I am King Grab

Hirelings! Come sing my praise!
Bulldoze Tom Humphreys
And crush him down
He's practiced honesty
Hence comes his poverty
Just the reverse with me
I wear a crown

And when I come to die
You need not wail or cry
Yourselves console
Know that I am to be
Throughout eternity
Where there's no scarcity
Or want of coal

"The *Times* is fast rivalling its ideal, the *Police Gazette*," the *Colonist* fumed. But if the *Times*'s near-hysterical attacks were irresponsible, so too was the swooning sycophancy with which the *Colonist* approached the "noble old man."

Unabashed supporters of their own particular cliques or parties, British Columbia's newspapers fought elections all year long, whipping themselves into a frenzy of bombast and hyperbole during the short campaigns. No publisher or editor saw his role as a true defender of the public good; investigative journalism did not exist. A notion persists that the press was inhibited by the alacrity with which Dunsmuir began libel actions. And it was true enough that he had the money to hire the best legal talent available and that the editors of the *Nanaimo Free Press*, *Westward Ho!*, the *Vancouver*

News Advertiser and the *Victoria Times* were each called upon to defend actions he had launched. But as Sir Matthew Baillie Begbie took care to point out when, as Judge of the Supreme Court, he heard evidence in such a case, the truth was the first line of defence against libel. All too often, however, when called upon to defend themselves, the newspapers were forced to admit that statements they had printed as fact were based on rumour rather than research and on appearances rather than reality.

On 19 October 1888 the *Victoria Times* printed an article that claimed Dunsmuir, and the government he controlled, were deliberately holding back the settlement of the lands in the vicinity of the mines he had opened at Comox. He was charging $3 an acre for the land, the *Times* said, and the government was refusing to extend public roads to the area. "Yet it is worthy of note that Mr. Dunsmuir has roads made to his mines, his stores and his railway stations—for is he not President of the Council and carries the government in his breeches pocket?"

For Dunsmuir that was the final straw. "Taking the public money for my private use! I would deserve to be hanged if I did," he exclaimed, and he went straight to his lawyer, the sitting attorney-general, to insist that he begin a legal action. "I instructed him to go right ahead," Dunsmuir said. "They had been at me for building a house and for many other things and I was ready for it."

The *Times* reacted by labelling the action "persecution rather than prosecution," but as the evidence unfolded it became clear just who was persecuting whom. Yes, Dunsmuir admitted, he had charged as much as $3 an acre, but only to speculators, men who lived in India or China and who had no intention of improving the land. For *bona fide* settlers the amount remained at a dollar an acre. He vehemently denied that he had benefited from the construction of public roads. Some roads, built on his own land, at his own expense, had later been taken over by the government; he had neither asked for nor received compensation for the monies expended or for the public right-of-way through his land.

William Templeman, editor of the *Times*, chose not to plead justification. As Judge Begbie put it to the jury, "The defendant, after the offensive nature of the passages is pointed out, makes no attempt to explain them." The jury took only twenty minutes to find the *Times* guilty of publishing a libel and awarded the plaintiff damages of $500.

In his opening statements on Dunsmuir's behalf, Theodore Davie had warned the jury that the *Times*'s article could produce dangerous results. "You are intelligent men, and know what credit to give to such an article, but there are many ignorant people in the place who do not. On common men the effect of such an article is to inflame the worst of passions in their minds, for they, seeing an article of this kind in the paper and hearing of a monopolist of this kind who is grinding down the working man, say at once, 'this is a monster who ought to be put down.'"

It might have sounded like lawyerly rhetoric, but Davie knew whereof he spoke. Just three months earlier his friend and client had begun receiving death threats.

The first letter had arrived on 3 August. Signed only with an ink-drawn black hand, it was written in a foreign language. "I looked at a Spanish dictionary," Dunsmuir said, "and made out that I was about to be killed."

"You have to die, by order of the Black Hand," the letter read. When he showed it to Davie, the attorney-general advised him to contact the police. But while he took the letter to the local police, he placed his faith in an outside agency—Mahoney's Detective Agency of San Francisco, to be precise.

Two days later a second letter arrived. Again it was signed with a black hand, but this time it was written in what appeared to be classical Greek. Dunsmuir regarded his correspondent as a harmless, if irritating, crank. He was prepared to shrug the matter off while his detectives searched for his harasser. But then, on 10 August a third letter arrived, and this one he decided to take more seriously—it contained the date of his death. Again it was written in Greek, but its message was clear, even in awkward translation. "On the 28th September we are going to kill you. It makes no difference if you have detectives. They are fools and cannot do anything. Prepare yourself. The time comes near when you will be no more."

So few Victorians were familiar with Greek that Black Hand's decision to use the language narrowed down the list of suspects, and soon Mahoney's men had a likely candidate in their sights. Dr. Gustavus Hamilton Griffin had arrived in town a few months earlier and had succeeded in attracting attention to himself almost immediately. Always dressed in black and with his glossy silk hat set squarely on his head, he had an aristocratic bearing and an appearance rendered all the more striking by his habit of waxing his narrow black moustache until it "stuck out like needles." He seemed well educated, and no one doubted him when he said that he was a graduate of an English university and that he had learned Italian in Rome, French in Paris and Greek in Athens.

Claiming that he was representing American business interests, he acquired the rights to several thousand acres of coal lands. No sooner had he bonded the land than he offered it to Dunsmuir, a coals to Newcastle proposition if ever there was one. "I have plenty of coal lands," Dunsmuir said, impatient with being bothered with so ludicrous a proposal. Smarting from being so perfunctorily dismissed, Griffin was reported to have said, "Dunsmuir is a dangerous man. A son-of-a-bitch."

On 1 September, Dunsmuir received a fourth letter. "Remember the 28th of this month. We have not forgotten anything. The time comes and is approaching very rapidly. Remember while reading the above, twenty-eight!"

The detectives kept Griffin under surveillance, but he did nothing to give himself away. However, he had not counted on Ben Atherton. Atherton had worked as his assistant in Los Angeles when he was running the California Land Bureau. When Griffin was charged with embezzlement, Atherton had posted his bail. Griffin had promptly decamped to Victoria, and Atherton had tracked him to the city in hopes of collecting the money he had lost. He was only too happy to sing like a bird when he was approached by Dunsmuir's detectives. He dredged his memory for any inflammatory statements Griffin might have made, and he readily agreed to break into Griffin's office to obtain samples of his handwriting, which several experts later testified was a match for Black Hand's.

Convicted of sending threatening letters, Griffin was sentenced to five years in jail. Some claimed that he had been railroaded by Dunsmuir's American detectives, that Atherton's testimony had been bought and paid for. But those charges seemed to stem from the notion that, for a man with Dunsmuir's wealth and power, anything was possible. As for Griffin, his subsequent behaviour suggests that the jury had been right. After serving out his sentence, he removed to Pittsburgh where he "figured in a giant swindling operation," and after doing time in an American jail, he turned up in England, where in 1908 he once again ran afoul of the law, and again for a gigantic swindle.

Nine

—

When the Queen's Honours List was announced on New Year's Day in 1889, it contained the name of only one British Columbian—Joseph Trutch.

"My dear Sir Joseph," Dunsmuir wrote. "I am glad that I now have the pleasure of addressing you as above, no one could be more gratified than I am at the Honor the Queen has been pleased to confer on you at last, and I trust that you may live many years to enjoy your well earned promotion."

Dunsmuir had delayed sending his congratulations until 22 February. "I know that I deserve a blowing up for being so dilatory in writing," he confessed, "it is not for the want of the heart to do so but pure laziness combined with quite a lot of business to think over ... it seems the older I get the more I have to do."

On 2 January, he had received a telegram from Wellington. The miners wanted an increase of 10 cents a ton; unless he came to Wellington before 7 January, they would go out on strike. Dunsmuir responded by shutting down the mines and sending a telegram of his own. "If you have a grievance to state, you will find me at my office in Victoria."

Wage rates, he maintained, had nothing to do with the dispute. "I believe that it is the not unusual result of a large body of well-intentioned men being misled by the influence of a handful of professional agitators, who want to take management of the mines out of my hands."

Dunsmuir knew whereof he spoke. As the deputation of miners who waited on him at his office on 9 January soon discovered, not a word was spoken at miners' meetings that did not reach his ears. To the four men who settled themselves uneasily into his comfortable office, he made his position clear. He was ready to meet with the men at any time to discuss any complaints or problems, but he would have no truck with standing grievance committees. Management was his business, his alone.

He was particularly piqued to learn that the miners at Wellington had dispatched two of their fellows to Comox to investigate claims that he had broken his promise and was employing Chinese at the newly opened Union Mine. "What difference is it to you?" he demanded. "It does not matter to you if I employ Hottentots up there as long as I do not send them down to *your* mines. I cannot see that you have anything to do with what I do 70 miles from you . . . you have no business to interfere with anything there."

He said he felt sorry for the old men, the practical miners who had been long-time employees. They had been swayed by agitators, by outsiders whom Dunsmuir regarded as the roving bandits of the labour movement. "You know that you are not all brothers and cousins up there. Sometimes a man has to lie down with a very different bedfellow. You know that very well."

When he closed down the mine, he had had the interests of the old men at heart, Dunsmuir said. He was determined to do away with strikes once and for all. "I have had two strikes and I will have no more."

"I suppose you do not know the reason I shut down the works," Dunsmuir demanded of Arthur Spencer, who was acting as the principal spokesman.

"Well, I have a pretty good idea," Spencer replied.

"I think that your idea is wider of the mark than you may think," Dunsmuir retorted. He reminded Spencer that he had sworn never to allow any striking miner back into the mines. If the men had walked off the job, he would have been forced to stand by that vow. "I have said so, and must keep my word . . . but I have some good men up there—as good men as ever went down a mine. I said to myself, 'If I allow those men to strike I never can take them back again' . . . I did not want it to be said that I had banished little children and women in the cold winter days without giving those who support them a chance, and so I shut down the workings for that reason and nothing else."

Not quite prepared to thank their boss for locking them out, the miners' delegation recognized that they had met an immovable object. But it may not have occurred to them that they had also fallen under the thrall of a skilled negotiator. He disarmed them by listening carefully to their grievances and then demonstrating that their complaints were either petty or easily solved. When told that the men had complained that the runners who moved the coal carts around the mine sometimes played favourites and passed them by, Dunsmuir easily defused the issue. "It may be that they do not speak to the runners fairly?" he asked. "If I were you I would speak to the runners fairly, and offer them a cigar now and then." And in spite of themselves, the miners laughed.

Without having a clear idea of how it had happened, the men soon found themselves arguing not over pay raises or improved working conditions but about the number of men who would be permitted to return to work at the old terms. He knew who the agitators were, Dunsmuir said, and nothing would induce him to rehire them.

At least one member of the delegation thought that that might be asking for trouble. Spencer began, "There *are* agitators, but still, at the same time . . . "

"Excuse me", Dunsmuir interrupted, "but I am not referring to you."

"No, but look here Mr. Dunsmuir," Spencer pressed on. "It is this way. If we say, when we get back to Wellington, that the men can go back to work, but that a certain few will be left out, it will create sympathy for them, and the rest might not like to go back . . . I know men who have large families that this will touch and it is really hard on them."

The men need not be told that the organizers would not be re-hired, Dunsmuir said. Simply say that anyone wishing to work had to report to Bryden; no one need know that Bryden would have a black list. "I don't suppose that men with families will be refused; men with families are not the worst."

He closed the meeting with a warning. "When you arrive, tell the men that I am a stubborn Scotchman, and that a multitude cannot coerce or drive me."

That message the men received loud and clear. There was some talk of holding firm, but the majority decided to return to work, and by 17 January, Wellington was back in operation.

"I had a strike on my hands at Wellington the first of the year," Dunsmuir confided to Trutch, "but I conquered at the end of 3 weeks, and the men are very sorry now, more so the ringleaders who I would not employ again on any account."

No sooner had he settled the Wellington strike than the men of the Union Mine at Comox walked off the job. "It seems I have not got quit of one strike, but another takes place at the Comox mines,"

Dunsmuir wrote wearily to Trutch. "Because the Superintendent sent 6 Chinamen down one of the mines to run out some boxes, every man quit work, and at present everything is at a stand [still] up there and will be until I get other men as not one of the old hands will earn a dollar at any of my works."

They were brave words, belying the tiredness from which he was suffering. Ordinarily, he enjoyed the repartee of the legislature. Nothing pleased him more than the opportunity to shout, "Bosh! It's all bosh!" in answer to Tom Humphreys's more outlandish statements.

Humphreys had supplied him with some of his best moments in the House. Since 1887 Dunsmuir had been serving as the president of the council, the most powerful position in the cabinet, and it was as president of the council that Humphreys addressed him during the tumultuous session of 1888.

During one question period, Humphreys rose to enquire of the Honourable President of the Council, "Is it the intention of the Esquimalt & Nanaimo Railway to construct and carry their railway to Comox?" After a calculated pause, Dunsmuir replied, "I, as president of the council, consulted the president of the Esquimalt & Nanaimo Railway, and the president of the company informed me as president of the council that I was to mind my own business. Therefore, I cannot answer the honorable member's question."

As the House erupted in laughter and applause, Humphreys sat tongue-tied, stunned into unaccustomed silence. After "gazing into space for a few moments," he responded feebly, "That is no answer at all." And Dunsmuir ended debate by saying, "It's a matter of private business. The question had no business to be asked."

Now, during the legislative session of 1889, Humphreys, like Dunsmuir, was feeling tired and ill. As Dunsmuir wrote to his friend Joe Trutch, "Everything in the Legislature very mild this session in fact nothing of any consequence to do. I am tired of it more so than ever. Alex Davie is keeping up well which is very surprising. That fellow Humphreys is a very sick man also, in fact looks worse than Davie."

Everyone knew that Davie was ill and that lengthy California holidays had done little to improve his health. Tom Humphreys, too, would seek the southern sun in hopes of curing the tuberculosis from which he suffered. But no matter how poor their health might have been, both men would outlive Dunsmuir.

By the time the legislature prorogued at the beginning of April, Dunsmuir seems to have become beset by feelings of doom. Encountering James Orr, a mainland member of the House, Dunsmuir bade him good-bye.

"I'll see you in a short time. I'm often in Victoria," Orr said, shaking his hand.

"Jamie, I don't think I'll ever see you again."

"Why not? Are you going to Europe?" Orr had heard that Dunsmuir was planning to join Trutch in England for a holiday.

"No, I don't think I'm going to live long," Dunsmuir replied.

"Nonsense," Orr protested. "You're good for another twenty years."

"Na, na. I dinna think that," Dunsmuir sighed.

On 5 April 1889 he took to his bed. He was suffering from what appeared to be a severe cold, and his doctors were confidently predicting a speedy recovery, when suddenly, on 10 April, he lapsed into a coma. Two days later, he opened his eyes to find his wife, Joan, and a Presbyterian minister anxiously bending over him.

"Do you see who has come to see you?" Joan asked.

"Yes, it is the minister."

Would you like to pray with me, the minister asked, and Robert folded his hands and uttered a few fervent prayers.

"I am praying for myself as well," he said. An hour later he was dead—poisoned by the uric acid his diseased kidneys could no longer filter from his body.

—

"With the rapidity of an electric spark the news of the death of the Hon. Robert Dunsmuir flashed over the city," the *Victoria Standard* reported. "As the sad intelligence became fully verified, a sense of personal loss was evident to all, and the universal expression was 'A true friend of the city and country has gone.'"

Sir Charles Tupper deemed his death to be "a public calamity." David Oppenheimer, the mayor of Vancouver, was quick to express his sympathies. "His name will forever live in the memory of his fellow citizens for his enterprising and upright spirit, and his loss will long be felt in our midst." The *Vancouver World* noted that flags throughout the city were flying at half-mast and that a great many Vancouverites were planning to attend the funeral.

On 16 April the mines at Wellington were shut down and over a thousand men and women took advantage of free railway passes to travel to Victoria to witness his funeral procession. They found a city plunged into mourning. Schools were closed. Businessmen and shopkeepers shut their doors and draped their premises in black.

Flags throughout the city hung at half-mast.

In the drawing room of Fairview, Robert Dunsmuir lay in a metal coffin, his head resting on a pillow of white roses. Mourners, peering through the coffin's plate-glass lid, saw a man who appeared to be at peace. "The genial kindly face, the finely chiseled lips and square determined chin, every feature, so well known and so long to be remembered, was perfect in its repose."

At two o'clock that afternoon, as every bell in every church began to toll, Dunsmuir's hearse, pulled by four coal-black horses, left Fairview to begin the largest public funeral procession the city had ever seen. Throughout the morning, marchers had been gathering on the lawns of the Parliament Buildings. Now, led by a military band, they set off—the Pioneer Society, the St. George's Society, the Ancient Order of Foresters, the St. Andrew's and Caledonian Society, a contingent of naval officers, the men of the police and fire departments, employees of the Albion Iron Works and the Canadian Pacific Navigation Company, and the miners of Wellington accompanied by their brass band—so many men that it took half an hour for them to pass. Twelve thousand people, a number that came close to equalling the entire population of the city, lined the route as the procession moved to St. Andrew's Church and then on to Ross Bay Cemetery.

As the sod fell upon the coffin and the Wellington band played "Nearer My God to Thee," the *Colonist*'s reporter began to compose the epitaph that would accompany his description of the day. "And so was laid to rest a man than whom no truer was ever born. A man who once a friend, was one until the end of time. A man of whom it may be said that he made his country and his friends his first and only thought. A man of iron will and gigantic intellect used for the benefit of his fellow men. A man such as the world knows seldom, and who by his life, his struggles and the good that he has done, has won for himself the first place in the hearts of British Columbians, and has earned an honored place in the world's history."

Not every British Columbian would have found himself in accord with so flattering an assessment of Robert Dunsmuir's character and career. But no one could deny his achievement. Thirty-eight years earlier he had arrived on Vancouver Island as an indentured $5-a-week miner for the Hudson's Bay Company. He had died the richest man in British Columbia, in sole control of a commercial empire worth an estimated $15 million.

But whatever his financial success, if his goal had been to establish a dynasty, he died a failure. He had chosen to dispose of his fortune by means of an unusual will. He may have thought that its terms would guarantee an orderly transition of power to his sons. Instead, it created havoc—speeding one son to an early grave, dividing the family into two warring camps, and eventually placing the Dunsmuir millions in the hands of the son who lacked the drive to increase the fortune or the wit to recognize the potential power it provided. If the Dunsmuirs went from prominence to obscurity in three generations, it was largely Robert Dunsmuir's fault.

Ten

—

"I know I can bring the undertaking out more successfully by not having too many voices in the matter," Robert Dunsmuir had said in 1871, and he had remained convinced that the key to his success was the sole and total control he exercised over every company in which he invested. He was loath to take on partners, reluctant to share power and authority, even with his sons.

Their father's insistence on remaining the only voice directing his corporate affairs placed James and Alexander in an unenviable position. They were working to increase the profits of Robert's companies and yet they received no set salaries, neither were they given any shares. Instead, they were permitted to take out of the business whatever living expenses they needed. "Take what you want," Robert said. "Just don't want too much." And so, while James and Alexander lived well, they lived cautiously, knowing that at any time he could cut off their income.

Robert's control weighed less heavily on his older son, James. He was settled and stable, content with his position as superintendent of the Departure Bay wharves and married to a woman of whom his parents approved. Laura Surles was a North Carolinian whom James had met and married while he was attending college in Virginia. When she had arrived as his bride in 1876, her southern charm won her instant acceptance in Nanaimo and Wellington, and her aristocratic ancestors made her a welcome addition to a family with growing social ambitions. Within the first ten years of their marriage, she provided James with six of the twelve children she would bear during their lives together—more than enough to provide her husband with a stabilizing influence in the unlikely event that James should ever have found himself in need of one.

For Alexander the situation was very different. He knew that his father considered him more capable than James. Over the years, Robert had made it abundantly clear that he viewed his younger son as his true successor. Whenever there were crises to be dealt with or honours to be savoured, he summoned Alex north from San Francisco while James was often left minding his own business at Departure Bay. But, despite his father's demonstrated faith in his abilities, Alex's future was even more tenuous than James's—for in California he was leading a double life.

Alex was just twenty-five when his father sent him to San Francisco. Unlike James who had no taste for whiskey and drank so little as to be considered almost unsociably abstemious, he had inherited his father's fondness for the bottle. A dour young man who lacked the easy bonhomie of a natural salesman, he soon made the welcome discovery that business in the city floated on a sea of whiskey and wine.

"Men drank cocktail after cocktail, sometimes ten, twelve or fourteen a day. That was the habit of San Francisco at that time," Richard Chandler recalled. Chandler had known Alex since 1858 when Alex was five years old and Chandler was a ship's captain carrying Fraser-bound gold miners across the strait from Nanaimo to the mainland. He took a fatherly interest in the younger man when he encountered him in San Francisco in 1876. "I saw him once or twice down at the dock drinking with some of the coal dealers down there," Chandler recalled. "I said, 'Alex that is a bad practice, I would not do that sort of thing if I was you, you are a young man, and I wouldn't fall into a bad habit.'"

Alex soon settled into a pattern that was to remain unchanged for most of his life. He would drop in at Dunsmuir, Diggle's East Street office in the morning and then wander over to the Merchants Exchange where San Francisco businessmen met to share gossip, make deals, study the stock quotations and drink more than was good for them before adjourning to one of the city's gentlemen's clubs to while away afternoons with cards and business and brandy.

It was at the Merchants Exchange that Alex formed a casual friendship with William Harrison, an Irish-born marine insurance salesman, who noted with approval, "Dunsmuir had a good Scotch head, and could drink what he wanted to without being much affected by it."

In 1878 Harrison was living on Eddy Street in a single room rented from the Wallaces. Wallie Wallace held down two jobs. By day he served as a clerk in a lawyer's office; by night he worked as an usher in the California Theatre. His wife, Josephine, cared for their two young children, Willie and Edna. Harrison had been living with the family for almost two years when Wallie asked him to do him a favour.

A walking match was being held at Pratt's Hall, the exhibition building at the corner of Bush and Montgomery streets. A test of endurance rather than speed, walking races lasted for almost a week. Day and night, contestants marched around and around the sawdust-covered floor of Pratt's Hall, the prize eventually going to the man who completed the most circuits during the six-day course of the race. "Mr. Wallace was anxious that Mrs. Wallace should see the walking match," Harrison recalled. But it wasn't the type of event that a woman could attend alone. Would Harrison agree to take her?

Harrison said he would, but, he warned Wallie, he couldn't stay. He would have to ask some friend to see her home. Moments after they arrived at the hall, Harrison spotted Alex.

Alex had never met anyone quite like Josephine before. Twenty-eight years old and three years Alex's senior, she was bright and vivacious, gifted with an unfailing optimism and an unaffected buoyant cheerfulness that impressed everyone she met. Quite aware that she was considered a beautiful woman, she took special care to always appear her best. She had, Alex noted appreciatively, "the finest figure of any woman in San Francisco."

Soon afterwards, Harrison's business took him to England for several months. When he returned, he went to Eddy Street to see if he could get his old room back. He couldn't, Josephine said. His room had been taken by Mr. Dunsmuir. Wallie Wallace had moved out, and Josephine had taken to describing herself as "keeping house for Mr. Dunsmuir." But she was doing rather more than that. On 15 December 1880 the Wallaces were divorced; Wallie took his son and his wounded pride to Oakland; and Josephine, who had won custody of Edna, remained in San Francisco, living with Alex while she waited for the day that he would be free to marry her.

Marrying Josephine was the farthest thing from Alex's mind. His parents would regard a penniless divorcee as an adventuress. That she had two children who might lay claim to the Dunsmuir estate only made matters worse, for as Robert's wealth had increased, so too had the suspicion with which he regarded outsiders and his fear that the fortune might slip from the family's hands. Alex's living arrangements might be an open secret among his friends in San Francisco, but he succeeded in keeping Josephine hidden from his family. Even his brother Jim was not taken into his confidence, and if business brought his father to the city, Alex simply booked a hotel room and remained there for the duration of his stay.

Not that he was not fond of Josephine. He gave her a pet name, "Peetie," and he doted on her little daughter Edna, a delightful child who had inherited her mother's vivacity and bubbly sense of fun. "I am going to take care of you and you are going to be my little girl," Alex promised her, and he carefully set aside an hour each evening to amuse her.

When Edna was nine, she was sent away to boarding school and Alex waited for school holidays with anticipation. "He was very kind and affectionate in every way, generous; and he amused me and played with me when I came home on vacations," Edna recalled.

She had been warned never to mention Alex to outsiders but rumours followed her from school to school, from San Mateo to Benicia to Oakland. She was in her third school in three years when she sadly noted that the other girls had begun to shun her and she was relieved when Josephine arrived one afternoon to pack her bags and take her home.

Alex moved them out of rented rooms into a little house on Post Street; Edna was enrolled as a day student at Van Ness Academy; and Josephine began calling herself "Mrs. Dunsmuir." But the wives of Alex's friends were aware of her true status and would have declined an invitation to Post Street had Josephine been so bold as to extend one.

Completely dependent on Alex, Josephine was in no position to criticize his behaviour, and during their years on Post Street she found herself standing by, incapable of protest, as he allowed alcohol to take an increasingly firm hold on his life. Twelve-year-old Edna noticed a change in him as soon as she arrived at the Post Street house. "Every Saturday and Sunday it became his custom to stay in bed and drink," she remembered. And his behaviour toward her was different now. A year before it had been marked by good-natured fun—like the time Edna had doused Alex with the garden hose and he had scooped her up and deposited her, clothes and all, into a bathtub full of water. But now, Edna recalled, "He would come home at night at one o'clock, two, three or four and he would come into my room ... he would come into my room and he would wake me up. If he was in a playful mood, he would bring me into his room to play. He would want me to lie along side of him and just pet me; then he would take another turn, and would have new games and would want me to play these games and various things."

Was Edna implying some kind of sexual contact? Seventeen years later, when she testified to these events, she was a worldly woman who had experienced one husband and several lovers. She was contesting Alex's will. It might have been to her advantage if she left the impression that he had behaved improperly. The questions Edna's testimony raised would hang unanswered in the courtroom, the impact of her story made all the more chilling when, after she was warned to recount only those incidents about which Josephine knew, Edna replied, "My mother was aware of everything."

But if ever a mother felt powerless to intervene, that woman was Josephine Wallace. A thirty-six-year-old divorcee, she had no standing in society and no money of her own. By 1886 she had invested eight years in her relationship with Alex, and she still clung to the hope that one day he would marry her. She told herself that he behaved badly only when he had been drinking; he was a different man when he was sober. But she had to admit that the days on which Alex could be considered even relatively sober were becoming fewer and fewer.

One evening at the Pacific Club, after sitting at an upstairs window idly watching the passersby, he suddenly threw up the sash and began to hurl the loose change from his pockets down into the street. Delighted by the size of the crowd that assembled, he called the steward for more coins. As a small fortune descended from the window, club members gathered around him, cheering him on and applauding the efforts of the eager boys who ducked and dived for the gold pieces raining down on their heads.

Possessed of an extraordinarily robust constitution, Alex was able to drink until four in the morning, sleep for five hours after being carried home in a hack, and still appear at the office by ten o'clock, clear-headed and able to conduct business with efficiency and despatch. It seemed he was indestructible. But then, sometime in the spring of 1886, Alex lost control.

The first night he failed to come home, Josephine was not too worried. It would not be the only time he had gone straight from the club to the office after having been revived by a restaurant breakfast on the way. But as his absence stretched to two and then three nights, she grew increasingly alarmed. On the fourth day, she threw caution to the winds and went to his office. Alex had not been there either. His clerk decided to take his disappearance seriously. He sent a telegram to James informing him that his brother was missing and, while James made plans to travel to San Francisco, he placed advertisements in the city's newspapers asking for information as to Alex's whereabouts.

He had been missing for more than ten days when suddenly he appeared, slumped in his chair at the Pacific Club. He was in a deplorable state when he was carried home to Post Street and the ministrations of Josephine, or "Alex's landlady" as she was carefully described to James.

Over the next few days, hovered over by doctors and restrained by two male nurses, Alex went through his first attack of *delirium tremens*. Warned by his doctors that he would surely die if he continued to drink, Alex rose from his bed a frightened man. He tried to make a fresh start. He moved Josephine and Edna to a new house on Ellis Street, and he promised to avoid the Pacific Club. That August when he journeyed north to take part in the last spike ceremonies on the E & N Railway, he was on his best behaviour and sobered by thoughts of his own mortality.

At the suggestion of Fred Crocker, he travelled part of the way along the newly laid tracks of the Crockers' California & Oregon line that would soon connect San Francisco and Portland. Five hundred miles north of San Francisco, the train paused to take on the pusher engine that would nudge it over the steep grade that lay ahead. Nestled deep in the mountain valley, a little town, with the inelegant name Pusher, had begun to grow along the railway siding. Alex was struck by the beauty of the setting. Here the Sacramento was a dancing trout stream; a few miles to the north, Mount Shasta towered over the valley's craggy peaks, its melting glaciers feeding springs that gave Pusher what some people said was the best drinking water on earth.

"If you change the name of this town from Pusher to Dunsmuir," Alex told Fred Crocker, "I'll donate a fountain for the town square." In January 1887, the little California town was renamed "Dunsmuir." Near the railway station on the town's main street an ornate three-tiered fountain appeared, bearing a small plaque, "Presented by Alexander Dunsmuir of the Wellington Collieries British Columbia," and Alex achieved some small claim to immortality.

For three years Alex managed to avoid the binge-drinking that had nearly killed him. He continued to be his father's right-hand man, spending half his time away from San Francisco—travelling to and from Victoria, meeting with his father, acting as a consultant and an advisor, and all the time preparing for the day when he would finally assume control. In April 1889 when he was summoned to his father's deathbed, Alex was thirty-six years old. He was, at least by his own standards, sober and steady, and as ready as he would ever be to step into his father's shoes.

But then Robert Dunsmuir's will was read. In a simple one-page document, the richest man in British Columbia left everything he possessed—his houses, his lands, his mines, his controlling shares in the railway, the ironworks and the steamship company, all his goods and all his chattels—to one person, his wife, Joan.

Alex and Jim were stunned. "It was R. Dunsmuir & *Sons*," Jim wailed. "Father always led us to believe it was going to be ours."

There must, they protested, be another more recent will. Yes, Joan agreed. There was another will, and its terms were just what the boys had been led to expect. But Robert had decided not to sign it. Instead, he had chosen to leave everything in her hands.

—

For most of the Dunsmuir saga, Joan remains a shadowy figure. She left no letters or diaries, and she figures only briefly in the letters or journals of others. Between 1847 and 1872 she gave birth to eleven children—a new baby almost every two years, and all born before the family could afford the luxuries of housemaids and nannies. Enough, one might suppose, to fully occupy her time. But from the scattered reminiscences of those who knew her, a clear and consistent picture emerges of a strong-willed, determined, fearless woman who was "the very backbone of the family" and the only real business partner her husband ever had.

"In the matter of business, her opinion was highly valued by her husband," one of Robert's associates recalled. "At all times he consulted and was guided by her advice."

The terms of Robert's will proved that testaments to her influence were more than empty praise. When the men with considerable estates who were his contemporaries wrote their wills, they demonstrated that they had little faith in the business acumen of their wives. Characteristically, they left their affairs in the hands of trustees who were charged with advancing the widow carefully directed payments from her lifetime interest in her husband's estate. For a woman to be entrusted with the largest fortune that had ever been generated in British Columbia was an extraordinary vote of confidence in her abilities. Not yet prepared to believe that Alex and James could be trusted with his estate, he had left it to Joan to study her sons and to decide when, and if, they would assume control.

For both boys, but most particularly for Alex, the next few years would be a nightmare.

Eleven

Within a month of Robert Dunsmuir's death, his widow had his corporate empire firmly in hand. Alexander and James would share their father's corporate directorships, but the shares those positions represented would remain in her control. Jim was made president of the Wellington Collieries; Alex became president of the E & N. Alex would remain in San Francisco; Jim would move to Victoria where he would take his father's place at the Store Street office. She would turn Fairview over to Jim and his family, and since Craigdarroch was still little more than an empty shell, she and her younger daughters would go abroad. After signing a power of attorney giving James and Alexander temporary authority to sign documents on her behalf, Joan sailed for Europe, leaving to her sons the melancholy job of completing Robert's castle and trusting them to manage the mines without deviating from the policies he had established.

Robert Dunsmuir had refused to recognize any attempt by organized labour to extend its influence to Wellington. His view had prevailed, partly because of the respect with which the men regarded him and partly because of the empathy he was able to project when he met the miners face to face. But another key ingredient in his successful campaign to keep Wellington free of unions was the miners' lack of leadership. And that was about to change.

At first glance, there seemed to be nothing that set Tully Boyce apart from the other men who were prepared to spend their lives underground hewing another man's coal. Like many of the miners, he was an American; before moving to Vancouver Island in 1888, he had worked in mines in Pennsylvania and Wyoming. But while Boyce might appear to be a typical working miner, he was also "a most determined man," a man who "would sell all he had and imperil those who are most dear to him to carry his points."

Boyce found it galling that the concessions American miners had won from their bosses were unheard of in British Columbia. In February 1890 he called together a meeting of all miners in the district to lay before them the possibility of forming an industry-wide union. He received near unanimous support. When the meeting ended, the Miners' and Mine Labourers' Protective Association had been formed. By May, nine hundred men had been signed up; Boyce had been elected president of the association; several blacklisted Wellington men had won positions on the union's executive, and a list of demands had been prepared to present to company management. From Sam Robins, superintendent of the Vancouver Company's mines, the association received a sympathetic response. John Bryden's answer was very different. True to Dunsmuir's long-established policy, he refused to recognize the union. He would meet with only Wellington men.

Tully Boyce responded to Bryden's rebuff by calling for a mass meeting. On Saturday, 17 May, six hundred Nanaimo men, marching shoulder to shoulder, waving flags and banners and singing "revolutionary" songs, paraded to a field outside Wellington where they were met by several hundred Wellington men. Bryden was a tyrant, Boyce told them. "The day is past when we must go to the rich man's door and beg." They must unite to fight the bosses. The Nanaimo men had won an eight-hour day; the Wellington miners must now demand the same.

The length of a shift a miner worked was not so relevant as it might first appear. The men were paid by the piece rather than by the hour or the day. Shifts of a standard length were required so that when hoists were lowered and raised, they were carrying a full complement of workers. In Dunsmuir mines, the men spent only eight hours actually working at the pit face, not counting a half-hour lunch break when the mine machinery was shut down and the mules were fed and rested. But from the time they arrived at the pithead at shortly after six in the morning until the end of the shift when they were returned to the mine opening, more than nine hours could pass. Sam Robins had agreed to begin calculating the length of a shift from the moment the men gathered at the pithead and he also agreed to do away with the lunch break, allowing men to eat while they worked. The Wellington men must demand the same concessions from the Dunsmuirs, the meeting was told.

A delegation, made up exclusively of Wellington men, was selected to take their demands to Bryden. He had, Bryden told them, neither the authority nor the inclination to acknowledge the association, nor was he empowered to recognize the pit committees elected by association members, nor was he prepared to accede to their demand for an eight-hour working day. Come back in a week, he told them. Give him some time to confer with the owners.

James Dunsmuir was in Victoria, less than three hours away. But the real figures of authority were somewhere in the middle of the Continent, and neither he nor Bryden was inclined to act until Joan Dunsmuir and Alex arrived on the scene.

A few weeks earlier, Jim and Alex had received word that their mother had fallen ill. "Alex came to England for us," his sister Maude recalled. "He was very kind to mother." But something less than devotion had prompted Alex to hurry to his mother's side. The news that Joan was ill must have sliced through him like a knife. How sick was she? Had she written a will? Might she die without having settled Robert's estate, and would that mean he and his brother would be forced to share everything with their sisters? He was relieved to discover that Joan was not as sick as he had feared. Now he and his mother were on their way home and not expected to arrive until 26 May.

As far as Tully Boyce was concerned, the union was being treated to a typical Bryden stonewall. The time had come for union men to flex their muscles and take matters into their own hands. The following Monday morning, the union members, who made up more than half of Wellington's day shift, dallied at home for nearly an hour, determined to delay reporting for work until seven o'clock. They arrived to find the gates locked. You can go to work tomorrow if you report at the usual time, they were told. That they refused to do—and the longest work stoppage Wellington would ever experience was on.

As soon as she returned to Victoria, Joan Dunsmuir took charge. Within hours of her arrival she was aboard a special train bound for Wellington. With Alex acting as her spokesman, she made her position clear. No one would tell her how to run the mine; no industry-wide union would be recognized at Wellington. On 30 May, Bryden, "acting on behalf of Mrs. J. O. Dunsmuir," issued eviction notices to the striking workers who occupied company cottages.

Boyce took his campaign to San Francisco. On 13 June he appeared before a meeting of the Council of Federated Trades, a powerful organization that claimed to represent 37,000 workers in two hundred trades in California, Oregon and Washington. Encouraged by the council's sympathetic response, Boyce sailed for home, but not before he had littered the town with circulars addressed "To the People of San Francisco."

> Boycott Wellington coal, mined by Dunsmuir & Sons. Boycott all coal handled by Dunsmuir & Sons. Boycott all dealers who buy coal of Dunsmuir & Sons.
>
> These purse-proud autocrats refuse to allow their miners to work for living wages, and are at present engaged in starving them into submission . . . Humanity demands that they be taught a lesson in common decency.

With his call for a boycott enthusiastically endorsed by the Council of Federated Trades, Boyce was convinced that the Dunsmuirs' submission was only a matter of time. But he had misjudged the tenacity of his opponents. Stubbornness was a Dunsmuir family trait. Immovability was strength; compromise was weakness. Neither had Boyce taken into account the Union Mine at Comox which was moving into full production and which could easily elude any Wellington boycott. Nor had he foreseen the wavering resolve that would soon beset half the Wellington workforce.

On 4 August the mine's whistle sounded for the first time in six weeks. The men who chose to answer its call were greeted by seventy-five striking miners who, according to the *Colonist*, "howled and jeered" and sang the "Marseillaise" and "other revolutionary songs." As quitting time neared, the mob reassembled to hiss and hoot at the men as they emerged from the mine. "One man, a foreigner, was particularly noticeable for his excesses," the *Colonist*'s man wrote. "Indeed, it may be said that three-quarters to seven-eighths, perhaps, of the demonstrators were other than English-speaking."

By painting a picture of right-thinking Wellington men being set upon by a horde of wild-eyed foreign revolutionaries, the *Colonist* was preparing its readers for the thud of the next shoe that was about to drop. The Dunsmuirs had decided to call in the militia.

In Victoria, that very night, three magistrates signed the necessary requisition, and by the afternoon of the following day, fifty armed militiamen were on their way to Wellington. They were greeted with stunned surprise. When asked why the militia had been ordered in, the *Colonist*'s man answered, "I'm blest if I know." In answer to a similar question, one of the special constables hired to protect the mines replied, "Well, you see, yesterday a lot of them got together and marched up and down the street, yelling and singing. They called the men who had gone to work a lot of blackleg sons of bitches and made considerable noise."

"Did they use violence?" he was asked. "Well, no, but they might have done so. They are a very excitable lot of men are those Belgians and there are very few constables."

The union leaders did not deny that intemperate language had been used. Miner Tom Carter, a member of the union's executive, was prepared to admit that much to the Dunsmuirs themselves. Yes, he said, one or two of the men had gone too far.

"Didn't a hundred of them yell like that?" James demanded.

"No sir, they did not—only one or two," Carter replied.

"Yes, they did," James insisted.

"If they did, I didn't hear it." And before he could continue, Alex interjected with a more pertinent question. "What are you men making the parades for?"

"Well, just to keep together," Carter hedged.

"And not to intimidate those who might wish to go to work?"

"No, not in the slightest. We don't want to intimidate anyone. If your men wish to go to work, they can walk down this road and no one will molest them or even speak to them."

Alex was becoming impatient. "But what is the object of these parades if it is not intimidation?"

"Well, it's not that anyway," Carter struggled.

"Well, what is it then?" Alex demanded. "Why do you parade here with flags, singing and marching?"

A miner named Suggett came to Carter's rescue. "Will you allow me to answer that question?" he asked.

"Yes," Alex said, turning toward him.

"Well, then, it's none of your business why we parade."

"That's straight, if it is cheeky," Jim laughed. "But it isn't a reason."

"Well," Suggett said. "I'll tell you why we parade. It is to show to the public that there are men locked out at these mines. We are willing to go to work but are not allowed."

"Not while you remain union men," Alex agreed. "And what are you going to do when other men take the vacant places?"

"Time will tell," Suggett said.

For the present, at least, time seemed to be on the union's side. The weather was warm and dry. The striking miners were under canvas, encamped with their families along the Nanaimo road, in so many tents that observers were reminded of an army bivouac. No one was going hungry, for the union members who were at work in other island mines had volunteered to donate 10 per cent of their pay to support their striking brethren. Even with the protection of the militia, only seventy-five men could be coaxed back to work, far too few to replace the four hundred men required for the full operation of the mine. And soon an encouraging rumour would reach Tully Boyce, a rumour that suggested that the Dunsmuirs were losing the heart to continue their fight against the union.

On 18 September, Joan Dunsmuir took up residence in her husband's castle and dropped a bombshell. She had decided to sell the Wellington Colliery. It was true, she said, that Robert Dunsmuir had always made it clear that one day the San Francisco business, the railway shares and the Union Mine would go to the boys. But his promise had never included the Wellington Colliery. Neither Alex nor Jim had been involved in the development of the first mine. Wellington was distinctly and uniquely hers.

She summoned Dennis Harris to Craigdarroch and detailed her terms. Harris, a partner in Lowenberg & Harris, the city's "phenomenally successful" real estate and insurance brokers, was given twelve months to sell the colliery. She would agree to a selling price of $2.6 million—one million at the time of sale, a second million a year later, and the balance within two years. She wasn't giving him much time to come up with a buyer with that much cash, Harris worried. "Do the best you can," Joan said, and she sent him on his way.

If Tully Boyce hoped that an impending sale of her colliery might weaken Joan Dunsmuir's resolve, she soon proved him wrong. She had no intention of seeking a compromise. The lockout dragged on for months and months, through the winter of 1890, the spring and summer of 1891, and into the fall. The Dunsmuirs stubbornly refused to recognize the association; the men refused to return to work on any other terms.

With the coming of October and the prospect of another bleak winter, the miners' determination began to crumble. When the dispute had begun, as much as $1,000 a week bolstered the strike fund. Now donations had dwindled to a meagre $400, and the miners of Nanaimo were beginning to lose the fire that had warmed them to the idea of making voluntary contributions. In November 1891 a vote was taken. The time had come, the majority decided, for the Wellington men to concede defeat.

The miners' decision to return to work was a victory for the Dunsmuirs, and James would certainly continue to see the defeat of the union as a vindication of the tough labour policies his mother and his father had pursued. But it was a victory from which the Dunsmuir brothers could take only the coldest comfort. Their mother had been unable to find a buyer for the Wellington Colliery, but she remained determined to sell, and even now her agent was in England pursuing potential purchasers.

By November 1891, James was forty years old and Alexander thirty-eight. Their working lives had been spent increasing the family fortune, but still they had no protected status, no money or property they could really call their own. All the profits produced by the companies they managed went directly to their mother. That was bad enough. Worse was the fact that Joan had no intention of using those millions to expand and diversify. Instead, she seemed determined to invest her income in acquiring for her daughters the best husbands Dunsmuir dollars could buy.

Twelve

—

By 1891, six of Joan's eight daughters had found husbands. Only one of them had chosen a man Jim and Alex considered to be of any consequence. Elizabeth's husband, John Bryden, had been Robert's friend as well as a trusted employee, and he continued to enjoy a special relationship with Robert's sons. The other men who had married into the family, the Dunsmuir brothers regarded with feelings ranging from disinterest to contempt.

In James Harvey, the coalminer turned shopkeeper, Agnes Dunsmuir had found a mate whom her brothers had come to view as an old friend and a pleasant nonentity. A hard-drinking man's man who had a passion for hunting and fishing and who relished his role in the militia, taking particular pride in his skill as a marksman, Jim Harvey had married Agnes before her father had become a wealthy man. When the Dunsmuirs moved to Victoria, they had turned Ardoon over to Agnes and Jim, and with that display of munificence, Harvey seemed to have been content. But even if he had itched to get his hands on the family purse, by 1891 he posed no threat, for he had obliged Jim and Alex by removing himself from contention.

On 15 September 1889, five months after her father's death, forty-year-old Agnes succumbed to typhoid fever. Described as being "dangerously ill from the same cause," Harvey discovered that, after Agnes's death, the Dunsmuirs lost all interest in him. In November, when he decided to travel to California to continue his convalescence, he was forced to mortgage his shop to finance the trip. He died in Pasadena three months later, and while the Dunsmuirs paid the freight to bring back his emaciated body to Nanaimo, no one stepped forward to make good his debts. When his mortgage fell due later that year, his property was conveyed to the lender and the contents of his store were sold at public auction.

As Robert's fortune increased, his daughters were able to attract a better class of man. And, Jim and Alex noted, the higher their social class, the less able they were to earn a living and the more they depended on Dunsmuir money to support them in the style their status deserved.

As for Marion's husband, the only good thing that Jim or Alex could say in his favour was that he had managed to stumble into a paying job. Born near Dublin into an Anglo-Irish family, Charles Frederick Houghton had joined the British Army in 1856 when he was seventeen. He seems to have made a success as a soldier, being raised to a captaincy before he was twenty-four, but in 1863 he decided to sell his commission and take up land in British Columbia. He settled on 1,000 acres at the head of Okanagan Lake, and there he discovered that he badly missed the life of an army officer. He was quick to volunteer when he learned that Governor Douglas was looking for a man to lead an exploratory party to investigate the rumours that gold was to be found along Cherry Creek, 35 miles east of his holdings.

Douglas, who took Houghton up on his offer, would later note that the gallant captain, who had come so highly recommended, was quite amazingly incompetent. On his first foray up the creek, one of his horses starved to death because he had failed to bring along enough feed. On the second, he allowed himself to be trapped, without shelter, in a two-day blizzard and was forced to limp back to his ranch with badly frostbitten feet.

In 1872 Houghton found himself catapulted to Ottawa by one of the oddest parliamentary elections British Columbia would ever experience. When British Columbia had entered Confederation in 1871, a special election was held to select the province's six representatives in the House of Commons.

Arthur Bushby, the postmaster at Yale, the little town that clung to the steep banks of the Fraser River 100 miles from its mouth, had allowed the election to slip his mind until a friend reminded Bushby that he was the returning officer for the district. Bushby rummaged through his desk and, finding the papers, discovered that nominations would close at midnight of that very day. He called to George, his man of all work.

"George, this is nomination day. Go down and rustle up as many of the boys as you can to come to a meeting and nominate a candidate. Tell them all to be sure and come and to hurry."

George returned with two men, the blacksmith and "a barroom hanger on."

Several names as candidates were suggested and rejected for one reason or another. Then the blacksmith remembered the rancher from the Okanagan who was always "liberal with his purse" when he brought his horse to be shoed. He placed Houghton's name in nomination; it was quickly seconded and Bushby declared nominations closed.

Houghton manfully shouldered the honour that had befallen him. By March 1872 he had been declared the winner of the uncontested election and was on his way to Ottawa. There he made a discovery that warmed his soldier's heart—the Militia Act of 1868 now applied to British Columbia. Canada had no corps of professional soldiers. After the withdrawal of British troops, the country was protected by a volunteer militia. British Columbia would now become Military District 11. Houghton determinedly pursued the position of deputy adjutant general in the province. In 1873 he happily abandoned his political career to accept the rank of lieutenant-colonel and the responsibility of organizing the B.C. militia.

When he moved to militia headquarters in Victoria, he made a calculated decision—he left his wife and children behind. In 1869 he had married, "by the custom of the country," Sophie N'kwala, a high-born Indian woman who had borne him two children: a daughter, Marie, in 1870 and a son, Edward, two years later. "My brother and I went to live with our grandmother," Marie recalled. "And my mother died of a broken heart."

Punctuated by episodes of near-disaster, Houghton's career was marked by exceptionally good luck. In 1877 he led the militia to Wellington to suppress the "anticipated riot." The success of that operation was somewhat marred when the steamer carrying the troops back to Victoria struck a rock and threatened to sink, leaving the lieutenant-colonel and his men to spend an uncomfortable night perched on a rocky islet. But Houghton must have felt his luck was holding when, as a result of the Wellington action, he was invited to Ardoon and discovered that Robert Dunsmuir's third daughter was unmarried and unattached.

Marion might be tight-lipped and bad-tempered, but with deep-set pale eyes and long dark hair coiled high on her head, she possessed a kind of petulant attractiveness. And she was young, fifteen years Houghton's junior. That she was the daughter of a rich and influential man only added to her allure. They were married on 27 March

1879 and, after a European honeymoon, settled in Victoria in a square brick house near the city's business district. They had been there for only a year when Marion received distressing news—her husband had been transferred to Manitoba. But if Marion regretted having to leave Victoria and her family, Lieut.-Col. Charles Frederick Houghton could not have been happier. With any luck at all, he would see some real military action at last.

In 1870 Manitoba had been the scene of armed rebellion by the Metis, the children and grandchildren of French-Canadian fur traders and their Indian wives, who had developed a distinct identity, a unique culture that combined both their French and Indian heritage. When the Canadian government began to speak confidently about colonizing the plains, the Metis had begun to feel distinctly uneasy. They had found a leader in Louis Riel, a charismatic, Quebec-educated Metis. Their rebellion had been put down before it really began and Riel had been forced into exile in the United States. But in 1881 when Houghton was transferred to Winnipeg, trouble continued to brew.

By 1884, Riel had returned to the northwest and was preparing to lead another protest. Aware of the simmering discontent, the prime minister, Sir John A. Macdonald, wrote to his son, Hugh, a Winnipeg lawyer, asking him to assess the strength of Houghton's militia. Hugh Macdonald's confidential report, posted to his father on 8 July 1884, suggested that the competency of the lieutenant-colonel had not improved with age.

"Col. Houghton is getting along fairly well as Deputy Adjutant General," Hugh wrote. "He does not go on sprees and I have never seen him under the influence of liquor though I think that day in and day out he drinks more than is good for him . . . I should say that he had plenty of pluck and determination and would make a capital *fighting officer*, but I must frankly admit I don't think he would be a capable commander as he has not much head and still less judgement."

Houghton failed to distinguish himself in either of the two skirmishes that made up the major battles of the North-West campaign. At Fish Creek, he blundered about on his conspicuous white horse, leading one rush toward the enemy with such reckless impetuosity that he found himself well in advance of his troops. "Lt. Col. Houghton is absolutely useless, and I wish I could find some excuse to get rid of him," his commanding officer complained. And soon Houghton found himself transferred to Montreal.

In 1891, when Houghton accompanied his ailing wife home to

Victoria, he was welcomed into his mother-in-law's home as a member of the family. But after Marion died at Craigdarroch on 13 February 1892 in her thirty-sixth year, he was cast adrift by his Dunsmuir relations. For Houghton, becoming a Dunsmuir *persona non grata* was not without its benefits. His marriage to Marion had been childless. Now, with nothing to fear by exposing the secret of his country marriage, he summoned his twenty-two-year-old daughter Marie to Montreal.

In 1898 Marie was residing with him on McGill College Avenue when he was informed by his doctors that he had cancer of the throat. Told that there was nothing they could do and that he would surely die, Houghton was overcome with a yearning to see an old friend. Charles Vernon was a fellow Irishman who had come out with Houghton to take up land in the Okanagan thirty-five years earlier. Now he had settled in Victoria and Houghton spent an agonizingly long week jolting across the country aboard the train. He died in hospital on 13 August, just over a month after he had arrived in the city. His body was claimed by his friend, and it was in Charles Vernon's parlour that he lay until his funeral.

"The attendance of friends was large, and many beautiful flowers were sent," the *Colonist* reported. No members of the Dunsmuir family chose to attend.

"The deceased was known and respected from one end of Canada to the other," the *Colonist* continued, conscientiously detailing Houghton's career but carefully avoiding any reference to his connection to the province's most powerful family.

—

Born in 1862, Robert Dunsmuir's fourth daughter, Mary Jean, reached young adulthood late enough in her father's career to enjoy some of the advantages increasing wealth could bring. Thought to be the brightest of the girls, she was sent to study at Mills Seminary in Berkeley, California, where she lived up to family expectations by graduating sixth in a class of eighty-one. She accompanied her parents when they toured Europe in 1882, and she was the first of the girls to be launched from Fairview. All of which helped her become the first Dunsmuir daughter to land a husband who could call himself a gentleman.

Tall and elegantly slim, with high cheekbones and a finely chiselled nose, Harry Croft certainly looked the part. The youngest of three children, he was born at "Mount Adelaide," a country house on Woomooloo Hill on the outskirts of Sydney, Australia. Taken to

England after his mother died when he was just a year old, Harry spent a lonely childhood. He developed a passionate interest in genealogy, and after completing his studies at Rugby and training as an engineer at the Derby School of Mines, he set off to pick up the threads of his family's past, travelling first to Australia where he worked for several years before moving on to the Pacific Northwest where his brother, Ted, had taken up farming.

Washington Territory was abuzz with news of the soon-to-be-built island railway, and it occurred to Harry that a railway would need timber for bridges and railway ties. By the summer of 1883, he had moved to Vancouver Island. With a partner, he acquired almost 500 waterfront acres at Chemainus, about halfway between Nanaimo and Victoria, where he established a lumber mill.

Doing business with Robert Dunsmuir by providing timbers for the E & N gave Croft an entree to Fairview and an introduction to Dunsmuir's twenty-one-year-old daughter Mary. They were married in the drawing room of Fairview on 1 July 1885 and before leaving for a California honeymoon took delivery of two rather special wedding presents—a grand piano from the bride's mother and from her father a cheque that, rumour had it, ran as high as $25,000. But Robert Dunsmuir might not have been quite so generous as he seemed. Less than a year later, an indebtedness of precisely that amount was registered against the Chemainus mill by Harry's father-in-law.

With the completion of the E & N, demand for Croft's lumber fell off. For Croft, the mill might have become a losing proposition, but Dunsmuir recognized an opportunity to turn a tidy profit. Selling the mill would give him a chance to offload some of the "worthless" timber lands he had received as part of the E & N land grant. By 21 January 1889 Robert Dunsmuir had become the sole owner of Croft's mill and he had found a purchaser, but Robert died before the sale was completed, and Croft's mill fell into his mother-in-law's hands.

After her father's death, Mary, who was possessed of an imperious nature, which her friends chose to describe as "outstanding gifts of leadership," took her mother's domestic arrangements in hand. She sergeant-majored her trip to Europe and spent several months touring the Continent before settling her mother and her younger sisters in Switzerland and sailing for home. Meanwhile, Harry began thinking about another career.

Real estate in Victoria was booming. Spurred by a continent-wide period of optimism and expansion, the city's population was growing apace. Between 1881 and 1891, the town of six thousand would bloom into a city with almost seventeen thousand residents. To provide homes for thousands of new Victorians, speculators were carving large pieces of property into small residential lots and filling the newspapers with excited advertisements extolling the virtues of their new subdivisions.

In November 1889 Harry purchased 19 acres on the waterfront between Esquimalt and Victoria. He had what seemed to be a foolproof plan. Three of those acres, he would subdivide into eighty-six building lots. With the profits he received from the sale of those lots, he would construct a fine house on the remaining 16 acres. At first everything proceeded nicely. By January 1891 he had found buyers for forty-three lots, and his house, christened "Mount Adelaide" after his Australian birthplace, was nearly finished.

"When the stables and other buildings are completed and the grounds are laid out, Mr. Croft will possess one of the handsomest and certainly the best situated residences in Victoria," the *Times* assured its readers. But soon one of Victoria's handsomest houses would be encumbered by one of the city's largest mortgages. By February, Croft was $45,000 in debt. He had needed money to buy speculative land on Salt Spring Island; he was still trying to develop the land he held in the "townsite" at Chemainus; he had underestimated the amount of time it would take to sell the remaining Esquimalt lots; and he had not counted on just how much it would cost to build a huge two-storey house "treated very liberally in the seventeenth century style of architecture." Harry was tottering on the brink of financial ruin when his recently acquired business partner, Francis Bourchier, pushed him over the edge.

A more experienced and less trusting man than Harry Croft might have sensed that there was something not quite right about the energetic Mr. Bourchier. Francis Sydney Bourchier had been plain old Frank Bees and a wine merchant in Bristol when he informed his wife, Clara, that they were going to search out greener pastures. In 1885 they arrived in Victoria with Frank sporting a new name and new profession. "Francis S. Bourchier, Real Estate and Insurance," his business card read. In 1890 he decided to expand his office, and who better to invite to join him than Harry Croft, a man already bitten by the speculative bug and intimately connected with the province's richest family.

In the summer of 1892 Bourchier's carefully constructed façade began to crumble. He suggested to his wife, Clara, that her health might benefit from several weeks of mountain air. Soon after Clara left for Banff, congratulating herself for having so solicitous a husband, Bertha Genns moved in. Victorians had scarcely recovered from that shock when Bourchier took Bertha camping at the nearby holiday resort of Cadboro Bay. No one within a mile of the Bay missed the fact that Mr. Bourchier and Miss Genns shared the same tent.

Clara returned to find her husband gone. Gone too was Bertha Genns, and missing from the real estate offices of Bourchier & Croft was $50,000. Harry Croft would never see his partner or his money again.

Whatever status Croft might have enjoyed in the Dunsmuir family, he lost when his partner decamped with the firm's assets. Two months after Bourchier's departure, Croft was forced to go to his mother-in-law for money. Joan agreed to advance him $20,000, but not in the form of a gift or a personal loan. Instead, she charged him the going rate of interest, and she added her name to the list of creditors lining up to claim Mount Adelaide if Croft failed to meet his commitments.

Three years later, with Croft owing a full $58,000 and with no hope of ever paying it off, the axe fell. Harry was insolvent. Mount Adelaide became the property of the Pemberton Trust, his principal creditor. Joan Dunsmuir entered into a private arrangement with the trustees. In return for her guarantee that she would, sometime in the future, pay off Harry's mortgage, they agreed not to sell the house. In the meantime, Mary and Harry could remain at Mount Adelaide— but only by renting it from the trustees. And since Harry was now penniless, any legal documents would have to be signed by his wife.

Mary signed the rent agreement, and she never let Harry forget that he was a failure, an assessment that her brothers shared. But at least Harry possessed the attributes of a true gentleman. He was quiet and courtly and kind. And that was considerably more than could be said about the man Emily Ellen introduced to the family.

—

On 14 July 1886 when she was twenty-two years old, Emily Ellen became the bride of a twenty-six-year-old captain in the local militia who gloried in the name Northing Pinckney Snowden—the only obvious asset he brought to the family. Describing himself as having been born in Yorkshire—at Hutton More House, which did have a nice country-house ring to it—Snowden had reached Victoria in 1881, taken rooms at the Union Club, and gone to work at Lowenberg & Harris as a real estate agent. Soon he became an indispensable man at Fairview. He served as Harry Croft's best man in July 1885, and six months later he was singled out as one of the more important of the hundred guests who gathered at Fairview for an elaborate fancy dress party deemed to be *the* social event of the season. Emily's sisters, nineteen-year-old Jessie and thirteen-year-old Maude, were disguised as Italian peasant girls while Emily herself drifted about looking ethereally chilly in swansdown and frosted moss in a costume she described as "Winter." Snowden dressed appropriately for a man with romance on his mind. He was a Turkish pasha, he explained as he cast admiring glances toward Emily.

After their marriage, Emily and her new husband settled in the Houghtons' Quadra Street house while Snowden sought out an appropriately spectacular site for the mansion they intended to build. By 1889 he had acquired 12 waterfront acres and construction had begun on "Ashnola," an imposing brick house that would cost $25,000 and rank as the most expensive residence built in the city during the year. Three years later, Ashnola was quietly transferred to Emily's name. By then it had become apparent that Snowden had come to the marriage with a distinct liability. He was suffering from syphilis.

He may well have sought out mercury treatments and considered himself cured when he married Emily, but instead of being vanquished, his disease had entered a latent stage, lying undetected for several years before it re-emerged to attack his brain. Snowden's increasingly erratic behaviour became impossible to ignore. When the time came to remove a potential embarrassment from the bosom of the family, the Snowdens slipped away to England. In 1898 Emily sold Ashnola, and at least some of the money she received was devoted to her husband's care in the Holloway Sanitorium where he died, insane, on 1 April 1904. The *Colonist*, in reporting his death, noted that he was a former resident of the city but discreetly avoided any mention of his connection to Emily and her family.

—

Jessie Sophia, the sixth Dunsmuir daughter, was twenty-four and still unmarried when she moved into Craigdarroch with her mother and two younger sisters in September 1890. The gloriously overdecorated eighteen-room mansion soon proved that a castle could be most effective as husband-bait. Within a year it had helped Jessie entrap an aristocrat and become the first of the Dunsmuir girls to merit an entry in *Debrett's Peerage*.

Sir Richard John Musgrave of Tourin, Cappoquin, County Waterford, came from an old, distinguished Irish family, the first Sir Richard, "a strong Protestant and Loyalist," having been rewarded with a baronetcy in 1782. Jessie's husband, the fifth baronet, who had assumed the title in 1874 when he was just twenty-four years old, had no taste for politics. Neither was he much interested in the management of his family's 8,000-acre Waterford estate. Instead, he developed a passion for fishing. To the end of his days, he would recall as the proudest moment of his life the autumn afternoon on Vancouver Island's Salmon River when he had landed a 70-pound salmon, "the biggest salmon ever killed on a rod and line."

Sir Richard, who was known to have a bad relationship with his mother, welcomed the obsession that allowed him to spend months away from Ireland and his responsibilities. After 1884, when his uncle Edward took up sheep farming on Salt Spring Island, he became a familiar figure on Vancouver Island, quite content to spend weeks and months waist-deep in rivers and streams and more than happy to leave his mother to deal with any problems that might arise on the estate.

In 1885 he was planning to enjoy the Christmas season at his uncle's sheep ranch when bad news from Ireland called him home. A poor crop year had left his tenants unable to pay their rents. He found he had little choice but to fall in line with other landlords who had agreed to a general rent reduction and, as a result, he came to think of himself as being "pretty impecunious." Not so poor that he felt compelled to forego his fishing expeditions. However, he did come to recognize that it might be prudent to take time off from casting for salmon to troll for a rich wife.

He must have counted himself fortunate when he attracted the attention of Jessie Dunsmuir. As well as being an heiress, she was an attractive young woman, sixteen years his junior. She had a flair for music and she sat a horse well, a not inconsiderable talent if she was to fit in with Sir Richard's fox-hunting friends.

Despite the fact that he was already possessed of a fiancee who was waiting patiently in London for his return, Sir Richard pressed his suit. After Joan Dunsmuir agreed to settle several hundred thousand dollars on her daughter, their engagement was announced, and Victorians prepared for the most fashionable wedding the city had ever seen—a spectacularly excessive ceremony, at which Jessie was accompanied down the aisle by twenty-seven bridesmaids and flower girls.

"The whole wedding arrangements were perfect, weather included," a guest reported. "Even Sir Richard managed to make the most of himself and behaved very well."

No one, it seems, had a particularly high opinion of "the Bart," and perhaps it was not too surprising that Jessie found her first years in Ireland rather forlorn. "You seem to be very gay in Victoria this summer," she wrote wistfully to a friend in 1892. "It is dreadfully quiet here . . . We have been having horrid wet weather lately." Still, she kept her part of the bargain, pouring thousands of Dunsmuir dollars into the Musgrave estate. She built a new wing on the house and she financed the "tremendously expensive" life the Musgraves enjoyed, with thirteen live-in servants in their Irish house and with a townhouse on Great Cumberland Place which Jessie purchased to serve as a *pied à terre* during the London season.

As Lady Musgrave, Jessie had entrée to the Court of St. James and to the Vice-Regal Court in Dublin. She hurled herself into society, entertaining with a will and accepting every invitation that came her way. She and her money created quite a stir when they arrived in Ireland, and not a few members of the land-poor aristocracy were intrigued to learn that she had two younger sisters—delightfully rich "black diamonds"—whom Jessie would soon be launching into their midst.

Thirteen

—

For Alexander Dunsmuir, the spring and summer months of 1891 were particularly bleak. The strike at Wellington was moving into its second year; his mother was prepared to sell the colliery the instant her agent found a buyer, and Sir Richard Musgrave was setting a new standard in expensive brothers-in-law. Drinking heavily, Alex had already set out along the path of irrecoverable alcoholism when Edna nudged him further along the way.

Four years old when Alex had become her mother's paramour, Edna was a winsome and willful seventeen in May 1891 when she delivered her ultimatum. Either Alex married her mother or she would leave home; she would go to New York and make her own way on the stage.

Alex begged her not to go. "He offered me anything," Edna said. He would buy a yacht and take them on a cruise around the world. "He said I could have anything under the sun if only I would stay with him."

If she went to New York, she would be on her own, Alex threatened. "He said that he would not help me, that he would do everything he could to prevent me from going," Edna said. "He would stop my allowance and not give me any money."

Throughout the rest of his life, Alex's feelings toward Edna would be a jumble of contradictions. Sometimes he would think of her as a little girl and shower her with presents—dainty dresses, a doll, tiny shoes—more appropriate for a child of seven or eight. At other times he would recognize the sophisticated woman she had become and insist that she accept expensive gifts of diamonds and pearls. Whatever their earlier relationship may have been, Edna was important to Alex. But still he could not bring himself to marry Josephine.

Edna's success in New York was instantaneous. A petite girl, not quite five feet tall, she was saucily pretty, bursting with energy and equipped with a *joie de vivre* and a breezy outgoing friendliness that drew people to her. On 17 August 1891, only three months after she left San Francisco, she made her stage debut playing Mabel Douglas in *The Club Friend* at the Star Theatre. She caught the attention of Charles Frohman, and when she returned to San Francisco in 1892, she came as a professional actress and a valued member of Frohman's touring company.

—

By the winter of 1893, Alex had, once again, drunk himself to the doors of death. Josephine had never seen him in so bad a condition. She felt she had no choice but to inform his office manager, John Lowe. Lowe summoned a doctor and, after hearing his prognosis, he sent a telegram to James, asking him to come at once and warning him that his brother was not expected to live.

Dr. Cornelius Buckley was appalled by Alex's condition. "He was perfectly delirious, perfectly insane," Buckley said. "He was also suffering from bad kidney trouble. Upon one occasion he did not pass water for 48 hours. I did not expect that he could possibly live."

Tied to the bed, trembling, thrashing about and wracked by convulsions, Alex could not be calmed by the narcotics Buckley administered. Finally, after more than a week had passed, and then only after James had arrived to give his permission, the doctor resorted to chloroform.

Buckley, who had been confidently predicting his patient's imminent demise, was astonished by the rapidity of Alex's recovery. After noting that Alex was in "tolerably good condition," he issued a stern warning. "I ordered him abroad. I gave him strict instructions to avoid alcoholic stimulants of every kind and form for the balance of his life. I cautioned him that if he did drink, he would lapse into the same condition and not live very long."

Hovering near his brother's bedside until the crisis passed, Jim received the first inkling that the woman whom he had understood to be Alex's landlady might have been playing a rather different role in his life. Assuming that Josephine had taken advantage of Alex's condition to insinuate herself into his life, he wrote to his brother, promising to do everything he could to help him get rid of her.

My Dear Alex

I am sorry to write what I am going to, but I have known it for a long
time + never said anything about it, that is the reason I asked you
before you went down this time if it was a woman's troubles that was
troubling you. I knew it was, but you said not, so I did not like to
come right out with it. I feel awful sorry + would help you all I can to
get rid of her. I think you should let me know the whole thing, so
that I could help you out of your troubles, if there is anyway that it
can be done, so far as money matters are concerned, or by advising a
way to get you out of it. I am your only brother + think it is your
place to let me know so that I can help you. Write me all about it, or I
will come down before you go to Mexico + talk it over, to see what is
best to be done. There are lots of men in the same fix as you and
surely there is a way out of it, and settle down to life in a different
way than you have been living for all these years. It is bound to worry
you, so I want to help you out of it if I can.
    Mother and all of us are well.
    Hope that you will be better than ever after your sickness + get rid
of the thing that is troubling you.

Your affect. Brother
James Dunsmuir

Alex followed at least some of his doctor's orders. He left San
Francisco, spent two weeks drying out in the Mexican sun and then
made plans to sail for Europe, where he would spend a year making
the rounds of health spas. But, contrary to Jim's expectations, he did
not for a moment consider making the trip without Josephine. They
were en route to the Continent when they paused in New York to
celebrate Christmas of 1893 with Edna and her new husband.
    The previous January, just eleven days after her nineteenth birth-
day, Edna had married DeWolf Hopper, the most popular comic actor of his day and a resounding success as the featured player in his
own touring company. A giant of a man, broad-shouldered and well
over six feet tall, with a commanding presence and a deep melliflu-
ous voice, Hopper was devastatingly attractive to women. Aware of
his appeal, he revelled in his reputation as "the roué's roué," a status he would continue to enjoy into old age. John Barrymore, the es-
teemed actor and notorious rake, said of Hopper, "I hate to admit
this, but if that old bastard and I saw a girl at the same time and had

the same idea, I learned to sadly bow out. And I'll be damned—so did my father before me."

On Christmas night 1893 when Hopper invited Alexander and Josephine to dinner at New York's Imperial Hotel, he and Edna had been married for only a year; Edna had joined his company and, as his co-star in *Panjandrum*, was demonstrating that she had a flair for musical comedy.

Hopper was taken aback when, within moments of being introduced, Alex leaned forward and murmured confidentially, "I've been very ill. I nearly died. The doctors tell me that if I ever drink again it will kill me." Hopper hesitated before ordering wine with dinner. "Oh well, I will drink a little," Alex said when the bottle appeared.

Edna, who thought Alex appeared "very feeble and shaky," asked him why he was drinking when he knew it would kill him.

"Oh, this little bit won't hurt me," Alex said.

"That little bit might lead to a great deal more," Edna retorted. And of course she was right.

During the year that Alex and Josephine spent abroad, he continued to drink. They were in Lucerne when he collapsed with yet another attack of *delirium* that once again brought him near death and left him hospitalized for three months.

It was in Lucerne, thousands of miles from home, that the tenuousness of her position suddenly overwhelmed Josephine. "What if he had died?" she asked a friend soon after their return to San Francisco. "What if I had been left in Europe without a dollar? See the shape I would have been in then." She became obsessed with the necessity of "getting Mrs. D. to her name." And Alex, perhaps finally concluding that marriage to Josephine might ease his mind and aid in his recovery, agreed to do what he could.

In January 1895, soon after they returned from Europe, he went to Victoria to talk to Jim. For the first time, he told his brother that Josephine had been his mistress for fifteen years, and he asked Jim to do him a favour. "He wanted to know if I would not go up and ask mother if she would not give her consent for him to marry Mrs. Wallace," James recalled. "I thought that if Alex married her it would be better for him. He would not drink so much. We all knew that he drank."

James broached the subject when he called on his mother at Craigdarroch. She reacted angrily. "If you advised him to marry, then you are as bad as he is," she hissed. "I would rather see Alex in his grave than married to that woman."

Alex was forty-one years old, and still he could not marry without his mother's permission. However, now that his family knew of Josephine's existence, he was no longer forced to keep her hidden away. He took two suites of rooms, joined by a connecting door, on the first floor of San Francisco's aptly named Grand Hotel. But he continued to drink.

Six years had passed since Robert Dunsmuir's death. With their mother apparently no closer to relinquishing her control of R. Dunsmuir & Sons, Alex and Jim decided that the time had come to inch their way to independence. Their father had never concerned himself with the San Francisco operation, they argued. And furthermore, R. Dunsmuir & Sons, San Francisco, had few assets; the office, the wharves and the coal bins were located on leased land. If she was not prepared to sign over the mines and the railway, might she at least give them control of the San Francisco sales office?

By 19 June 1896 their arguments had worn her down. She put her signature on a bill of sale. For a token payment of $10, she conveyed R. Dunsmuir & Sons to a new company to be known as R. Dunsmuir's Sons—a small but significant change.

That much accomplished, the brothers shifted their attention to the Union Colliery and the E & N. "We always understood they belonged to us; Mother told us they *did* belong to us," James said. "Mother had always promised, and Father had, that the Union Colliery and the E & N were to go to the boys. And in the will it was so."

For six months they hammered their arguments home. The time had come for her to carry out the provisions of their father's unsigned will, they insisted. And finally Joan agreed. On 10 December 1896 she conveyed her shares in the Union Colliery and the railway to her sons. Now only the Wellington Colliery and the Victoria sales office remained outside their control.

Their sisters charged them with having coerced their mother into signing, a notion James dismissed out of hand. "You put a document before my mother, and if she don't want to sign it, she won't sign."

But in the weeks following the creation of R. Dunsmuir's Sons, Joan began to wonder if she had been too hasty. As James recalled, "Mother worried that if Alex should die, that woman—she called her—would step in and cause some trouble in San Francisco." What Joan wanted from James and Alex was an agreement that if either of them predeceased her, his half-interest in R. Dunsmuir's Sons would revert to her. James asked Charles Pooley, the Victoria lawyer who represented both him and his mother, to draw up the agreement. He signed it and promptly forgot about it, never thinking for a moment that either of them would die before their mother. "I never thought about Alex dying," Jim said. "Never gave it a thought, Alex dying."

Alexander should now have been enjoying at least some peace of mind. But he had gone past the point of redemption. Every day, champagne, wine punches and whiskey slipped down his throat in enormous quantities. "That man had the power of consuming a quantity of alcohol that would simply have been fatal to another man," a friend recalled. "Three bottles he would usually get away with; sometimes two; sometimes one and a half. We considered him on his best behaviour when he only got away with one and a half."

Alex had learned to fine tune his consumption, and although he was never strictly sober, he remained reasonably alert and able to conduct business. "I found him particularly sharp and shrewd," Harry Bullen, a Victoria shipbuilder recalled. But every two or three weeks, his control would slip and he would be off on one of his sprees, drinking steadily day and night until his stomach rebelled and he began to vomit.

Josephine led a miserable existence. By nature sociable and out-going, she had few friends and few opportunities to leave her suite as she felt that she should spend every waking hour keeping vigil over Alex. "She wore herself out in the service of that man," a doctor who attended her asserted. She sat beside him, her fist firmly planted in the small of his back, trying to keep him steady as he sagged and wavered. She read him the morning papers when he was too bleary-eyed to focus. She wrapped his head in ice-filled towels when he complained of "a very peculiar feeling . . . as if something was cracked in his brain." When his hand shook so badly that he could not eat, she fed him spoonful by spoonful. She kept a supply of pepsinated milk on hand and insisted that he use it to dilute his whiskey. And she worried about him constantly.

The one time Josephine took a few hours for herself, the results proved disastrous. In the summer of 1897, Edna was once again in San Francisco. When the run of her play ended, Josephine was suddenly overcome with loneliness. Anxious to prolong her hours with her daughter, she decided to risk leaving Alex while she travelled to Sacramento to see Edna off on the Chicago-bound train. She left him in the care of Mrs. Jacques who had been hired as a seamstress but who had become more of a paid companion, spending every day at the Grand before escaping to the sanity of her own home in the evening.

Josephine asked Mrs. Jacques to do the impossible. "Don't give him any liquor while I'm away," she warned, and poor Mrs. Jacques felt duty-bound to take those instructions seriously. Alex became enraged.

"He became so unmanageable that he stepped out into the hall and demanded whiskey anyway." Mrs. Jacques was mortified. "His pajamas were in a condition that any gentleman would not appear in a public hall," she recalled with a shudder. "They were badly soiled. He had lost control of his bowels."

His whiskey provided by an ever-helpful bellboy, Alex ordered her to leave and bolted the door behind her. She met Josephine at the Oakland station the next morning. "It's pretty bad," she warned. "He's been drinking all day and all night. He'll be in a pretty bad state."

"I was on my way downstairs," bellboy Harry Smith recalled. "I heard Mrs. Wallace run out greatly excited and call me to hurry up and get a doctor, 'Quick, for God's sake.' Mr. Dunsmuir was in his bed screaming and screeching."

"I found him suffering from the effects of a debauch," Dr. Walter Thorne reported. Like every doctor who had attended Alex since 1886, Thorne told him that if he continued to drink, he would die. But unlike the others, he theorized that Alex had been using alcohol as a pain suppressant. "This man had, and had had for a long time prior, hemorrhoids and ulceration of the rectum which rendered him very unhappy."

When Alex recovered from the effects of his spree, Thorne recommended an operation. Alex's convalescence was slow. Six weeks after his surgery, just as he was beginning to feel well again, he was hit by a severe attack of shingles, the nerve ends of his chest and back erupting in fiery welts. "He was quite dilapidated and pulled down from this painful, distressing disease and then he begged me for a drink," Thorne said.

Having nothing but sympathy for his patient, the doctor gave in. "It was going to be a long, tedious convalescence," he reasoned, "and so I allowed him liquor in moderation." Alex began by taking a little sherry, but as Thorne was forced to admit, "He soon switched to something stronger."

By the spring of 1898, Alex was fully recovered, out of bed, back to his old habits and determined to convince his mother to loose her grip on the Wellington Colliery, the last vestige of Robert Dunsmuir's empire that she continued to control. Hiring Louis Ginter, a bellboy from the Grand, to act as his valet, he travelled to Victoria that August. They stayed at Craigdarroch, and Alex lowered his guns on his mother and subjected her to a near-constant barrage.

With Joan having failed to find a buyer for Wellington, both Alex and his brother had became obsessed with the notion that the colliery was rightfully theirs. They knew that after thirty years of operation, the mine was nearly played out. In fact they had already decided to abandon it and shift their attention to the Union mine at Comox and the Extension mine south of Nanaimo. But the reputation of Wellington coal still excited the confidence of consumers; the right to market Union coal under the corporate banner of the Wellington Colliery was reason enough to try to induce their mother to sign it over.

Joan had a weakness for her younger son. She had shared her husband's opinion that Alex was a better businessman than James. He might have won her over if he had made an attempt to remain sober during his visit. But he did not. And his determination to settle the matter only increased with the amount of alcohol he consumed. One night he barged into his mother's room. Swaying at the foot of her bed and raising his voice so that everyone in the house could hear, he began to harangue her. "Mother, you must sign," he demanded. "You must. I won't leave this room until you do. You must."

More than a match for her drunken, wild-eyed son, Joan reacted with anger. "Get out of my room," she ordered. "You're mad. Get out of my room and go back to bed."

One evening at dinner, his courage bolstered after a day spent in the barroom of the Driard Hotel, he decided to tackle her once again. "Eat your dinner," Joan said. "If you won't eat, then go to bed."

"No!" Alex screamed, and pushing himself away from the table, he lurched toward the door. Louis Ginter found him sprawled on the castle's steps, unconscious and with a bad gash on his forehead. Called to dress the wound, Dr. Davie quickly sized up the situation. He ordered Alex confined to bed and he warned Ginter to make sure that he had no access to alcohol.

Once again Alex suffered from hallucinations. "He would think there was somebody listening, somebody behind the curtains, somebody at the door, somebody at the window," his sister Mary, who had taken charge of his convalescence, recalled. But after only two days, the crisis passed, and by the third day Alex was feeling quite himself again. So superhuman were his powers of recuperation that, two weeks after Dr. Davie had first been summoned, his patient was strong enough to leave on a fishing trip.

That voyage aboard the *Thistle* would be Alexander's last truly happy time on earth. Used by the Dunsmuirs to carry coal and freight, and fitted out to accommodate fifty passengers, the *Thistle* was diverted from her regular duties to carry Alex and his party to favoured fishing haunts. Surrounded by men with whom he felt at ease—his brother-in-law John Bryden and, from San Francisco, his personal physician Dr. Thorne and his office manager John Lowe, Alex sailed through lingering summer days, heady with memories of his boyhood and youth. The thick muddy smell of clam beaches at low tide; morning fog clinging to quiet still waters; sun-warmed afternoons hazy with the smoke of distant fires; evening air sharp with hints of autumn.

He was in his element—shooting seabirds from the *Thistle*'s deck, scrambling easily up and down the shipside ladder, negotiating in Chinook for Indian canoes and paddlers, spending afternoons wading into salmon streams, and roaring with laughter when, during one stormy night, his valet became seasick.

"Land me somewhere," Ginter moaned. "For God's sake, Mr. Dunsmuir, let me die." And Alex responded by playing valet to his valet, ordering him up on deck, wrapping him in coats and blankets and, once Ginter had been made as comfortable as possible, standing by him until he fell asleep.

Alex was refreshed, alert and sober when he returned to Craigdarroch. During the last two weeks of September, he occupied himself with business, and as usual when there was a disagreement between the brothers, Jim deferred to Alex. "I always gave way to my brother," James said. "He knew more about business than I did."

James had become involved in litigation with Joseph Boscowitz over the *Czar*, a powerful steamer leased by the Union mine to tow sailing ships from Esquimalt up the straits to the Comox mines. Boscowitz, who had recently acquired the *Czar*, had chosen not to honour the Dunsmuirs' lease. Jim had wanted to fight it out in court. "No, we'll settle the matter," Alex decreed, and as treasurer of the Union mine, he wrote out a cheque for $22,000, waved it under Boscowitz's nose and took possession of the vessel.

James continued to bow to his brother's business acumen, despite the obvious fact that within days of returning to Victoria, Alex had taken to drink. When his brother was unable to drag himself to the office, Jim waited on him at the castle. Alex was in bed—"I expect he had been drinking the night before," Jim said—when suddenly he interrupted their discussion to introduce the subject of his will.

"Look in my pocket, Jim," he said. "You'll find my will. You read it, Jim."

Signed a day or two earlier, Alex's will left everything to his brother. "Put it in your safe," Alex said. And after Jim promised to provide Josephine with a $12,000 annuity, and after he agreed to give each of their sisters $50,000 when he could afford to do so without "embarrassing" himself, Alex sank back in bed. "I will trust you," he said. Like his father, Alex could not bring himself to divide his estate.

Alex was due to leave Victoria by the middle of October to join Josephine and Edna in New York. His ticket had been purchased and the steamer was about to leave, but Alex was nowhere to be found. As sailing time approached, Jim went in search of him. He found him in the billiard room of the Union Club. Staggering and incoherent, Alex waved him away. It took three men to manhandle him out of the club and pour him aboard the steamer. For Louis Ginter, the train trip to New York was a nightmare. "There was a time there when he was out of his mind," Louis recalled.

"Louis, Louis, what are those snakes doing up there?" Alex quavered.

"That's not a snake. That's the bell-cord," Ginter assured him.

"No, no, it can't be the bell-cord—it can't be—call the porter," Alex shrieked. The porter gave him the same answer.

"It's rot, rot," Alex cried.

"What's the matter with him. Is he crazy?" the porter asked.

"No, just drunk," Louis sighed.

Fourteen

When Alex joined Josephine and Edna, he gave every indication of a man suffering from a guilty conscience. His newly signed will excluded both women from any direct share in his estate. Josephine and Edna might have been Alex's family for almost twenty years, but still he was capable of regarding them as outsiders. He was determined to prevent them from making trouble in the event of his death. And, by leaving it up to Jim to take care of Josephine, he had done just that.

But now, in New York, surrounded by the solicitous attentions of Josephine and her daughter, he might have felt a twinge of remorse. He certainly became uncharacteristically generous. He led the two surprised women to the city's most elegant shops. He bought hats and bodices and fancy-waists and all manner of extravagant things—$75 handkerchiefs from Stearns and from Tiffany's a $22,000 pearl collarette for Edna. He took them to a toy shop where he bought Edna a doll. Don't wrap it, he said. She'll carry it out. "You are my little girl," he told the twenty-four-year-old Edna. "You should carry your dolly with you."

When they returned to San Francisco, Josephine discovered that Alex's philanthropy had not been left in New York. He decided to buy her a home—a fine place in the country—that would be registered in her name alone.

In November 1898 he found Souther Farm and an owner who could not have been more anxious to sell. Gilbert Tompkins had decided to go into the business of raising trotting horses on a grand scale. He had invested heavily, building a racetrack and paddocks and spending thousands of dollars "in all sorts of foolish ways." But then the bottom had dropped out of the trotting horse market, and Tompkins had been delighted to accept Alex's offer of $80,000 for his 315 mortgaged acres.

Alex had made a canny investment. Souther Farm was in San Leandro in Alameda County a few miles south of Berkeley and Oakland, the genteel San Francisco suburbs that climbed the shoulders of the Coast Range, providing fog-free days and plenty of elbow-room for the leisured rich to indulge in the building of wildly exuberant Victorian mansions.

But Alex had been attracted to Souther Farm not by its prestigious setting alone. He had been won over by the privacy it offered and by its potential to turn a profit as a working farm, providing Josephine with an income and relieving James of some of the responsibilities he had agreed to shoulder. By the time he was finished, Alex would spend an additional $150,000 on the farm, plowing under the racetrack, tearing down many of the barns and replacing the small, wood-frame farmhouse with something more appropriate to San Leandro's blossoming status.

Chronically suspicious of strangers, Alex chose Eugene Freeman as his architect. A practising architect for only nine years, Freeman might not have been the most experienced man in San Francisco, but he enjoyed a distinct advantage. He came from a family that had been intimately connected with the Dunsmuirs for many years. His father was Capt. Joshua Freeman, the master of the *Glory of the Seas*.

The *Glory* and her captain were legends on the Pacific coast. "She often went down the coast under full sail, with timbers, spars and rigging creaking and groaning. The *Glory* under full sail was a sight to warm the heart," sea-going men recalled. In January 1886 the *Glory* had begun carrying coal from Departure Bay to San Francisco, and although she would be chartered by other concerns from time to time, the Dunsmuirs remained her best customers. Before each trip northward, Freeman negotiated the rate he would receive with Alex. "He was pretty sharp, kept me down to the lowest rate he could possibly get, and he was well-posted on what rates were going," Freeman said.

A stern, demanding man, he developed a respect for the younger Dunsmuir and became one of his closest friends—so close that in 1896, soon after he moved into the Grand, Alex introduced him to Josephine. And Josephine, achingly grateful for Freeman's fatherly concern, bombarded him with confidences, poured out her fears, shared her secrets and enlisted him as her principal aide in the campaign to keep Alex alive. By February 1899 Freeman had become so devoted an ally that when Alex was suffering through a bout of drink-induced nausea, the captain held his head while he retched and strained, and then obediently carried the basin to Josephine so that she could examine the vomitus for traces of blood.

That relationship was more than enough to recommend Freeman's son to Alex, but by the time he realized that he had made a mistake, it was too late. After surveying the property, Freeman decided that the old farmhouse occupied the best building site. While it was being moved, he prepared plans for a house that he estimated might cost as much as $20,000 to build. He was astonished to discover that the lowest bid he received was for $26,000. That was too high, Alex told him. If that was the price he had to pay, then he would not build. In the end Josephine won Alex over, and by the time she had finished fine tuning Freeman's plans—adding beamed ceilings, mahogany panelling and ornate mantelpieces—the San Leandro house set Alex back $40,000. Freeman had produced an otherwise pleasantly proportioned house dominated by three massive pillars that supported a fragile-looking pediment and threw the whole structure off balance. And, Alex grumbled, one of those huge pillars was positioned directly in front of the entrance, effectively blocking the grand sweep of the stairs.

—

What would become of the San Leandro estate after Josephine's death was a subject that Alex had not considered, but it became a question of some moment when Edna arrived for a visit and invited a reporter from the *San Francisco Examiner* to come calling.

"Hatless, She Wanders the Fields. A Summer Day with Edna Wallace Hopper," the *Examiner* headlined its feature article. Edna led the *Examiner*'s man all over the estate—to the stables and cow barns, to the kitchen garden and the orchard, through the nearly completed mansion and then into the farmhouse, sending Alex scuttling out the back door.

There seemed to be no limit to Edna's indiscretion. She introduced the two ponies. "Aren't they cute little fellows," she cried. "Here's Toddy."

"Toddy was named after J. Todd Sloan, the jockey, between whom and Mrs. Hopper there exists a warm friendship," the *Examiner*'s man deadpanned. He might also have added that J. Todd Sloan had been named co-respondent in Edna's divorce, for she had been so indelicate as to name the pony after the man who had put DeWolf

Hopper through "the acid test of cuckoldry."

Hopper had been whiling away an afternoon with a group of fellow actors at the Lambs Club, when, on the spur of the moment, he invited them to tour the elegant New York townhouse he and Edna had recently rented. Their visit became a Broadway legend.

On entering the place, he expatiated on the wonders of the first floor, then he took his friends upstairs. Flinging open an imposing door, he intoned, 'This is the bedroom.' The Lambs duly filed in, to stop aghast. In the four-poster bed, deliciously nude, was Edna Wallace. Beside her, equally nude, sprawled the jockey, Tod Sloan. Both were fast asleep, obviously exhausted from the transports of rapturous love. The Lambs swivelled horrified eyes to huge De Wolf. What would he do about this ultimate in manly disgrace? Hopper slowly walked to the side of the bed and peered down like a connoisseur at the two small, naked, perfectly formed bodies. 'Aren't they beautiful?' he quietly asked.

Edna's lack of subtlety was monumental. She claimed that Souther Farm belonged to her. She revealed financial details—"It has not been a bad investment," she confided, adding that the estate received $2,000 a year from the rental of its orchards and pastures. And she risked public exposure of Alex's role in her mother's life.

"Mr. Dunsmuir was pretty cross," one of Alex's associates recalled. "He said he didn't want any newspaper people out there; he didn't want any notoriety at all; that Mrs. Hopper was doing it all for notoriety and he didn't want it done there."

Just how annoying Alex found the episode became apparent a few days later. Josephine, who had been feeling vaguely unwell, suffering from what seemed to be a pinched nerve in her neck, decided to write a will. She would leave the San Leandro estate to her two children. When she showed her will to Alex, he threw it in the fire. "He didn't want either Willie Wallace or Edna Wallace to have a cent of his money. He wanted that property deeded back to him in the case of her death." When all was said and done, Alex was nothing if not his father's son.

—

While Alex had been occupied with the improvements to the San Leandro estate, James had kept up the pressure on Joan to sign over the Wellington mine. Seventy-one years old and in failing health, she had taken to spending most days in her second-floor sitting room and bedroom, peacefully removed from the comings and goings in the house below. Every time James came to call, she found herself repeating her position over and over again. She had given the boys enough, she said. If she failed to find a buyer, Wellington would be theirs after her death. The only condition attached to the bequest would be the establishment of trust funds for their sisters. In the meantime, she had to think of the girls. If Jim and Alex wanted Wellington so badly, why didn't they buy it?

Thousands of tons of coal and $5 million in profits had been taken out of the mine since she had set her first price in 1890. Now, she told James, she would be prepared to accept $500,000. That was too much, Jim argued. The mine was nearly played out.

They were still at an impasse in August 1899 when Joan received an anonymous letter. James was treating her unfairly, her correspondent claimed. He had begun the process of dismantling the mine; rails had been taken up and machinery had been removed from the shafts. Joan was incensed. He had not reported any of this to her. What was he up to, she demanded. Was he deliberately devaluing the mine?

Don't listen to tittle-tattle, Jim said. And he placed before her, once again, the papers that required only her signature for the mine to be theirs.

At that point, Dr. Hannington arrived to find his elderly patient in a high state of agitation. He ordered James from the room. His mother's intransigence had brought Jim to the breaking point. He wheeled on the doctor, told him to mind his own business and threatened to throw him out the window.

"Leave my house at once," Joan demanded, and Jim stormed out. It was the last time he would see his mother alive.

He remained determined to possess Wellington, but now negotiations with his mother were conducted only through their lawyers. By October 1899 Joan, acting on the advice of John Bryden, had dropped her asking price to $410,000, and James, who respected Bryden's expertise, agreed to accept what he recognized to be his mother's final price.

For their money the brothers received the buildings near the E & N's Store Street station which housed the Dunsmuirs' Victoria offices, the colliers *Wellington* and *Bristol*, and the tugs *Pilot* and *Lorne*. James estimated the total worth of the buildings and the steamers to be no higher than $225,000. That meant they were paying $185,000 for a mine that they had already decided to abandon.

"Don't give the girls anything now," Alex said as he added his signature to the document. "Mother can pay them out of that $400,000."

—

Since 1896, when Joan had signed over her shares in the E & N and the Union Colliery, Alex had been a wealthy man, free to live his own life with nothing to fear from his mother's disapproval. But the possession of the Wellington Colliery had loomed so large that it was not until the sale was complete that he made plans to marry Josephine.

The ceremony took place on 22 December 1899 in the sitting room of an inn, "one of those little old California country hotels" hidden away in the countryside, far away from the prying eyes of San Francisco reporters. Alex gave his age as forty-six, but Josephine brushed away more than a decade and declared herself to be thirty-eight. She had waited twenty-two years to "get Mrs. D. to her name," and it was hard to admit that she had become a grandmotherly fifty years old before that day finally arrived.

James came down from Victoria to witness his brother's marriage; he was the only family member to attend. Supporting the bride was Emily Agnew, Josephine's only friend. John Lowe, the manager of the San Francisco office, and James Taylor, a coal dealer who had known Alex since 1877, made up the remainder of the party. They had been invited for a very special reason—Alex needed them to witness his will.

According to California law, any will he had signed before his marriage would be invalidated once Josephine became his wife; if he should die without drafting a new one, his widow would automatically inherit his estate. And so Alex had come to the ceremony prepared. As he exchanged vows with Josephine, a new will, naming James his sole heir, was nestled in his pocket, where it waited to be signed as soon as possible after the ceremony.

The wedding feast at the Agnews' modest East Oakland home was a melancholy affair. "It was a rather dry wedding," a guest remarked. The men engaged in desultory conversation as they sat together in the sitting room. They shifted closer to the coal stove, banked high in an unsuccessful attempt to combat the December chill. "Well, we know it can't be Wellington coal," James observed, and the others laughed weakly and lapsed into silence.

The following day, Alex and Josephine boarded an eastbound train to begin the honeymoon for which Josephine had been waiting more than two decades. Alex was not on his best behaviour. "They had a quart bottle with some in it when they came aboard," the porter Henry Sample noticed as he made up Alex's bed and lowered him into it. And soon Sample's bell was ringing—Alex wanted more whiskey.

They reached Chicago on Christmas morning. Alex had to be roused to be transferred to the New York train. "I put his clothes on for him," Sample said. "It seemed to me he had no control over his bowels. He had soiled his linen and himself. I sponged him off first, put his underwear on, and socks and shoes on, put the buttons on his shirt."

When Alex signed the register of New York's gracious Imperial Hotel, he could manage only an unrecognizable scrawl. His time was running out; he now had fewer than five weeks to live.

So accustomed were they to seeing Alex suffering from the effects of one of his sprees that neither Josephine nor Edna, who was in the city for the Broadway debut of her latest play, recognized the seriousness of his condition. They dragged him out of bed, forced him into his clothes and insisted that he attend the New Year's Day debut performance. Wedged upright in the centre box at the Victoria Theatre, Alex could not concentrate on the play, did not recognize Edna when she appeared on stage and had little understanding of where he was or why he was there. By the time the intermission arrived, he had become an embarrassment. Edward Crowninshield, a young man from an aristocratic East coast family, who was so besotted with Edna that he was prepared to take on any chore if only to be near her, heaved Alex out of his chair. "Don't come with us. It will only attract attention," he whispered to Josephine as he prepared to manoeuvre Alex out of the theatre.

Alex managed to leave his hotel room only once again, on 17 January, Edna's birthday. "He wanted to buy some pearls for me," Edna recalled. "And he went down to Tiffany's and got as far as the private office when he sank in a chair and could not move; they had to send out and get whiskey for him and he was taken out and assisted into a carriage and driven up to the hotel and put to bed and that was the last time he ever got out."

For the next two weeks, Alexander was delirious. The team of doctors summoned by Josephine diagnosed alcoholic dementia. They experimented with depriving him of liquor, but that only made him more irritable and restless. Hoping to stabilize his condition, they prescribed one ounce of whiskey every two hours. But his heart continued to beat erratically, pumping madly for a time and then becoming weak and fluttery. On 31 January 1900, forty days after making Josephine his wife, Alexander Dunsmuir died.

—

Alex was not the only patient to be examined by the doctors. Josephine had begun to suspect that the pain shooting down her arm had a sinister cause. Finding a large and almost certainly cancerous growth in her right breast, Dr. Culbert recommended an immediate operation. "I told her that she was risking her life by delaying a single day," he said. "Postpone the funeral," he insisted. "Have the body put in a vault." And at first Josephine agreed. But James Dunsmuir, who had arrived to collect his brother's body, did not.

Dr. Culbert was appalled. "I told him that this was a serious condition; that it had already been allowed to go too far—that it had involved the axillary glands, and that it had to be operated on at once, immediately, without delay—every day she waited, the longer she waited, every day counted against her."

But James was determined to bury his brother, and he was equally determined that Alex be interred in a west coast cemetery. In that case, Dr. Culbert insisted, Josephine should not go west with the body. "Oh well, we will see," James said. But it was clear that he thought it was Josephine's duty to remain by his brother's side.

"It will be better for her to come out and see her husband buried," James said. "After that she can come back if she wants to and be operated on." And Josephine, anxious to please, succumbed to his arguments. As Dr. Culbert said, shaking his head in disbelief, "She felt it was her duty to go, if her husband was to go."

—

Even in the face of his brother's death, James demonstrated customary Dunsmuir wariness when it came to spending money. Alex's body would be transported to the west coast by train. "They want $4000 for a casket and box," James complained to Crowninshield. "Go down there and see if you can do better."

Crowninshield haggled with the undertaker, and after getting him to agree to $700, he arranged to have Alex's body removed from the hotel and loaded aboard the train. James arrived a few minutes before the train was due to depart. "Is my brother aboard?" he asked.

"Yes, I drove up behind the remains and saw the coffin put on the train," Crowninshield said, and he handed James the train tickets. Expecting to be thanked for the trouble he had taken, he was astonished when Jim demanded, "What's this extra ticket for?"

"Well," Crowninshield replied uneasily. "It's for the body."

"What?" James exclaimed. "You agreed to pay *full fare* for the body?"

———

Money remained uppermost in James's mind during the journey across the plains. It was extremely important that Josephine be given no reason to contest his brother's will. Alex had asked him to give her a thousand dollars a month, but, James declared expansively, he didn't think that that was enough. And with the easy magnanimity of a man who was offering an annuity to a dying woman, he promised to raise the payment to $2,000 a month. He noted with relief that Josephine seemed quite pleased. Her only concern was that he put his promise in writing.

"James, I can trust you, but if anything happened to you, what would happen to me?" she asked.

"Josephine, I don't want to sign an agreement," James said. "My word is as good as an agreement."

Josephine later confided to her lawyer the reason for her concern. James was often involved in disputes with the men who worked his mines. He might be assassinated, and without an agreement binding his estate, she would be left with only the income from the San Leandro farm. But James, afraid that a written contract might be interpreted as an acknowledgement that Josephine had a legal claim to Alex's estate, remained firm. It took many months before she winkled a written agreement out of her brother-in-law, and by then it was too late.

———

In spite of her doctors' warnings, Josephine remained on the west coast for several weeks. She saw Alex buried in the cemetery in East Oakland and then, with James and his wife, Laura, she travelled to Victoria. For the first time she saw Craigdarroch, standing high above the city, dominating the skyline as its mistress had dominated her husband's life. She had entertained a faint hope that some day she might be accepted within its walls. Alex had had a plan. After honeymooning in New York, they would visit Victoria. He would send his mother a telegram from the train, announcing their time of arrival. If they found her carriage waiting for them when they stepped off the steamer, then they would know that she had accepted their marriage. Now, there would be no opportunity to put Joan to the test.

Laura, who had accompanied her husband to New York and who

knew all about Josephine's condition, called in Dr. Davie to examine her. The doctor confided his findings to Laura. He had discovered a very advanced cancer of the breast. The operation had been delayed too long; he would be surprised if she lived as long as twelve or eighteen months. There is no evidence to suggest that Laura shared Davie's bleak prognosis with Josephine—for still she dallied, warmed by the welcome she had received in James and Laura's home and by her sister-in-law's friendship and concern. She would later state that a strange dream, in which Alex appeared at the window begging her to have the operation, convinced her to return to New York.

More than six weeks had passed before she presented herself to Dr. Culbert once again. He noticed a sharp deterioration in her condition. "She was more emaciated than when she went away; she was weaker and quite a bit more irritable." Dr. Abbe, the surgeon who had examined Josephine in January and who would now perform the long-delayed surgery, found "a marked progress in the disease, a very marked progress."

"She had been suffering more than she had been when I first met her—very materially. There was much darting pain at night, worse during the past month so that she was losing sleep."

Abbe removed her breast, the underlying muscle, and the hardened, cancerous glands in her armpit. He found no reason for optimism. And neither did Josephine. The bubbly, cheerful woman emerged from the surgery irritable and restless, depressed at the extent of the wound and by the fact that she had lost the use of her right arm. "At times she was in a desperate state of mind," Dr. Culbert recalled.

By the end of the year, she knew that the cancer had returned. She would go to New York for a second operation, but first she would sign the agreement her lawyers had coaxed out of James—an agreement that might have been finalized much sooner if Josephine had threatened to contest Alex's will. But as her lawyer, Mountford Wilson said, "She spent a good many years trying to get back a respectable name." For years she had called herself "Mrs. Dunsmuir." Litigation would mean full disclosure of her true relationship with Alex and her reputation would be in tatters. That would have been enough to keep Josephine out of court. But an even more compelling reason was her need to remain on good terms with James and his family.

In September 1900 she had been delighted to learn that James and Laura with five of their children were planning a visit. "She was crazy for them to come down," her maid recalled. During the week they stayed at San Leandro, the house came alive. Captain Freeman and his wife came to call and to invite Josephine and her in-laws to dine aboard the *Glory of the Seas*. She missed them badly when they had gone. Other than Edna, whose visits were infrequent, they were the only society Josephine enjoyed. To lose them by launching a lawsuit was beyond contemplating.

James, fully aware of Josephine's dependence, had postponed signing a settlement. Every month $2,000 was deposited in Josephine's account, and every month he refused to bind himself with a signed agreement. But by December 1900, almost a year after Alex's death, Josephine and her lawyer had finally worn him down.

"She was bothering me about it all the time," James said. "And Wilson got me to make it $25,000 a year; and then after that, Wilson got me to give one half the profit, which I did not want to give at all. I did not want to give it."

He really need not have worried. The agreement granted to Josephine "half of the net income from the property owned by Alexander Dunsmuir in California." But that net income was to be calculated "only after the R. Dunsmuir's Sons Company, a California corporation, shall have paid to R. Dunsmuir Company of British Columbia the present existing indebtedness due from it to the latter corporation."

Shortly before Alex's death, the two brothers had decided to buy the San Francisco property that they had been leasing. The $300,000 required to make the purchase had come from the Victoria office. Until that amount was repaid, the San Francisco office would show no net profit and therefore there would be no share for Josephine, unless by some miracle she managed to survive until R. Dunsmuir's Sons was free of debt. In return for a half-share she could never hope to see, Josephine agreed "expressly to waive, relinquish and renounce" any further claims on her husband's estate for herself and her heirs.

Josephine had become thin—emaciated, some people said. Her hair had gone grey; she was tortured by constant pain. She trusted James implicitly. "I know I will get my share in two years," she told Edna. "You see there is a large debt; James says there is a large debt to pay, and if I would be patient and wait until everything is all right, why then I will have my share of the estate."

"She thought she was going to get everything at the end of two years," her maid observed. "And at the same time everybody knew that she was not going to live two years."

When Josephine returned to New York in January 1901, Dr. Abbe found her in a terrible state. So hopeless was her condition that he was reluctant to perform any further surgery. "It was so extensive that on many people I would rather refuse to operate, but she *desired* it and I felt that if nothing was done she would be in a more demoralized condition than she already was." He held out no hope of recovery. But he was glad he had decided to operate when he saw the improvement in his patient's morale.

—

Josephine returned to San Leandro that spring. She died there on 22 June 1901, outliving her husband by only eighteen months. It had cost James Dunsmuir only $36,000 to buy her cooperation and to ensure his retention of his brother's million-dollar estate.

PART TWO

James Dunsmuir

James Dunsmuir in his formal attire as lieutenant-governor of British Columbia.

Fifteen

—

With his brother's death, James Dunsmuir became "the greatest landed and colliery proprietor in Canada, and one of its richest men." His mother, Joan, continued to hold Robert's shares in the ironworks and the navigation company, and she retained possession of his personal real estate holdings—Craigdarroch, Fairview, the Victoria Theatre and a tangled collection of titles to land in Nanaimo, Esquimalt and Victoria. The millions she had taken out of the mines were hers to invest. She had several hundred thousand dollars scattered about in mortgages—$150,000 to the Driard Hotel, and similar amounts to the water works and the electric railway. And she was establishing handsome trusts, some as high as $200,000, for her daughters. But James had the mines and the controlling interest in the railway—and the profits they generated were his alone.

Without ever intending to, the Dunsmuirs had followed the rule of primogeniture, the system of inheritance that seeks to preserve a family's wealth by consolidating it in the hands of the eldest son. To outside observers, the fortune seemed to be in good hands. Middle age suited James Dunsmuir. Flecks of white sprinkled through his red-brown beard gave him a distinguished air, and the benefits of a life of moderation were evident in his clear, sharply focussed eyes. A burly, heavy-set man, he carried his weight well. The extra pounds that had settled over his belly only added to his aura of prosperity, providing a solid expanse on which to display his heavy gold watch chain. He appeared to be the very model of a successful turn-of-the-century capitalist.

But in James's case, appearances were decidedly deceiving. Unlike his father, who had welcomed opportunities to display his quick wit and sharp tongue, James was a quiet retiring man. Where Robert had been outgoing and friendly, James was cautious and wary. Uneasy with repartee, he was gruff and short-spoken. To disguise the fact that he had become deaf in one ear, he often remained stolidly silent rather than admit that he had not caught a comment or question. By all but his closest friends, he was regarded as cold and haughty, a tough-minded businessman—impatient, imperious and demanding.

But the power and prestige that came with the Dunsmuir name were a burden to Robert's eldest son. A simple-minded man and modest in his ambitions, he had no desire to outdo his father. With his brother, he had struggled to gain control of the Dunsmuir empire, but after Alex's death the little heart he had for running the railway and the mines deserted him. As one of his contemporaries observed, "The weight of heavy responsibilities, recognized and accepted as such, has rested upon him ever since he reached man's estate." Now, he wanted nothing more than to be rid of those responsibilities. A plan had already begun to form. He would sell off his holdings; the money he received, he would husband cautiously, buying government bonds and seeking out other low risk, nonspeculative investments.

He yearned for the life of a country gentleman. A life of simple manly pleasures—an estate to run, woods to prowl and game to shoot, a life of tweeds and fishing tackle and a manor house designed to appear as if it had been standing for generations.

Before the decade was out, he would achieve his goal. But the years that passed before he became the master of "Hatley" would be the most turbulent of his life. He would be dragged into court, first by his mother and then by Alex's stepdaughter. He would hear himself described as scheming and unscrupulous, and he would suffer agonies of public humiliation as the sordid details of Alex's alcoholism were paraded before his friends and enemies in banner headlines.

Cunning politicians, hoping to rally support behind the Dunsmuir name, would coax him into assuming the role of their party leader, and he would find himself, reluctantly and uneasily, filling the office of premier of the province. And later, he would bow to the social ambitions of his wife and accept appointment as British Columbia's lieutenant-governor.

———

The Conservative-minded clique, of which Robert Dunsmuir had been part, continued to hold power into the spring of 1898. But as British Columbia newspapers came to a boil in anticipation of the July election, it occurred to the premier, John Herbert Turner, that, while his own Victoria seat might be safe enough, some of his supporters were facing almost certain defeat. Turner had enjoyed a long political career, but still he conducted the business of the premier's office with a genial naiveté—a personally endearing but politically dangerous way of doing business, since the legislature had become an unsavoury stew of antagonistic philosophies and bitter regional discontent. By 1898 "Turnerism" had come to stand for "favoritism, a lax civil service, extravagance in the expenditure of public monies, looseness of administration, sectionalism, increasing indebtedness, encouragement of speculators and promoters at the expense of public assets, recklessness in railway charters, lack of definite and comprehensive policies, non-sympathy with labor aspirations"—and almost anything else suitably disagreeable that oppositionists could think of.

Against this background, James Dunsmuir reluctantly allowed himself to be persuaded to step upon the political stage as a government candidate. "He did not care for politics," an associate recalled. "He did not like publicity of any kind, being essentially retiring and domestic in his tastes, but it was almost inevitable ... that he should enter the Legislature."

And inevitable it probably was. Like his father before him, James Dunsmuir had come to see that the best place to defend his rights as the province's largest employer was in the provincial legislature. The government was facing defeat; and oppositionists were determined to enact anti-Oriental legislation that threatened to undermine his profits.

In 1897 the Alien Labour Act had been introduced in the House as a private member's bill and succeeded in winning approval despite Turner and his cabinet voting against it. That act, which would have prohibited the employment of Chinese in any provincially chartered company, was stalled when the lieutenant-governor questioned its constitutionality and refused to sign it. Reintroduced the following year with little changed beyond its title, the Labour Regulation Act speedily cleared the desk of the new lieutenant-governor, Thomas McInnes, who was ready to sign into law any piece of anti-Chinese legislation placed before him.

For James Dunsmuir, the passage of anti-Chinese legislation was very bad news indeed. Within days of learning that his colliery manager had been charged with eleven counts of "allowing Chinese to be in the Union Colliery Mines for the purpose of employment," James allowed himself to be nominated as a government supporter.

"Alex did not want me to go in," Jim admitted. "He said they were pulling my leg. I did not think so at the time." But later, he would confess, "I think they were pulling my leg a good deal."

When he announced that he would seek election in Comox, the riding which had within its boundaries the Union mine and its illegally employed Chinese, the *Colonist* was ecstatic. Dunsmuir was "inspired by a sense of public duty," the editor rhapsodized. Dunsmuir glided to an easy victory. The same could not be said for the Turner administration. When the final ballots were counted, the results were a deadlock. In the thirty-eight-member House, the government and the opposition each claimed nineteen supporters.

In the ordinary course of events, Turner would have been allowed to meet with the House and survive or fall on the first vote taken. But Lieutenant-Governor Thomas McInnes had other ideas. He took the extraordinary course of dismissing the Turner ministry and then did a more remarkable thing still. Ignoring the elected members of the opposition, he called upon Robert Beaven to form a government.

Beaven was only too happy to accept. He had served as leader of the opposition from 1883 until he lost his seat in the election of 1894. Defeated once again in 1898, he possessed no seat in the House and no status in any existing party. "In the whole province of British Columbia he could not be said to represent anyone but himself," one commentator observed.

British Columbians were given no chance to savour the novelty of being governed by a premier so recently repudiated at the polls, for no "gentlemen of standing" could be found to serve in Beaven's cabinet. Four days after accepting the lieutenant-governor's invitation, he asked to be relieved of the office.

McInnes now turned to Charles Augustus Semlin, the leader of the opposition. Semlin struggled through one legislative session and might have survived a second if it had not been for his attorney general, "Fighting Joe" Martin. On 21 June 1899 Martin attended a banquet in Rossland to honour one of the town's more adventurous speculators. And at that banquet he either became very drunk or went out of his way to prove that he could live up to his reputation for rashness and open indiscretion even when sober. On 3 July Semlin asked for his resignation. Martin reluctantly complied, vowed to get even and became an "active and effective" opponent of the government.

His majority reduced by Martin's defection, Semlin was hanging by a thread. On 23 February 1900 a member, previously a government supporter, voted with the opposition. The house was adjourned while Semlin scurried about trying to form a new coalition. Believing he had enough support to survive a confidence motion, he called on the lieutenant-governor, asking leave to meet with the House. He left feeling his arguments had won McInnes over, and he was stunned the following morning when he received notice of dismissal. There was worse to come. The lieutenant-governor called upon Joseph Martin, who "stood absolutely alone in the House," to be the new premier.

—

At two o'clock on the morning of 1 March 1900, the *Colonist* received a joyous telegram from London. "Ladysmith is Relieved." Victorians, who had been following the news out of South Africa with some anxiety, were swept with relief as they read the banner headline in the morning paper. The city erupted in spontaneous celebration. Flags flew; bunting fluttered; the day was loud with the crackle of fireworks; and the members of the legislature were feeling quite giddy when they gathered that afternoon to hear the lieutenant-governor prorogue the current session and introduce them to their new premier.

They had just passed a motion stating their want of confidence in Joe Martin, when Lieutenant-Governor McInnes entered the chamber. "Simultaneously Mr. Dunsmuir rose and led the way to the lobby, the members of both parties and all interests ... trooping after him," the *Colonist* reported.

The cheers that rocked the public galleries as the members marched out turned to hisses and cat-calls as McInnes began to speak. Pale and nervously clasping and unclasping his hands, he waited a full two minutes for the hubbub to subside. With Joseph Martin the only member there to hear his remarks, he delivered a brief speech rejoicing in the victory in South Africa and praying that the war would soon come to a satisfactory end. Then to the thirty-seven vacant chairs ranged before him, he said, "I now release you from further attendance" and escaped to his carriage.

As he hurried away, the members of the just-prorogued house burst into the chamber. "We are the people. And we must be respected," one member cried as he reached his seat with a bound and flung his hat in the air. Cheers from the floor and the galleries rocked the House and echoed after McInnes as his carriage pulled silently away. And the "strangest scene ever enacted" within the

British Columbia parliament ended with a ringing rendition of "God Save the Queen."

To be singled out as the man who had led the protest against an unpopular and autocratic lieutenant-governor would have been regarded as something approaching a gift from God by any ambitious politician. By that single act of defiance, James Dunsmuir established himself as a natural leader and won for himself a degree of popularity beyond what he could have ordinarily expected. But James, who always insisted that he was no politician, now went out of his way to prove it. Instead of seizing the advantage, he quickly moved to correct the report.

Walking out on McInnes had been prearranged rather than spontaneous, Dunsmuir insisted. He had had no part in formulating the plan. He had first heard of it while he was taking his seat in the House. "I do not wish to be held responsible for an act which I did not advise and which I would not have recommended if I had been consulted."

Dunsmuir was as good as his word. He was certainly no politician. No matter. What he was not prepared to do for himself, Joe Martin was quite capable of doing for him.

As the new premier, Martin faced the same problem that had confronted Beaven two years earlier. No elected member would agree to serve with him. It took him a month to round up a cabinet. And the appointments of men who were "not in politics, had never held a seat in the Legislature, and were practically unknown outside their own respective places of abode" were regarded as a joke. His four cabinet colleagues hung like albatrosses around Martin's neck as he prepared to fight the election that would be necessary before he dared face the House.

That election was scheduled for 9 June, and once again James Dunsmuir offered himself as a candidate. Not in Comox this time, but in the South Nanaimo riding, which included his Extension Colliery, opened two years earlier, and the wharves and bunkers of Oyster Harbour, the company town that he had recently renamed Ladysmith in celebration of the happy news from South Africa.

Trotting out a campaign promise that would stand decades of British Columbia politicians in good stead, he pledged to "urge upon the government the necessity of better roads in your district." And then he turned his attention to wooing the miners without whose support he could not be elected. "I will do all I can to bring about a better feeling between capital and labor," he vowed. "I will do away with all Chinese labor in the coal mines under my control, just as soon as I can find white men to replace them." James was following his father's example, forestalling government control by volunteering to institute change. If no law dictated his management policies, then when agitation for reform subsided, he could gradually slide back to the old way of doing things.

By now, the courts had dismissed the province's anti-Chinese legislation as *ultra vires*, or outside provincial authority. James was promising to do voluntarily what the highest court in the land had said he could not be forced to do. The Liberal-leaning *Victoria Times* was impressed. "When the resolution of Mr. Dunsmuir is carried into effect we shall have made a long stride forward in making British Columbia a white man's country."

The enthusiasm with which the miners at Extension greeted the news was evident when he stood before them at a packed election rally in South Wellington. "I make no claim to be an orator," he warned his audience. "I only ask your patience for a few minutes." And after reading from his list of minor campaign promises, he got down to business.

"Here comes what interests you all," he alerted his listeners. "I shall replace Chinese employed underground with white men so soon as I can get them." He was interrupted by a burst of applause. "I have said that I'll take them out of the mines, and I'm going to do it." More applause. "And I'll go further still—I'll give you my word that so soon as the other industries of the province do away with them, I'll get rid of them altogether."

"Speechmaking isn't my business," Dunsmuir said in conclusion. "Mining is my business."

"Ever punch a mule?" a voice from the audience sang out.

"Yes. I've driven a mule and an engine," James retorted. "And I've put up brattice and can fix a curtain." And to loud applause, he resumed his seat.

He had given the men what they wanted to hear, and more than that, he underlined the genuineness of his promise by advertising throughout the province for "500 White Miners and Helpers for the Wellington, Extension and Comox Mines to supersede all the Chinese in our mines. Apply at once."

James Dunsmuir won election, the 249 voters who supported him giving him a 24-vote majority. His detractors claimed that he had assured his victory by running in a coal-mining district in which the majority of voters were men who depended on him for their jobs. His supporters claimed that in winning election, he had demonstrated that most of his men endorsed his management policies and that criticism had come only from the excited executive of the miners' union. The niceties of that debate mattered little to the lieutenant-governor as he surveyed the total confusion the election had produced.

The Martinites had been trounced. That much was clear. The premier had retained his seat, but only five members-elect were pledged to support him. The anti-Martin forces held thirty-two of the thirty-eight seats, but were united only by their opposition to the premier. And who among this hodge-podge of mainlanders and islanders, of Conservatives, Liberals, Independents and Socialists would be capable of forging a majority in the House? The answer to that question, McInnes decided, was James Dunsmuir.

Except for an overriding determination to protect his own interests, Dunsmuir was regarded as being nonpartisan. It was no secret that he made financial contributions to both federal Liberal and Conservative parties—an understandable largesse from a man whose investments could easily be affected by federal legislation. As the wealthiest man in the province, Dunsmuir had the most to lose if governmental chaos continued and the most to gain from a return to stability and order. Even the most rabidly sectarian politicians were beginning to realize that the time had come to call a temporary ceasefire; battle lines could be redrawn after the province was set on a more orderly course. And after all, one could easily argue that, for the time being at least, the interests of Dunsmuir and the province were the same. If anyone could command a majority in the legislature, that man was James Dunsmuir. On 14 June 1900, the lieutenant-governor accepted Martin's resignation and invited Dunsmuir to pay him a call.

For Dunsmuir to accept the lieutenant-governor's invitation was evidence that he considered the business of the province to be severely affected by continuing uncertainty. If his becoming premier would set things straight, then he was prepared to assume the burden—even though his elevation to the province's highest office could hardly have come at a worse time. Alexander had been in his grave for only six months, and by his own account, James missed his brother's advice and counsel. Now he not only had the San Francisco business to worry about but also he had assumed Alex's role as president of the railroad—a job for which he had few qualifications and little enthusiasm. But, he told himself, his term as premier would be brief. He had no intention of clinging to power. Once he was sure that provincial affairs were being conducted on a businesslike basis, he would be happy to step aside.

At last McInnes had made an acceptable choice. Even the *Victoria Times* reacted with enthusiasm. "The knowledge that a gentleman with the business reputation of Mr. Dunsmuir is to be at the head of the government will do very much to restore the confidence of the business community . . . there is good reason to believe that our provincial affairs will become settled and British Columbia generally go speeding along the road to prosperity."

With that sentiment, the twenty-four anti-Martinites who gathered with the new premier on 18 June at the Hotel Vancouver to hammer out a government policy heartily agreed. Satisfied that they were part of a large government majority, the members got down to business—the first item being a motion condemning the actions of Lieutenant-Governor McInnes.

In calling on Joseph Martin to form a ministry and by allowing him to select a cabinet "unendorsed by the electorate," McInnes had acted "contrary to the principles, usages and customs of constitutional government." That motion received unanimous approval, Dunsmuir and his ministerial colleagues adding their names to the telegram that would soon be winging its way to Ottawa and the desk of the prime minister, Sir Wilfrid Laurier.

Laurier acted immediately. Within two days, the deed was done. McInnes, who stubbornly refused to resign, was peremptorily dismissed, and a new lieutenant-governor, Sir Henri Gustave Joly de Lotbinière, was sworn in.

"A new era has dawned for British Columbia," the *Colonist* sighed.

Sixteen

It seems not to have occurred to James Dunsmuir that he might be accused of accepting the premiership only to serve his own ends. The entire notion of conflict of interest he found quite incomprehensible. To him, it was all very simple. What was good for him was good for the province, and vice versa.

"I consider when I am watching the people's interests, I am watching my own," he said. "I have very large interests here and, if I don't look after the interests of the country, my own interests will not be looked after."

He knew that his personal interests might suffer when he was distracted by the demands of the premiership, but the unstable political situation had been so bad for business that he was prepared to sacrifice temporarily both his profits and his peace of mind to bring about governmental orderliness. He expected to be praised for his unselfish dedication to the provincial good. When he was accused of formulating railway policies designed to boost the profits of the E & N rather than to benefit the province as a whole, he was flabbergasted. And he was equally surprised and not a little chagrined when the management of his coal mines was placed under a political microscope.

By 1900, the year he became premier, James had already decided to abandon Wellington, the only mine that he owned outright, and concentrate his efforts on Union, Alexandra and Extension, the mines that had been opened within the E & N land grant, and the profits of which he shared with the railway's American partners.

Of the three, only the Union mines predated the railroad. As early as 1881 Robert Dunsmuir had begun to acquire coal lands in the Comox Valley. In 1888 he had sold those lands to the E & N—a tidy little transaction in which he pocketed $200,000—and then set to work developing the mine as president of the railroad. By the turn of the century, the Union Colliery was a going concern with over a thousand employees, more than half of whom were Orientals, and with an annual output of more than 250,000 tons.

Robert Dunsmuir had also been responsible for the opening of the Alexandra mine, established in 1884 after coal was discovered near the E & N tracks a few miles south of Nanaimo. The coal was of good quality, but the seams proved to be irregular, and in 1885 he had shut down operation. Alexandra sat idle for a decade, until a stunning discovery was made on land a few short miles away.

Ephraim Hodgson was wandering through the woods on E & N land on the south slope of Mount Benson when he came across a fallen tree with shiny black coal clinging to its upturned roots. James Dunsmuir paid a handsome reward for the information and threw himself into an aggressive development program. Within six months, a 600-foot slope had been burrowed into Mount Benson. At the surface the coal was 9 feet thick; the deeper the slope descended, the thicker the seam became. Near the banks of the Nanaimo River, two and a half miles away, a second outcrop was discovered, and a bore revealed that here, too, the seam was thick and regular. "There must be a great many square miles in this new coal field," the mines inspector concluded. Even more encouraging was the quality of the coal, for tests revealed it to be an extension of the Wellington seam—the best coal Vancouver Island produced.

It was the discovery at Extension, and in particular the extent and quality of the seam, that had encouraged the Dunsmuir brothers to redouble their efforts to coax their mother into assigning them her controlling interest in the E & N. And it was their desire to capitalize on the Wellington name that had finally persuaded them to pay an inflated price for the original colliery. Once their title to their father's first mine was secure, they had begun in earnest the work of dismantling Wellington—tracks, machinery, equipment, even the little company-owned cottages, were carried down to the new Extension mine. By January 1900 Wellington was a ghost town and Departure Bay had been abandoned; Extension was fully operational and new wharves had been constructed 12 miles away at Oyster Harbour.

Each of the collieries James managed for the E & N—Union,

Alexandra and Extension—would be beset by problems during his tenure as premier. His handling of those problems, complicated by his political role, would earn for him the reputation of being ruthlessly unfair and stubbornly antilabour.

—

Within two weeks of being sworn in as premier, James made it clear his major campaign promise had been no mere idle boast. As the *Vancouver Province* reported with some surprise, "The last Chinaman in the Alexandra and Extension mines has not only been ordered to go, but has gone."

Frank Little, who had superintended the development of Comox coal and who had recently been promoted to the position of general manager of all Dunsmuir mines, thought it was a mistake to make business decisions based on political promises. "Mr. Dunsmuir wants to change," he grumbled. "I do not agree with this new idea of his."

Dunsmuir had declared that he intended to hire only "the best element of Canadian coal miners," but he soon discovered that, after a brief flurry of applications, most of the newly available positions remained unfilled. He was left with little choice but to recruit men from the Old Country.

Two hundred Scottish miners were found, each of whom agreed to work for at least as long as it took to repay the $70 it would cost the company to bring him out. "They were no good," Little complained. A few months after their arrival, only twenty remained. As for the others, "I do not know where they went to and I don't care," Little muttered. "I do not think one-third of them ever dug coal in their life . . . Very few paid their passage . . . Many of them went to Seattle at once. They never came here at all. Mr. Dunsmuir spent $15,000 on them. I do not think he got $3000 back. I paid $3 a day for a $1 day's work to some of them. I was longing for the Chinamen."

And so undoubtedly was James Dunsmuir. But his political position made their reintroduction all but impossible. His attitude to the miners' union now hardened. The difficulty in recruiting local white labour had made nonsense of the union's claim that the Chinese were depriving willing workers of jobs. He was also facing higher production costs, while at the same time coal prices in San Francisco were once again in a slump. The miners, he decided, would have to accept a cut in pay.

He began his campaign with Alexandra, the least profitable of the three mines. He proposed a wage reduction of 25 per cent. When the miners protested, he shut down the mine, throwing two hundred men out of work two weeks before Christmas. Pressed for an explanation, he maintained that the labour dispute had nothing to do with the closure. The decision to shut the mine had been taken some time ago, he said, and had been based only on the lack of shipping facilities at Alexandra.

Lionel Terry, secretary of the Alexandra Miners' Protective Association, did not believe that for a moment. He was convinced that Dunsmuir was trying to starve the men into accepting "Chinaman's wages." Terry calculated that Dunsmuir's political position would give the union a tactical advantage. He bided his time for six weeks, until the premier was in Ottawa for a much-publicized meeting with the prime minister. On 21 January 1901 he wrote a letter to the *Ottawa Citizen*, designed to embarrass Dunsmuir into submission. "Mr. Dunsmuir ... attempted to force a reduction of wages in Alexandra, which attempt being resisted, the present lockout is the result. Nearly 200 men, many with wives and families, are thus thrown out of employment in the depth of winter, and as the mine has now been closed down for six weeks, the bare necessities of life are beginning to be regarded as luxuries."

The *Citizen* found Dunsmuir comfortably ensconced in the Russell Hotel. "I want to see my employees satisfied," he said. "I believe they are and have little use for professional agitators. I think the laborers of British Columbia are better off and better paid than elsewhere in Canada." And changing his story, he now insisted that a sales slump had forced him to shut the mine. "I hope to find a market for the coal and as soon as I do, the mines will be reopened."

Three weeks later, Dunsmuir was aboard the train returning to Victoria, and no doubt contemplating the welcome Terry might be preparing for him, when all hell broke loose at the Union mine.

———

William Roy, a "hale and shrewd old miner," had worked in pits in Scotland, Nova Scotia and Ohio, then at Nanaimo and Wellington. When Wellington had been shut down, he had moved on to Union and settled in Cumberland, the little town that encircled the entrance to No. 6 pit. From the first day he reported for work, he had been uneasy about No. 6.

"Man and boy, I've worked in coal mines all my life, but No. 6 was the gassiest I've ever seen and that is saying a good deal," Roy said, shaking his head. He had saved his money, bought a farm and quit the mine. "I knew that she would blow up some day, and at my time of life there was no use tempting fate too much, so I left the job."

On Friday, 15 February 1901, more than sixty men reported for work on the mine's day shift. As usual the pit boss, Will Walker, began his day by inspecting every section of the mine. A cautious, thorough man whose teenage son, William, worked with him on the day shift, he was prepared to order the men aloft if he sensed any trouble.

It was young James Allison's first day in the mine. He had been hired as a mule-driver, but the man Walker had counted on to train him was sick with the flu and had not reported for work. The pit boss decided to enlist the aid of his sixteen-year-old son, George, who had recently graduated from mule-driving to become a member of No. 6's night shift. Walker returned to the surface, roused his sleeping son and together they made their way back to the mine. On their way to the pit entrance, they encountered David Roy.

David Roy had finally decided to take his father's advice. "I warned him every day, until, thank God, he decided to quit, and quit he did," the elder Roy sighed with relief. David had reached his decision the night before. He had resigned that morning and now all that was left was for him to descend the mine one last time to collect his tools.

David was following the Walkers to the pit-head when he stopped to exchange a few words with a friend. By the time he reached the mine entrance, the cage had already begun its 600-foot descent.

"Oh well," he told himself. "It doesn't matter. I'll catch the next one." A few minutes later, he heard a deep ominous roar and felt the ground tremble under his feet. A plume of dust and debris, rising 100 feet in the air, shot from the pit mouth. As Cumberland's residents hurled themselves toward the entrance to No. 6, the sound of a second, and then a third, explosion rumbled from below. Thick black smoke began to billow from the air shaft. No. 6 was on fire! If any of the sixty-four men below ground had survived the explosions, they would now be burned alive.

An hour later, James Dunsmuir, on his way back from Ottawa aboard his private railway car, received word of the Cumberland horror. "Mr. Dunsmuir did not look well at all," an observer noted.

—

No one in No. 6 pit survived. Five days after the explosion, only seven bodies had been recovered. They were, reported the *Province*, "nearly cooked." Three weeks after the accident, the body of the last remaining white man, young George Walker, was discovered buried under a fall of rock. The bodies of seven Chinese were now left below and, so devastating had the explosions been, that weeks would slip into months before the last one was recovered.

Everyone knew that No. 6 was a dangerous mine. Small "blows" were experienced when metal hammers sparked as they met the coal face. In some places, the air was so bad that men often found the flame of their safety lamps flickering out; and sometimes they were forced to work lying prone to catch the fresher air that settled near the floor of the tunnel. Lionel Terry should have had the wit to recognize that the Cumberland disaster had dealt the Miners' Protective Association a strong hand—an opportunity to win sympathy by attacking Dunsmuir for his laxness in failing to guarantee adequate ventilation and an opportunity to win support for an industry-wide union. But, caught up by the anti-Oriental mood of the times, he led off with his weakest suit, in a letter he addressed to the *Nanaimo Free Press*.

> Whereas the immigrants of China and Japan, employed in coal mines in this province, represent the lowest class of the people of those nations, we submit that the employment of these immigrants . . . constitutes a grave menace to the safety of the mining community.
>
> With regard to the fatal explosion at Cumberland . . . we submit that better precautions would have been adopted by management if the men employed at No. 6 mine had been all white men, and we believe the explosion would not have occurred had no mongolians been working in the mine.

Any suggestion that Dunsmuir considered the Chinese expendable would, no doubt, have been greeted with nodding assent. But twenty-seven of the Cumberland victims had been white, and it seemed ludicrous to argue that management had been cavalier with their safety simply because they shared the pit with Chinese.

Terry missed his second chance when he was invited to attend a meeting of the Nanaimo Miners' Protective Association. Variously described as a union and an association, the MPA was fragmented. Each mine elected its own executive; no overall organization bound those executive committees together. Surely, with the Cumberland deaths so fresh in their minds, the time had come to galvanize them into becoming part of an industry-wide movement. But Terry issued no rallying cry, no call for solidarity. Instead, he dealt only with the problems at Alexandra.

As colliery president, James Dunsmuir had little to fear from the miners' associations, but as premier, he would soon suffer the slings and arrows of political opponents. James Hawthornthwaite, an avowed Socialist, a member of the MPA and the newly elected member for Nanaimo, treated the House to the "liveliest session" the Dunsmuir regime had witnessed. The premier was not amused. As the press gallery reporter for the *Province* noted, "The delivery of the speech was made notable, not only because of the newness of the speaker to the house, but because of the persistent interruptions of the premier, who does not appear to love the representative of the Nanaimo miners."

There was little to love about a man who was proposing an amendment to the Coal Mines Regulation Act—even though that amendment was nothing if not moderate, its most contentious clause being a requirement that all men who worked below ground hold certificates of competency.

"At present, experience is not necessary for employment," Hawthornthwaite informed an attentive House. "A petty boss may employ anyone he desires. The bulk of accidents occur at the working face where a shot placed by an inexperienced man in too-solid coal goes off like a gun, and if there is any gas in the vicinity, causes an explosion."

"If the Bill becomes law, it will exclude Chinese from the working-face. I want to be perfectly frank about that," he assured his listeners. "It will have the same effect upon whites without experience, but there is no doubt that Chinese were the unfortunate cause of the greater number of explosions."

"You have got to prove that," Dunsmuir shouted.

"If you hadn't believed that the Chinese were the cause of accidents, you wouldn't have ceased to employ them at Alexandra and Extension," Hawthornthwaite shot back.

Dunsmuir's breath quite taken away by the injustice of that conclusion, Charles Pooley leapt to the premier's defence. "That's not so," he hollered.

"I never met a miner of intelligence and independence and who was not dominated by his boss who did not give it as his frank and honest opinion that they were the cause," Hawthornthwaite countered.

Hawthornthwaite continued by contrasting "the beautiful chamber in which the members sat and the dangerous quarters in which the miners worked."

"I would rather be there than sit here," Dunsmuir called.

"A great number of coal miners in this province heartily wish he was in that position than where he is," Hawthornthwaite pressed on.

"I've been there. I understand it," Dunsmuir shouted back.

"The premier doesn't understand the horrors attached to an explosion," Hawthornthwaite insisted.

"I know what I am talking about and you don't," Dunsmuir thundered.

But Hawthornthwaite had the muse on his side. For the members of the House, he painted a graphic picture of mine accidents—the terror of an explosion—the distress of seeing the blackened bodies of friends being carried out of the pit. "I think," he concluded, "in view of these things you will be inclined to listen to their petition with me, and not laugh with the premier."

A majority of the House, stirred by his oratory and touched by the miners' plight, voted in support of the amendment.

It was not the first battle Dunsmuir had lost; and, if anything, it renewed his determination to win the war. What little empathy he had had with the men now deserted him. He was convinced that they had fallen under the thrall of professional agitators. A smarter man might have attempted to undermine union influence by treating his employees with fairness and consideration. Dunsmuir dug in his heels.

—

Unlike his father who had had the confidence to shrug off criticism, James was capable of behaving like a petulant schoolboy when he was challenged. His handling of the controversy that grew out the colliery's refusal to sell land within the Wellington townsite clearly demonstrated the difference between the two men.

When Robert had first opened the Wellington Colliery, he had intended to subdivide some of his land and establish an adjacent townsite. But soon he reversed that decision. Perhaps he had come to see that it would be to the company's advantage if his men lived in colliery-owned cottages. But perhaps his motivation had been a humane one. When the easily accessible coal had been removed, colliery operations would shift to more profitable sites, and the town of Wellington would cease to exist. "In my father's time he would not sell any lots knowing that some day the whole thing would be worked out," James said.

Believing that his father's first consideration had been the miners' welfare, James's conscience was clear when, during the strike of 1890, he had found himself under attack. "The *Free Press* in Nanaimo said we would not sell town lots—that we wanted to keep the town lots." James recalled. "It made me angry." Rather than defend his company's policy, he reacted with spitefulness. "I had a survey made and sold so many lots to the miners. Now as soon as the mines are worked out they lose everything." And, he no doubt thought, it served them right.

And so, while the men who had worked for Robert Dunsmuir had been able to tell each other, "No one can say the old man ain't fair," the miners who worked for his son came to suspect that decisions were being made based on considerations that had nothing to do with their welfare, or, for that matter, the profitable operation of the mines. James Dunsmuir was determined to resist unionism in his mines, but his treatment of the men at Alexandra and Extension guaranteed its introduction.

—

When he first began operations at Extension, he had supposed that the townsite would be sited as close as possible to the pit-head. It had been an unpleasant surprise to discover that the surface rights were in the possession of a farmer named Bramley, and that Bramley was not prepared to accept the $2,000 Dunsmuir offered him for his land.

"Extension was not a fit place for a town," James decided. The water was poor; drainage was bad; he had been warned to expect an outbreak of typhoid fever. In April 1896, only a few months after work on the mine had begun, he had purchased 320 acres on the shores of Oyster Harbour. It would be "better for the men" if they lived at Ladysmith, the town he had decided to build at the shipping point.

In 1899 when the men dismantled their Wellington cottages—cottages that Dunsmuir had allowed them to buy even though he knew that the mine would be abandoned within the decade—they re-erected them at Extension on land they leased from Bramley. By the spring of 1901, two hundred families had settled near the Extension pit, and Mrs. Bailey's Temperance Hotel had opened its doors to single miners.

At that point Dunsmuir decided to make it clear that Ladysmith was more than simply his preference. He announced that the men would no longer be paid at Extension. Instead, the only pay office would be located at Ladysmith—12 long miles from the mine. Some of the men agreed with Dunsmuir's contention that Extension was "not a health resort" and obediently moved their cottages once again, but most preferred to stay where they were. A delegation waited on the premier to plead with him to change his mind. But that he was not prepared to do, Dunsmuir informed them. He intended to build up Ladysmith.

Two months later, with the miners still clinging to their Extension homes, he tried a little friendly persuasion. He announced that two hundred Ladysmith town lots would be made available to miners who agreed to build there at once. But despite that, and despite the report that Extension residents were "genuinely alarmed by the sanitary conditions of the town," fewer than seventy men took Dunsmuir up on his offer.

Seven months later, their place of residence and the location of the pay office continued to be contentious issues. Shortly before Christmas 1901, two men were selected by the Extension miners' association to approach Dunsmuir with a renewed request that the men be paid at Extension. The meeting did not go well. Ushered into the premier's office, they introduced themselves as representing the union, whereupon Dunsmuir roared, "To hell with the union! To hell with the committee! To hell with the men!" and showed them the door.

"The Extension men will continue to travel twelve miles to Ladysmith every pay day, wait eight hours for a return train, and return home minus that portion of their earnings which has gone to enrich the keepers of the half dozen saloons down there," the *Province* sympathized. But at least the Extension men had earnings to splurge. That was more than could be said for the miners at Alexandra.

———

The Alexandra "trouble" was well into its twelfth month and Extension miners were threatening to hold a sympathy strike when the federal deputy minister of labour, William Lyon Mackenzie King, decided to intervene. In November 1901, King, who would later serve twenty-one years as Canada's prime minister, was approaching his twenty-fifth birthday and thoroughly enjoying the fact that he was "probably the youngest Deputy Minister ever appointed in Canada." He saw his role as one of peacemaker, and in the sixteen months that he had been in office he had received recognition as a skilled conciliator. He decided to try his hand at Alexandra.

He succeeded in getting Dunsmuir and the men to agree to a compromise. The miners would return to work for $3 a day; meanwhile

King would convene a series of meetings during which the final terms of a wage settlement would be hammered out. On 29 November the strike was called off, the lockout was raised, and work was "being rushed" at Alexandra.

Eleven days later, Dunsmuir arrived at the mine to find a notice posted by the Miners' Protective Association, informing the men that the mine would be closed for the day so that they could attend a union meeting at Nanaimo. Dunsmuir was furious. The mine, he announced, would be closed, not for one day but permanently. And this time he meant it. More than twenty years would pass and the mine would be under new ownership before Alexandra was reopened.

—

Organizers at the Denver headquarters of the Western Federation of Miners, an American union that was looking for a Canadian toehold, recognized an opportunity for expansion in the growing animosity between Dunsmuir and his men. James Baker was dispatched to Vancouver Island to woo the men with visions of the power that would be theirs if they became members of an international union. "I gave $300 to start a Ladysmith band, and the first man serenaded was Mr. Baker," Dunsmuir noted indignantly.

On 8 March 1903 at a mass meeting held at Ladysmith, miners voted to join the "radical" American union. Two days later, notices appeared in town and at the pit-head.

> From the first of April, 1903, Extension mines will be closed down.
> All workmen are requested to return their tools to the storekeeper at Extension.
>
> JAMES DUNSMUIR
> PRESIDENT

The news "came like a bomb," not only to the miners but also to officials of the colliery and the railway, and to the shopkeepers of Ladysmith. One thousand men were being thrown out of work at a time when coal markets were improving. The effect on Ladysmith would be disastrous. Anyone who had invested in the town's future would be faced with bankruptcy. Dunsmuir was imperilling his own large investment, for without the mines, Ladysmith's expensive bunkers and wharves would become useless.

But he was prepared to pay the price. "I will never recognize the affiliation of my miners with the Western Federation of Miners," he said. "Rather than submit to it, I will close the mines and keep them closed for two years."

On 5 April, James Baker took his crusade to Cumberland. "I came here to organize a union, and am going to today," Baker declared. By the end of a meeting which most participants agreed was heated and stormy, he had scored only a partial success. Of 600 white miners, 110 joined the union.

Dunsmuir chose to regard the results as encouraging. "Mr. Dunsmuir does not anticipate that the union will make any marked progress among his permanent miners at Comox," the *Colonist* dutifully reported. "On the contrary, these men who have worked for years for him and who have drawn good wages will, he feels satisfied, refuse to join the union." And should that prediction prove to be overly optimistic, he had other plans in mind.

"If there is a strike, I will close the mine down, just as I did at Extension and keep them closed—for ten years if need be—before I will submit to this tyranny."

The situation now was becoming extremely serious. Ladysmith was reeling from the effects of the lockout. If the lockout spread to Cumberland, the entire island would begin to feel an economic pinch. And the trouble was not confined to Vancouver Island. Throughout the province, labour was beginning to flex its muscle and capital was feeling increasingly embattled and wary. The situation called for the talents of Mackenzie King. In April 1903 the Ottawa government appointed him secretary to a royal commission and dispatched him to British Columbia to investigate the cause of the "recent and present labor trouble in the province."

"What can they do in the Extension trouble?" Dunsmuir demanded when he learned of the commission's appointment. "What is there to arbitrate? I have said I will not recognize the Western Federation of Miners—that is all there is to it."

Mackenzie King made no secret of the fact that his sympathies were with the workingman. After satisfying himself that the two commissioners, Chief Justice Hunter and the Reverend Dr. Rowe, were "inclined to sympathize with labouring men," he arranged for the commission to begin its hearings at Ladysmith. One of the first witnesses was James Baker. "He made a splendid witness, answering important questions frankly & directly," King confided in his diary. "The fellow appears to me a hero, one who is leading an honest struggle for his fellow men, in an intelligent and thoughtful way."

With Baker's performance still in his mind, King spent his evenings contemplating the "greed & tyranny of capital." And after he heard the testimony of a score of Extension men, he experienced a growing distaste for the "millionaire monopolist" who had shut down the mines. "One after the other told how he had built a little home for himself & family and had been obliged to tear it down & rebuild at Ladysmith, a distance of 13 miles from his work. It is a piece of the worst tyranny I have ever known & is hard to believe." This assessment was shared by Chief Justice Hunter, who privately swore that he found Dunsmuir's treatment of his men "a damnable outrage."

On 10 May, after the first week of testimony had been concluded, King attempted to summarize his feelings.

> The situation as I see it is this. A selfish millionaire has become something of a tyrannical autocrat. To satisfy a prejudice or greed he has undertaken to make serfs of a lot [of] free men by compelling them to live at a place of his own dictation miles away from their work. Owning everything and possessing all but absolute power, he will let his men possess as little as possible. Every attempt they have made to form a union he had frustrated by dismissing leaders. To be more secure in their position these men have at last joined the Western Federat'n of Miners, to have a moral & financial backing. For this the mines of the owner have been closed. To my mind the right to live where a man pleases & the right to join a lawful organiz'n are legal rights, which for an employer to deny because of monopolistic power is a social wrong. To be free from Individual Autocracy, these men are embracing Socialism. It is a natural and inevitable step.

On 18 May he heard the testimony of the man he had come to see as the chief architect of local labour strife. In spite of himself, he was quite disarmed. "Mr. Dunsmuir, the owner of about 1/3 of this Island . . . gave his evidence in good form. It was straight from the shoulder, no hesitation. He wd. have nothing to do with Unions, wd. hire who and where he liked, wd. treat his men well but as he pleased. There was no equivocation. One cld. see that in his view he might think his course eminently just."

King had expected the commission to hear from a power-mad autocrat. Instead, they had encountered a plain-talking man, as simple as he was stubborn; a man who was incapable of seeing the wider picture. Dunsmuir "carried his overbearing attitude too far," King mused. His absolute refusal to have anything to do with the union "displayed a power of defiance which is too great for any individual to possess." But, at the same time, Dunsmuir demonstrated honest puzzlement when he asked, "Haven't I as much right to refuse to recognize a union among my men as Baker has to tell them if they

176

do not join the union, they will be blacklisted all over the North American continent?"

As it turned out, the report of the royal commission gave Dunsmuir little to worry about. Unions of the "revolutionary socialist" stripe would be outlawed, while the formation of employee associations would be encouraged. With that recommendation, Dunsmuir could live. He had always been prepared to meet with his men—provided of course that they never mentioned having been selected by an association or a union.

Nothing had changed. All the trouble had been caused by "foreign revolutionaries"—aided and abetted by his political opponents, whose only interest had been to bring down the government he controlled. That was what he believed. And if he needed proof that he was a victim of politics, he could always cite the slamming he had taken over his railway policies.

Seventeen

—

Railways! Railways! Railways! Sometimes it seemed as if turn-of-the-century politicians could think of little else. But British Columbians had good reason for focussing on the subject. In a land of mountain ranges and tumbling rivers, railways were the only practical means of transportation and, as such, they held the key to provincial prosperity. British Columbia was a mineral treasure-house. Each new discovery—whether it was silver or copper or iron ore—brought a flurry of excited speculation and a new demand for a railroad. Promoters sprang up like weeds and dispatched their lobbyists to Victoria to compete for government favours.

Railways, or more particularly their financing, quickly became the most compelling issue of the Dunsmuir administration. Promoters argued that British Columbia's rugged topography made construction costs so prohibitively high that no line could be built without government assistance.

With that point of view, Dunsmuir found himself in sympathy. When a promoter offered to build a hundred miles of track in return for a subsidy of 12,000 acres per mile, Dunsmuir announced that he thought it was "a pretty good proposition" and admitted that he would have happily signed the contract if it had not been for adverse public reaction. "The people," he noted with some surprise, "were against giving away the land."

If the public rejected the notion of land subsidies, then cash subsidies would have to be the answer. But could the province afford those cash subsidies? And even if it could, was it not the responsibility of the federal government to assume a share of the burden? It was not for nothing that British Columbia had become known as the "spoilt child of Confederation." Almost from the moment the Terms of Union were signed, British Columbians had begun to whine.

"How," Dunsmuir asked, "are we to build all the railways, bonus shipbuilding, and open up and develop all the immense country . . . if the Terms of Union are not readjusted, and we are not to receive a much larger share of what we contribute to the Dominion?" Dunsmuir decided to argue the provincial case in person. In January 1901, six months after having been sworn into office, he set off for Ottawa and a meeting with the prime minister, Sir Wilfrid Laurier.

To Easterners, the millionaire-premier was something of a novelty. Leading Toronto businessmen lined up to meet with him. He created quite the right impression when he allowed as how "British Columbia wants more business and less politics." And he certainly impressed the *Ottawa Citizen*. "It is not generally known that he gives his service gratis to the people of the Pacific province," the paper burbled. "Every month he forwards the check for his salary as a cabinet minister to some deserving charity."

But from the prime minister, he received little more than a sympathetic hearing and a vague promise that British Columbia's arguments would be considered at some unspecified time in the future. Still, Dunsmuir felt he had done his best and was expecting to be congratulated for his efforts. Instead, he returned to Victoria to find himself accused of having gone to Ottawa only to do his best for the E & N.

"The premier has not disclosed the fact that the chief thing he wanted when there was a grant of $10,000 a mile for 250 miles of road on Vancouver Island in which he himself is directly interested," a disgruntled member of Parliament confided to the *Vancouver World*. He had pursued the issue so doggedly that he had "paid comparatively little attention to other matters while in Ottawa."

Dunsmuir immediately telegraphed Laurier, asking him to refute the report. The prime minister tried to be helpful. "During your stay in Ottawa," he wired back, "you pressed all claims of the province and presented your memorial with earnestness and good faith." That was as far as Laurier was prepared to go, for, as Dunsmuir himself admitted, the extension of the E & N *had* been an important topic of conversation.

—

The E & N possessed a charter allowing it to extend its tracks from Comox to Cape Scott on Vancouver Island's northern tip. Dunsmuir was eager to get that extension built. But, he explained, he would have argued in favour of federal subsidies even if he had not been the railway's major shareholder. "I haven't got nothing that I know of to hide from the public," he insisted.

Even more puzzling for him was the reaction his railway policy received when it was presented to the House. "I look on the country in much the same light as a big corporation in which the electors are the shareholders and the government the board of directors," he said. And, in this case, that point of view stood him in good stead, for he developed a fresh new policy that seemed both rational and fair. Subsidization was necessary; no doubt about that. But cash grants should go only to schemes that promised to produce real benefits for the province. In other words, railways running south into Washington State or east into Alberta would be met with parsimonious indifference, but purse strings might be loosened if a promoter planned to run a line from the Kootenay mines to smelters near Vancouver or New Westminster. Provincial subsidies, contingent on the railway receiving matching grants from the federal government, would be limited to $5,000 a mile. In return, the province would expect to receive two per cent of the railway's profits until the grants had been repaid; freight rates would be government-controlled; and after twenty years, the province would have the option of purchasing any line it had subsidized.

Promoters of the latest scheme to build a Coast-Kootenay line had expected to do considerably better than that. They charged that Dunsmuir's policy had been formulated only to shut them out and to leave the field open for himself and his friends.

On 21 March 1901 at an opposition rally held in the Victoria Theatre, E. V. Bodwell, King's Counsel and chief lobbyist for the Coast-Kootenay line, leapt to his feet to charge that Dunsmuir and his cabinet were under the domination of the CPR—a not unreasonable accusation since, six months earlier, the CPR had acquired control of Canadian Pacific Navigation, a steamship company in which Dunsmuir held a large interest. They were determined, Bodwell shrieked, to continue the monopoly that that railway enjoyed by preventing the construction of competing lines.

When Dunsmuir rose in the House to refute Bodwell's charges, even his supporters were surprised by the depth of his anger. Usually when he addressed the House, he read from a carefully typewritten page, but that day there were no papers before him. In tones of ringing indignation that penetrated every part of the chamber, he repudiated the charges as utterly false.

"There is only one interest I have in this House and that is the interest of British Columbia," he bellowed. "My holdings in the province are so large that it makes me take an interest in it, but I would not sell the province of British Columbia for all the corporations or companies in it!"

The members of the House, reacting to so passionate a response from a man usually "so sparing in his speech and so reserved in his manner," greeted his speech with wild applause. The bill passed; the Dunsmuir government survived.

So rich were the rewards that even after the new railway policy was in place, the legislature continued to be besieged by promoters and their lobbyists. Seventeen private bills, calling for the charter of as many railways, were introduced in the House. The proposal submitted by the Canadian Northern Railway, Dunsmuir found particularly interesting. The Canadian Northern had transcontinental ambitions, and even more significantly, intended to bring the tracks through to Victoria.

—

The dream that one day Victoria would become a great terminal city had refused to die. Vancouver, which had been little more than a wilderness shantytown before the first CPR train arrived, had become a commercial metropolis. In 1898 during the Klondike excitement, Victoria's businessmen had been reminded of the benefits of becoming a commercial clearing-house and their wistful longing for a railway turned to headlong pursuit. They struck a Committee of Fifty and instructed them to court railway men by dangling before them the promise of possible subsidies.

On 1 May 1899 James Dunsmuir, the elected member for Comox but not yet premier, had tendered a proposal as vice-president of the Esquimalt & Nanaimo Railroad. He pledged to unite the island line with the CPR. In Vancouver, passenger and freight cars would be rolled aboard a fast ferry boat, carried to a point on the E & N line near Chemainus, and then wheeled onto the E & N tracks for quick passage to Victoria. From terminal to terminal the trip would take no longer than three-and-a-half hours, Dunsmuir promised, adding that he intended to schedule two round trips a day. It would be an expensive proposition, he warned. Initially an outlay of $1.5 million would be required to build the ferry, to buy land for the Vancouver terminus, to lay additional track and to construct terminal buildings. Because the whole idea was to encourage the commercial growth of the island, he intended to keep freight rates low. Many years would pass before the connection could be expected to make a profit.

Dunsmuir wanted the Songhees Indian Reserve, 20 acres of land on the Victoria waterfront. In addition, he required permission to build a bridge across the entrance of the Inner Harbour. And that bridge, together with the terminal buildings and all the railway lands within the city limits, must be free of municipal taxation. Finally, an outright cash subsidy of $700,000 would be required.

While the Committee of Fifty retired to consider the financial realities of railway construction, pencils were being sharpened in Washington State. Three days after the Dunsmuir proposal arrived on their desks, the committee was presented with an alternative proposal. The shareholders of the Port Angeles Eastern Railway Company would run a ferry between Victoria and Port Angeles. From there the line would run to Olympia, the state capital, where it would connect with the Northern Pacific Railroad. It too would require a subsidy, but compared to Dunsmuir's it was modest— $350,000 to be paid in annual instalments of $17,500.

Dunsmuir promptly withdrew his offer. He had been stung by the criticism his request for subsidies had received. His only interest was Victoria, he said. He wanted a railway—any railway. If the Americans could do it, well then, good for them.

The Committee of Fifty dipped their toes into the waters of city-financed subsidies and suddenly got very cold feet. After one member threw them a lifeline by questioning the legality of civic subsidies, the committee voted to reject the Port Angeles proposal and settled back to await developments.

—

Two years later, Dunsmuir had become premier and, while Vancouver continued to boom, Victoria had begun to slip into a genteel decline, when the Canadian Northern proposal surfaced.

The Canadian Northern had decided to follow the route rejected by the CPR two decades earlier. Entering the province through the Yellowhead Pass and emerging on the sea at Bute Inlet, the tracks would cross Seymour Narrows to Vancouver Island and then turn south for the run down to Victoria.

Any premier might have welcomed a proposal that promised to jolt the island out of its economic slump. But a premier who also happened to be president of the E & N was capable of greeting the Canadian Northern's promoters with something more than cautious approval. In their first private tentative approach to the premier, the Canadian Northern won him over with an offer at which Dunsmuir was prepared to leap. They wanted to buy the E & N along with the

1.7 million "worthless" acres of its land grant that had not yet been sold. And they were prepared to pay $8 million.

—

Dunsmuir, who thought of himself as a mining man rather than a railroader, was weary of running the railway without his brother's advice. He was eager to sell, but the decision was not his alone to make. He held a controlling interest in the line, but half the shares were still in the hands of his father's American partners, who now operated under the corporate banner of the Pacific Improvements Association and whose affairs were conducted out of New York by Gen. Thomas Hubbard, president of the Southern Pacific Railroad.

The simplest solution seemed to be to buy out his American partners and free himself to entertain the Canadian Northern offer. Fortunately for Dunsmuir, his American partners were as eager as he to offload the railway. Yes, they would agree to allow Dunsmuir to buy them out; and yes, they would accept $4 million.

The premier was now prepared to present the Canadian Northern with a contract that made nonsense of his carefully considered, and hotly defended, railway policy. The provincial government would agree to cash subsidies as high as $5,000 a mile and, in return, would expect to receive two per cent of the railway's gross earning. So far so good. But Dunsmuir had agreed to an additional incentive that brought the opposition to their feet in howls of protest. The company would be granted 20,000 acres for every mile of track.

He had been "obliged to fall back" on the land grant to get the railway built, Dunsmuir shrugged.

The premier, it seems, had decided that the time had come to take the money and run. He had promised his supporters that he would serve for twelve months; he had now been in office for almost two years. His political debts were paid; he cared nothing about his personal political future. The Canadian Northern offer was almost too good to be true, and certainly too good to be refused.

He had perched himself at the end of a politically precarious limb, when the Canadian Northern negotiators arrived with a very sharp saw. They informed him that they had decided against buying the E & N's land holdings. Instead, they were interested in acquiring only the roadbed. And for that they were prepared to pay no more than $2 million.

Dunsmuir did some quick calculations. If he uncoupled the railway from the coal mines that had been developed on its land and treated it as a separate entity, he could demonstrate that the line was operating at a deficit. Between the years 1891 and 1900, it had lost over $1 million. Perhaps the new offer was not so bad after all. But in order to accept it, he would have to renege on his offer to buy out his American partners, and instead convince Hubbard to accept the Canadian Northern proposal.

On 7 March 1902 he dashed off an excited telegram to Hubbard. "Can sell the roadbed to Canadian Northern for two million dollars, they giving three per cent first mortgage bond. I am willing, are you? An answer by noon tomorrow, the eighth, is very important."

The general must have thought Dunsmuir had taken leave of his senses. Only a week earlier Hubbard had agreed to let him buy up all the shares. Now, he was being presented with a quite different proposal and being asked for an instant reply. "Cannot decide so important a matter off hand without information," he wired back.

The second telegram he received from Dunsmuir was hardly more informative. "Final offer two million dollars, three per cent first mortgage bonds, fifty years, quarter of a million cash in two years, and another quarter of million in three years. Sale depends on bill passing House, whether Canadian Northern come here or not. Full discussion tonight. I advise you very strongly to accept proposition, as we shall never get a better terms. You can depend on me protecting your interests. Answer immediately. Rush."

But General Hubbard was not about to be rushed. "Your second dispatch does not give much more information than the first, and certainly to my mind does not make the proposition any more attractive." And once again, he declined the offer.

—

Dunsmuir had good reason for demanding quick action from Hubbard. The Canadian Northern bill had already been introduced in the House, but now the promoters were refusing to sign a final contract with the government until the question of the E & N was settled. Rumours of the private deal that had been struck between the premier and the Canadian Northern had become the talk of the town. Dunsmuir, though braced for public criticism, was quite unprepared for the virulence of the attack.

"A Deal or a Steal," the *Victoria Times* headlined an editorial. "Is Dunsmuir selling his railway for the good of the country, or his country for the good of his railway?" others asked.

Victoria was in the midst of a by-election, and the premier's alleged collusion with the Canadian Northern became the election's single most important issue. Bodwell, determined to defeat the Canadian Northern bill and to bring down the Dunsmuir government, offered himself as the opposition candidate; running as the government supporter was Edward Prior. The former inspector of mines and a long-time friend of the Dunsmuir family, Prior set about defending the contract with a will.

"The railway is Victoria's salvation," he ventured. "I believe that the railway policy of the government is going to boom Victoria and send her well up to the position she ought to occupy as a shipping, commercial and manufacturing centre."

James Dunsmuir reluctantly mounted platforms to stand beside Prior and to repeat, over and over again, the principles that guided his conduct of government affairs. "My home is in British Columbia, my property is in British Columbia, and I know no other home than this, and I want to protect the interests of the province, instead of doing like some people who come to this province to make money and take it away . . . I have got the interests of Victoria at heart, and the interests of British Columbia at heart."

In one of the most hotly contested elections Victoria had ever seen, passions ran high. James's wife, Laura, received a letter warning her to keep her husband home. If he attended the political rally to be held at the Victoria Theatre, he would find a man with a revolver lying in wait. James went anyway. He had had so many similar threats, he said, that he really had no choice but ignore them. But he promised himself that this would be his last political fight.

Prior squeaked into office, his fifty-four-vote majority cold comfort to Dunsmuir. He had expected Victoria voters to overwhelmingly approve any scheme that would bring a transcontinental line to the city. Instead, the riding most likely to support him had come close to repudiating him.

A week after Prior's election, an opposition member rose in the House to formally accuse the premier of corruption, grave misconduct and gross and wilful neglect. His mandate slipping away, James had little choice but to agree to the appointment of a provincial inquiry. Over three gruelling days on the stand, he was faced with many prying questions regarding the conduct of his private business affairs, some of which he grudgingly answered, but most of which he cut off with the gruff response, "None of your business."

He flatly denied the truth of the accusations. "I had no desire to sell the road," he testified—a statement that General Hubbard would have found rather puzzling. "I never had any idea of selling the road for a big sum through the making of this contract. Self interest was never in my mind in the course of these negotiations. It was for the benefit of the whole of the province, and particularly that of Vancouver Island and the city of Victoria." He stood to make a profit, he agreed, but only as a property holder and only to the same extent as other property holders.

The inquiry concluded that the charges against him had not been proven and his majority held. But the Canadian Northern proposal faded away. The success of the contract depended on matching federal subsidies, and those federal subsidies were not forthcoming.

If he considered only the railway debacle, James Dunsmuir would have had good reason for declaring that he was thoroughly sick of politics. He suspected that the Canadian Northern contract might have breezed through the House and gone on to receive federal assistance if he had not been premier. Now he was left with an unprofitable railroad, and Victoria remained isolated from the rest of the continent. He had been a caretaker premier for two years, and those years had been much more trying than the men who had urged him to run had led him to expect. His brother Alex had been quite right; entering politics had been a mistake. And not only because of its impact on his coal mines and his railway, but also because his prominent political position had invited public scrutiny of his and his family's most private affairs.

Eighteen

PREMIER OF BRITISH COLUMBIA SUED BY HIS MOTHER. In November 1901 newspapers from New York to California and British Columbia headlined the news. Joan Dunsmuir was taking her son to court to challenge his possession of Alex's share of R. Dunsmuir's Sons, San Francisco. She was rich and she was old—seventy-four on her last birthday. She had little reason to pursue Alex's estate. Her daughters, however, found sufficient incentive.

For three of them, money had ceased to matter. Agnes, carried off by typhoid, had been in her grave for more than a decade. Marion had died in 1892. And their husbands, James Harvey and Charles Houghton, had likewise gone to a better place. Elizabeth, the oldest daughter, had died in Victoria earlier that year, "an estimable lady" of fifty-three years. Her husband, John Bryden, only recently retired from management of the Wellington Colliery, had settled into "Dalzellowlie," a handsome Tudor house near the Esquimalt waterfront and was doing very well for himself as his mother-in-law's most trusted advisor. But that left five daughters, and they were intensely interested in maximizing the benefits that would flow to them when their mother went to her final reward.

Emily Snowden had sold Ashnola, deposited her husband in an asylum for the insane in England and returned to Victoria, where she had become the "very good friend" of Harry Burroughes, a big, loud Colonel Blimp of an Englishman who had dabbled with the idea of exporting champagne to California but otherwise had no visible means of support.

Mary and her husband, Harry Croft, remained at Mount Adelaide, but Harry had yet to find a career that would allow him to crawl out from under the ignominy of having the house, and the style of living the house demanded, at the mercy of his mother-in-law's financial whim.

Jessie, the wife of Sir Richard Musgrave, had produced two daughters and built a new wing on the Lismore house. She had introduced her two younger sisters to Dublin's vice-regal court, a society enlived by the presence of unattached young English officers whose regiments were doing a tour of duty in Ireland. In June 1898 "Lady Musgrave's pretty sister" Maude had glided down the aisle of St. Peter's, Eaton Square, on Sir Richard's arm to become the bride of Reggie Chaplin, a polo-playing young officer in the 10th Hussars.

By 1901 even thirty-two-year-old Annie Euphemia, Joan's seventh daughter, had found a husband. The prettiest of all the sisters, Effie had thrown herself into Dublin's social whirl with a reckless abandonment. "She is as thin as a knife," a friend worried after encountering Effie in Dublin. "The people here seem to think she is rather mad to hunt all day and dance all night, any spare time being filled up by bicycling, at homes, dinners or skating!! . . . her appearance is quite sad and Jessie is worried about her."

There was a manic quality to Effie's Dublin season. Even after she had ridden all day and danced till four in the morning, her desperate energy refused to desert her and she sat up until dawn writing letters. Her family in Victoria became alarmed. Joan wrote to her daughter suggesting that it was time she came home, but Effie, who declared that she had never had such a good time in her life, demurred. She remained abroad until 1900 when she found a man who thought he could cope with her nervous fragility. Somerset Arthur Gough-Calthorpe was thirty-six years old. A serious-minded commander in the Royal Navy with "not one ounce of magnetism," he possessed a handsome house on the Isle of Wight and the prestige that came of being the second son of the seventh Baron Calthorpe. Joan Dunsmuir settled a $100,000 trust on Effie when she and Arthur announced their engagement. And after Sir Richard was trotted out to lead the bride down the aisle of St. George's, Hanover Square, a second $100,000 trust was established in Effie's name.

Joan's older daughters, Mary, Emily and Jessie, had been distinctly unhappy about their mother's decision to sign over her shares in the E & N and the Union Colliery. When they learned that Jim and Alex had convinced her to sell Wellington, they were appalled. So often did they insist that she had been coerced into signing that gradually Joan herself came to believe that perhaps they were right; perhaps it was true that her judgement, once so reliable, had failed her.

When Alex died, leaving his entire estate to Jim, the sisters declared war. Jim had taken advantage of Alex's condition; it was his doing that Alex had written a will that excluded all other members of the family. Their mother *must* do *something*.

But what could she do? The only part of his estate that might be recoverable was his half-interest in the San Francisco sales office. When she had signed R. Dunsmuir's Sons over to the boys, Joan had extracted a promise that if either of them predeceased her, his shares would revert to her. But there was a risk that, if she began a suit, Alex's widow might be stirred to take similar action. In June 1901 that roadblock was removed when Josephine died. On 30 October Joan filed an action against her son, James, "for delivery of 4,998 shares in the firm of R. Dunsmuir's Sons, in pursuance of an agreement between the plaintiff, the defendant, and the late Alexander Dunsmuir."

—

As the family divided into two hostile camps—James on one side, his mother and sisters on the other—Harry Croft found himself in a particularly precarious position. In 1899 he had signed on as manager and mining consultant for the Lenora Company, which was developing a copper claim on the slope of Mount Sicker north of Victoria. In that position, he had reached an agreement with James, acting in his role as vice-president of the E & N. Lenora was allowed a right-of-way through E & N property for the construction of a tramway connecting the mine with the railway; the E & N agreed to carry the ore to Ladysmith, to store it at the coal wharves and to load it aboard ore carriers for a set rate of one dollar a ton. But that arrangement had been concluded before Alex's death. Once his will was read and the family split apart, Harry was left with no doubt as to where his loyalties were expected to lie. It occurred to him that it might be prudent to sever his business connections with his brother-in-law.

The solution seemed to be to construct his own wharves and a copper smelter at nearby Osbourne Bay and avoid the E & N altogether. When Jim Dunsmuir got wind of Croft's plans, he responded by wooing the Tyee Mining Company, which held a competing copper claim on Mount Sicker. He bought shares in the company, squired its directors around Ladysmith, offered land for the site of a smelter and promised an unlimited supply of cheap coal.

Croft's back was against the wall. To get access to Osbourne Bay and the site of his proposed smelter, Lenora's tramway would have to cross the E & N tracks. Guessing that Dunsmuir would be in no mood to cooperate, he ordered the construction of false trestle work designed to appear as if he were planning a level crossing of the railway but actually intended to force Dunsmuir's hand.

"You will not cross my railway," Dunsmuir exploded.

Harry decided to apply a little pressure. In January 1902, with the premier already on the defensive over his alleged collusion with the Canadian Northern Railway, Croft took his problems to the *Victoria Times*, knowing that the opposition newspaper would be only too happy to make public his contention that Dunsmuir was determined to choke off all development within the railway belt.

Dunsmuir responded by taking to the pages of the *Colonist*. "Everything went on harmoniously until family affairs intervened, and after that, he endeavored by every means in his power to get out of his agreement with me ... I am as sure as I can be of anything that if it had not been for this trouble he would now be giving the railway his ore."

———

The public now had its first inkling that the trouble between James and his mother went deeper than a corporate disagreement, and the first hint that the Dunsmuirs' dirty linen was about to be hung out on banner headlines. Then, less than a week after James had given public voice to the family feud, Josephine's daughter, Edna Wallace Hopper, burst on the scene with the announcement that she had entered an action in the California courts to set aside Alexander's will.

Edna had been in New York, appearing as Lady Holyrood in *Florodora*, when she received word of Josephine's death. Unaware of the terms of the arrangement her mother had made with James, she hurried across the continent, thinking herself an heiress. She was horrified when she learned that all she stood to inherit was the San Leandro estate. But help was to hand. Edna was engaged to the son of Senator Elkins of New York. Her fiancé, a major shareholder in the Metropolitan Street Railway Company, was a wealthy man in his own right. For "sentimental reasons," he volunteered to provide Edna with an attorney, his company's solicitor, Judge Edward P. Coyne of New York.

On 16 July 1902 Edna Wallace Hopper, her maid and her legal advisor arrived in Victoria and checked into the Driard Hotel, which by a nice coincidence was now the property of Joan Dunsmuir, the former owners having defaulted on the mortgage she held. Encouraged by what she learned after interviewing potential witnesses, Edna decided to expand her legal battle to Victoria. That October, she began an action in the British Columbia Supreme Court to set aside both Alex's will and the agreement Josephine had signed six months before her death.

"Where all parties to the suit are so wealthy, there is no doubt that the prediction of a long and bitter fight is well founded," the *Province* noted with anticipation.

The case was scheduled to be heard before Mr. Justice Drake of the B.C. Supreme Court the following July. Edna's case rested on her ability to prove that for several years before his death Alex had been suffering from alcoholic dementia so severe as to have rendered him incapable of making rational decisions and that James had taken advantage of his condition to exercise undue influence in the matter of his will. She successfully petitioned for the right to have witnesses examined before the British consuls in New York and San Francisco, and in June 1903, as details of that testimony began to appear in newspapers on both coasts, it became apparent that the public was in for a rare treat.

In New York, Dr. William Culbert, who had attended Alexander at the Imperial Hotel, testified that he had found "a very sick man— delirious ... irritable and tumultuous ... the facial expression rather dragging; the jaw more or less depressed; the speech thick and unintelligible." Helen Stevens, who had met Josephine and Alexander in San Francisco in 1897, stated that he asked for a drink every twenty minutes, and if one were not brought to him, he resorted to baby talk. "He would say, 'I want a jinky, and if you don't give me a jinky, I am going to cry, and you don't love me if you don't give me a jinky.'"

In San Francisco, Dr. Buckley stated that in November 1893 he had found Alex "violently insane from alcoholic excesses." Herbert Yaeger, one of the male nurses who had seen Alex through his first attack of *delirium tremens*, confirmed the doctor's diagnosis. "Dunsmuir was violent and crazy most of the time," Yaeger recalled. "He was always seeing fish ... fish with remarkable colors seemed to appear before him very frequently and he did not want anyone to come near him for fear of disturbing them."

"Great interest is developing in the suit," the *Province* announced with considerable understatement.

In July attention shifted to Victoria, where the trial had entered the examination for discovery phase. On 6 July, James spent an uncomfortable day on the stand refusing to answer questions about the real value of Alexander's estate. Time enough to do that if she won the suit, he grumbled.

The following day produced much more titillating news. Sir

Charles Hibbert Tupper, whose father, as minister of railways, had encouraged Robert Dunsmuir to build the E & N, appeared at the courthouse to make an extraordinary announcement. His client, Joan Dunsmuir, intended to intervene in the action. The woman who had said that she would rather see Alex in his grave than married to Josephine was now joining hands with Josephine's daughter to become a party-plaintiff in the suit against her son.

No matter how distasteful it must have been—appearing to be in league with the daughter of Alex's paramour—Joan really had little choice. She had been contesting only her right to Alex's share of the San Francisco business; Edna was after everything. If Edna succeeded in having the will set aside, Alex would be judged to have died intestate. His entire estate would then flow to his natural heirs—to his wife, and through her to Edna, and perhaps to his mother, but only if she could successfully defend her interest. In addition, it had occurred to Joan that Edna's argument contained a potentially fatal flaw: if his will was invalid, then so was his marriage. By entering the action, Joan would be there to pick up the pieces and win for her daughters a share of Alex's estate, an estate that some estimates placed as high as $6 million.

———

The case, adjourned while the litigants sorted themselves out, finally came before Mr. Justice Drake in December 1903. And as the minutiae of Alex's troubled life were paraded before the judge and reported in scrupulous detail on the front pages of newspapers in British Columbia and California, there emerged a picture of two Alexander Dunsmuirs—one who drank liquor in such astonishing quantities that he had become a "gibbering idiot"; the other a clever businessman who always appeared clear-headed and capable of making sound judgements.

James Dunsmuir was able to produce more than a dozen prominent men who were prepared to testify that while Alex might have gone on the occasional spree, his drinking had never affected his ability to do business. Edward Palmer, the manager of the Victoria Lumber & Manufacturing Company, stated that he had found Alex to be "a bright, sharp, shrewd business man, looking for the best of the bargain in every little detail," and added that, when the two brothers were together, it was always Alex who transacted all the business.

Shipbuilder Fitzherbert Bullen agreed. "At all times Alexander Dunsmuir was the dominant one," he testified. "He looked like a man who drank," Bullen admitted. "He was a man who had a very red face always. And bleary eyes sometimes." But most of the time he was sober, Bullen said. Alex had often told him that he and his brother had built the business up and that he had no intention of "giving his money to his brothers-in-law to spend."

Charles Pooley, lawyer, Speaker of the House and firm friend of James Dunsmuir, stated that he had represented Robert Dunsmuir and later his widow and sons. On Alex's instructions he had drawn up a will for him in 1898; a year later, he had been asked to draft a new will. He admitted that he had done so at James's request and that James was the sole beneficiary. But, he carefully pointed out, the provisions of both wills were identical, the second being required only because Alex intended to marry.

Edna produced a small army of doctors, nurses, ladies' maids, bellboys and bartenders who were prepared to state that Alex had habitually drunk himself insensible and that he had displayed unmistakable symptoms of insanity. "He was never sober," Josephine's maid said. "He used to average two quart bottles of Canadian Club a day."

Uri McKee, a nightwatchman at Alex's hotel, told of the times he had found Alex stumbling about in the lobby, not knowing which way to turn for his room. "Mr. Dunsmuir, do you want to go to your room?" McKee would ask. "Yes sir, ain't I going to my room?" "No, you're going in the wrong direction," McKee would answer before taking him by the arm, guiding him down the corridor and unlocking his door.

Edna's maid, Mary Howe, remembered that Alex "had to be amused as a child, and dressed as a child, and put to bed as a child ... He had a little pillow which he used to put between his knees, and called it his baby."

Edna painted a graphic picture of Alexander's decline. "He talked baby talk ... he would call himself 'itty boy'. He would say, 'Itty boy want a jinky'. He would never ask for it in a sensible way." And she hinted darkly that, at times, his relationship with her had been something other than paternal.

James's sisters took the stand to bolster Edna's case. Maude Chaplin admitted that she had never seen Alex actually drunk but that she had found his behaviour decidedly odd.

Mary Croft recalled that from the time of their father's death, Alex drank very heavily and that James had become worried about his condition. "Mr. James Dunsmuir told me on several occasions that it was not safe to leave the San Francisco business in his hands," she testified. "He said that mother must do something, that

Alex was not responsible . . . He said that his drinking was affecting his brain."

Emily Snowden agreed that Alex was never the same after their father died. She too had encountered Alex at Craigdarroch in 1898. "He seemed stupid," she said. "He seemed very bent and feeble, very shaky."

For James Dunsmuir, the three days he spent on the stand were pure torture. As he struggled to explain the casual, off-the-cuff way in which he and his brother had conducted the affairs of their corporate empire, his own inadequacies became painfully apparent. Asked which of the two of them took a leading part, James answered, "My brother always did. I always gave way to my brother knowing that he knew more about business than I did . . . I had charge of the mining department of the business, and he had charge of the business department." He found it difficult to recall specifics. "I am not very good in making speeches, and all that, or reporting, not very . . . I have never had that education."

His worst moments came when Sir Charles Tupper rose to cross-examine him. "After you got all you could from your mother, you never went to see her again," Tupper challenged.

"I was told that if I went to see my mother, the door would be shut in my face," James quavered. "I waited, then, until my mother should send for me."

"Mother had always promised, and father had, that the Union Colliery and the E & N were to go to the boys, and in the will it was so," James testified. But his father had not signed that will. "He was sick at the time . . . It was too late."

And what had he and Alexander done for their parents that they should have expected so much, Tupper demanded.

"What did we do for our mother?" James wailed. "What did my brother and I do for our father? We had worked all our lives. I had worked 48 years before I got anything. I worked for my mother all my life and my father, and those were the promises from my father down to my mother."

———

The case ground on and on, with eighty witnesses giving testimony over forty-two days. Mr. Justice Drake had heard more than enough. "This case has taken a preposterous time," he grumbled. He brought down his decision—ten tightly typed pages—on 6 February 1904. He accepted the evidence that Alexander was a hard-drinking man, given to the occasional spree; but he could find nothing to suggest that he had been a less than capable businessman and nothing to suggest that James had exercised undue influence over his brother. He found in the defendant's favour and levied costs against Edna and Joan.

Thus ended what the *Vancouver Province* deemed "one of the most remarkable cases ever heard in a Canadian court." It was certainly one of the most expensive—both sides having spent an estimated $150,000 to prepare and present their arguments. But while James may have sighed with relief thinking it was over, for Joan Dunsmuir and Edna Wallace Hopper the bell had simply sounded on round one. He was given no chance to savour his victory before they launched an appeal.

On 30 November 1904 the appeal hearing began before the full court sitting in Vancouver. The case dragged on, through December, January and into February. During the trial, Edna had taken a sabbatical from the theatre and had attended every session. Now, in February 1905, she had returned to the stage and an imaginative manager had sent her on a tour of the west coast. Her Victoria performance lived up to all his expectations. "He reckoned on a full house, a fashionable house, a curious, interested, speculative house, and he reckoned rightly," the *Victoria Times* noted. "And tiny Edna Wallace Hopper—she was dainty, cute and coy; she had charming gowns and she was in the glare of the floodlights long enough to allow everybody equipped with a glass to take an inventory of her."

Interviewed by the press, Edna declared herself to be full of hope and in a state of "delicious suspense." Her suspense was to continue through two more months of testimony, and then for an additional eight months while the three Supreme Court Justices considered the evidence. It was not until 9 January 1906 that they rendered their decision. They found in favour of James Dunsmuir.

—

Joan Dunsmuir had unlimited funds to pursue further action, but by the beginning of 1906, Edna was in financial trouble. She had been fighting the case on two fronts—in California as well as British Columbia. And now her millionaire fiancé had lost interest in both Edna and her cause. She had won a small victory in her California action—on 27 March 1905 the California Superior Court decided that the British Columbia probate of the will had been illegal on the grounds that Alex had been a resident of California. But seven months later, that decision had been overturned. To keep the California case alive, Joan Dunsmuir entered the fray, and together they tried to find some new grounds for contesting the will.

Edna charged her mother's attorney with conspiracy. Mountford Wilson had acted as Josephine's counsel in the agreement she had reached with James; at the same time, and unbeknownst to Josephine, he had been accepting fees as James's attorney. Later, she would discover that Wilson had been paid handsomely to make sure that Alex's will avoided California probate. But with this, as with several other attempts to have the California courts examine the issue, she was unsuccessful.

There now was only one last hope—an appeal to the Privy Council in England. In April 1906 Sir Charles Tupper received leave from the B.C. Supreme Court to take the appeal to London. In June the law lords of the Privy Council agreed to hear the appeal. On 20 July, James received a telegram from his solicitor informing him that the Privy Council had dismissed his mother's appeal. The "most celebrated case ever tried in Western Canadian courts" was finally over.

Hopper v Dunsmuir had been before the courts in California, British Columbia and England for almost five years. The cost of the trial and the appeals had been astronomical, as much as a million dollars, some experts estimated. Edna had run out of money, and her mother's creditors had run out of patience. Josephine had left debts totalling $38,000, the result, according to the executor of her estate, of her fondness for purchasing books and art curios from expensive dealers. The San Leandro estate, valued at $500,000 and deemed to be one of the most beautiful country homes in the state, was ordered sold to pay for the expensive bric-a-brac that had been bought to adorn it.

But while Edna was prepared to declare herself beaten, James's sisters were not. On 18 September 1908 the *Victoria Times* reported that eighty-year-old Joan Dunsmuir was reviving the action she had begun seven years earlier. But she was not to meet her son in court. Fourteen days later, on 2 October, she died.

Joan Dunsmuir's funeral was not the public event her husband's had been. But still, several hundred spectators were gathered outside St. Andrew's Church when her hearse arrived. The *Colonist*'s reporter was able to find several "poorly clad" people anxious to talk about the "unremitting kindnesses" they had received. One old miner, who had walked 28 miles into town to attend the funeral, told of "benefactions that stretched back over half a century"; an old woman said that for twenty-three years she "had to thank Mrs. Dunsmuir every week for help and kindness."

At first James thought he would not attend the funeral. Almost a decade had passed since he had last spoken to his mother; he could hardly join his sisters as a principal mourner. But at the last moment he changed his mind. He took his place in the church, not as a grieving son, but in his official capacity as the lieutenant-governor of British Columbia, paying homage to one of the province's pioneers.

Halfway through the service, his shoulders began to heave, and the mourners who thronged the church shifted uncomfortably in their pews as the lieutenant-governor broke down and cried. "He so loved all his family," his youngest daughter recalled. ""My distasteful aunts duped my old grandmother and broke my father's heart."

Nineteen

For a woman who could afford the best legal and financial advice, Joan Dunsmuir left her affairs in a surprising muddle. When she had fallen out with James in 1899, she had lost the services of Charles Pooley, who had acted as attorney for Robert Dunsmuir and later for his widow and her sons. If anyone had a clear picture of Dunsmuir affairs—their landholdings, mortgages, shares and securities—that man was Charles Pooley. When forced to make a choice, he had thrown in his lot with James, and Joan had been compelled to entrust her affairs to other hands.

At first, while she was still mentally sharp and with John Bryden acting as her advisor, everything went smoothly. But then came the will case, and Bryden, who felt an equal allegiance to both sides of the family, found it convenient to absent himself from Victoria for extended periods of time. Meanwhile, Mary Croft, who was her mother's most devoted companion, calling at Craigdarroch almost daily, suggested that she seek the advice of John Samuel Henry Matson, an energetic young real estate and insurance broker.

After Matson took charge, Joan's estate quickly succumbed to his "too smart by half" manipulations. On 19 December 1905 Joan sold several properties including Fairview, her first Victoria home, to the Pemberton Trust—the notion apparently being to set the stage for an arm's length conveyance to her daughters. A year later, those same properties were sold to Matson for a dollar. So far so good. But less than two weeks later, on 8 November 1906, Joan Dunsmuir wrote her will. The bulk of her estate was to go to the girls, but she made special provision for her grandchildren. Two pieces of property, Craigdarroch and Fairview, were to be separated from the rest of her estate. The proceeds of their sale, or the income they produced, were to be divided into seven equal shares—one for each of her five surviving daughters, one for John Bryden and his children, and one for the three surviving children of her daughter Agnes Harvey.

Joan seems to have become confused. Fairview was no longer hers. Matson understood that he held the property "upon trust for and to the use of" the girls. But what was the point of trying to protect it from succession duties, and then including it in her will?

By the beginning of 1908, it had become obvious that Joan's health was failing. The time had come to make sure her affairs were in order. On 14 March, without amending the will she had executed two years earlier, Joan signed two documents. The first was an Indenture of Sale. Craigdarroch and its 28 acres, together with the Driard Hotel and the Colonist Building on Broad Street, two properties that had come into her possession when the former owners defaulted on mortgages totalling over $200,000, were conveyed to her daughters for the sum of $2 "in consideration of the natural love and affection the Vendor hath for the Purchasers." The second document was a private agreement, meant to accompany the sale and without which the sale should not have been completed. In it, Joan set up a trust of $326,387.77 in favour of her five daughters on condition that they agree to pay her an income of $1,000 a month. In addition, they agreed that, after her death, Craigdarroch would be sold, and that out of the proceeds of that sale $75,000 would be distributed to her grandchildren. Named as trustee, and no doubt the genius behind the agreement, was John Samuel Henry Matson.

It was only after Joan's death, and after her estate had started to wend its way through probate, that it became apparent that Matson had neglected to get the signature of Joan's daughter Effie—without it, the agreement was invalid and the trust did not exist. Nothing required Joan's daughters to distribute any part of the estate to her grandchildren.

The value of Joan's taxable estate shifted and changed as the probate office and the Supreme Court tried to sort out the mess—from $381,700 up to $854,000—and finally, in April 1909, six months after Joan's death, coming to rest at $794,000. Succession duties of $39,700 were paid—and then it was over. Mary, Jessie, Emily, Effie and Maude had got all that they would ever get from their parents' estates.

They were five very well-off women. While the complete details will probably never be known, it is safe to assume that in addition to their inheritance, each benefited from trusts and investments in excess of $250,000—more than $2.5 million by today's standards.

And so now they finally had the money, what would they do with it? Would they and their husbands squander the fortune, as James and Alexander had so confidently predicted? And what would happen to Craigdarroch, Robert Dunsmuir's monument to his success and the symbol of the wealth he and his family had so relentlessly pursued?

———

Robert Dunsmuir's dream castle was everyone else's white elephant—too big, too expensive for a single buyer. The sisters reached an unusual arrangement with land speculator Griffith Hughes. He agreed to pay them $30,000 for the castle and its 28 acres; in addition they would receive $1,750 for each of the 144 lots he intended to carve out of the estate. Hughes, who hoped to sell the lots for considerably more than that, set about promoting Craigdarroch as Victoria's most exclusive residential subdivision: "What the DERBY is to the racing world! What the MARATHON is to the athlete! Such is CRAIGDARROCH to the man who desires an absolutely perfect site for his residence or the sound investment of his money!!"

That was one of Hughes's more modest attempts to lure Victorians to Craigdarroch. But despite his aggressive advertising campaign, sales were slow. He decided to appeal to purchasers' gambling instincts. Prices were set at a flat $2,750 a lot. Each purchaser's name would then be entered in a lottery; he would not know which lot he owned until the evening of 26 March 1910, when a draw would be held. As an added incentive, Hughes announced that there would be a second draw. One of the lot-holders would win the castle.

The lucky winner was Solomon Cameron, who perhaps should have taken it as something of an omen that he had also drawn lot 13. Cameron mortgaged the castle to the hilt, invested his money in other properties and went broke. In 1919 the castle became the property of the Bank of Montreal, which was only too happy to lease it to the Department of Soldiers' Re-establishment for use as a hospital for veterans of the Great War.

Two years later, the castle became the home of Victoria College. The double drawing room, with blackboards blocking its fine gilt-touched fireplaces, became the purview of the history and English teachers. The dining room, crowded with slatted benches, became the mathematics classroom. French classes were conducted in one of the bedrooms. And the ballroom, a breathtaking seventy-one steps above the main floor, became the library.

After 1946 when the college moved to new premises and changed itself into the University of Victoria, there was talk of demolishing the castle. But it hung on, subdivided into school board offices and later divided into even smaller spaces as practice rooms for the Conservatory of Music.

When the conservatory departed, and the castle, half-heartedly run as a Dunsmuir museum, was finally opened to the public, the grandchildren of the men who had worked in Robert Dunsmuir's mines had an opportunity to view the fruits of their ancestors' labour. Some of them were not impressed. They sought to doom Dunsmuir's monument with their own particular curses. They need not have bothered.

The past has permeated the castle's walls. Not everyone has seen ghosts; not everyone hears the sound of the angeles-organ, Alexander's favourite instrument; not everyone has noticed the unmistakable odour of burning tallow, as if candles had just been extinguished, that sometimes seems to pervade Joan Dunsmuir's bedroom when the doors are thrown open in the morning. But few who have spent time there, at least since the castle became the home of Dunsmuir memorabilia, have escaped completely untouched from the mood of mean-spiritedness that seems to hang heavy in the air.

And what of Robert Dunsmuir's daughters?

Anne Euphemia—the madcap Effie who had danced into dawn with Dublin society—went mad. According to family legend, she lost her mind during her husband's tour of duty as naval attaché with the British legation in St. Petersburg. Effie, so the story goes, went out for a drive, found herself in the middle of a riot and became unhinged when a severed hand, tossed through the open window of her carriage, landed in her lap. And perhaps Effie's experience is more than an apocryphal tale; soon after the supposed event, her husband, Somerset Arthur Gough-Calthorpe, brought her home to Victoria. For a few months her name appeared as a guest at any number of society events, but by 1908 Effie was in England—residing in an asylum.

Gough-Calthorpe applied for a Certificate of Lunacy so that he might manage her affairs and succeeded in having her declared irrecoverably insane. She spent the rest of her life—an unfortunately long life, given the circumstances—in madhouses, half-forgotten by her relatives.

Shortly before Effie died, one of her nieces took it into her head to visit her. She was horrified when she encountered "a very smarmy doctor," sipping champagne and nibbling smoked salmon, who told her, "Effie loves to give parties."

She died in a nursing home on the Isle of Wight on 15 March 1952 of acute and chronic bronchitis at the age of eighty-four, having spent the last forty-four years of her life in institutions. Her trust funds—used to keep her doctors and nurses in salmon and champagne, her niece presumed—were almost gone. As her great-nephew recalled, "Aunt Effie died just in the nick of time to save a nasty family embarrassment."

———

Jessie and Sir Richard made the most of her money. Jessie had a domineering personality. Even her friends, who admired the fact that she went to hounds very well, found her a "very formidable woman"; and her servants regarded her as "something of a martinette" who ran the house "with a rod of iron." After a few stay-at-home years during which Jessie gave birth to two daughters, Joan in 1892 and Dorothy two years later, the Musgraves set off in pursuit of pleasure. The early months of the year they spent at the Hotel Metropole in Monte Carlo, with Sir Richard winning prizes for shooting clay pigeons while Jessie bided her time at the gaming tables. Early summer found them at their house in Ardmore, a little seaside village 20 miles from their Tourin estate. Late summers were spent on Vancouver Island, with Jessie visiting her sister Mary while Sir Richard reacquainted himself with the island's salmon streams. And then it was back to England for the London season.

By 1920 Jessie, who had left a considerable amount of her fortune in the casino at Monte Carlo, had begun to worry about money. When her daughter Joan announced that she was going to marry Thomas Ormsby Jameson, an all-round sportsman who had played cricket for England but who was not considered to be well-off, Jessie was furious that Joan did not have the sense to marry money. But as things turned out, it was Jameson who had to pay for his mother-in-law's keep rather than the other way round.

When Sir Richard died in 1930 in his eightieth year, his title went to his cousin, but the Tourin house and its surrounding acres became the responsibility of Joan and her husband. Jessie grumbled about spending money on an estate on which she was now living as a dowager rather than the lady of the house. But in 1932 she stopped complaining. Jessie, like thousands of others, had been won over by the salesmanship of promoter Ivar Kreuger, who had built an international financial empire on his Swedish Match Company and its boast that it controlled one-third of the world's production of matches. In 1932 Kreuger was revealed as a swindler and a forger, and promptly committed suicide. And, as Kreuger's corporations came tumbling down, Jessie lost what was left of her inheritance.

She was "virtually penniless," her grandson remembered. From then on, Jessie lived a more simple life. She devoted herself to the gardens at Tourin and Ardmore and to playing endless games of bridge with a small circle of friends. A heavy smoker, she amazed her grandchildren with her ability to keep her long, black cigarette holder clamped firmly in her teeth as the ash got longer and longer until it was almost the length of a cigarette.

In 1944 she fell getting out of the bathtub and broke her leg. Just as her recuperation was nearing its end, she suffered a stroke and remained bedridden until her death in 1946 in her seventy-ninth year.

———

If there was anything for which Jessie could be thankful during those difficult last years, it was the hovering presence of her sister Maude. Unlike her brothers and sisters, Robert Dunsmuir's youngest daughter, Henrietta Maude, was blessed with a sunny disposition. "She was a very kind sweet person," her great-nephew recalled. "Almost too good and innocent to be true."

And perhaps that was why she alone managed to remain on good terms with both sides of the family. She and her husband, Reggie Chaplin, had testified at the will case, but their statements had been so mild that James had had no reason to take offence, and when they visited Victoria, the Chaplins were as welcome aboard his yacht, the *Thistle*, as they were at Mary Croft's home, Mount Adelaide.

In the 1920s, when Reggie retired from the army as a lieutenant-colonel, they moved to Victoria, staying at Mount Adelaide while Maude nursed Mary through her last illness. In 1928, after Mary's death, the Chaplins settled in Vancouver, building a luxurious home, "Glen Lodge," on Belmont Street in the city's fashionable Point Grey district. They remained there for ten years, with Reggie becoming an enthusiastic member of a Vancouver polo team and a favourite in the city's shooting and hunting circles.

In 1939 they decided to move to South Africa, where Reggie had seen active service during the Boer War. While their furniture was making its way to Capetown, they travelled to Ireland so that Maude could visit her sister Jessie, and Reggie could join Sir Richard at his favourite fishing spots on the Blackwater River. War broke out while they were in Ireland, stranding them there. Reggie died at

Tourin the following year and was buried in the Ardmore cemetery.

After the war ended, Maude stayed on "as a sort of paying guest" and as a companion for her ailing sister. After Jessie's death in 1946, Maude's grandson made arrangements for her to join him in England. She died in 1950 in her seventy-ninth year, and she was buried in Ireland beside her husband.

—

For Emily, as well as Maude, Jessie's home became a kind of refuge. On 1 April 1904 her husband, Northing Pinckney Snowden, died, aged only forty-four, in the Holloway Sanitorium, and after waiting for a discreet six months, Emily married Harry Burroughes. They dipped into the capital of Emily's trust to buy an estate in Norfolk and lived "a pretty gracious life" until Harry "went bust rather spectacularly."

After moving to Ireland in rather straitened circumstances, they lived in a series of rented houses. Harry was deeply affected by his bankruptcy. "He never ever again owed anybody a penny for more than a week," an acquaintance recalled.

Harry was regarded as "a rather ridiculous old fellow," particularly by Lady Charles Cavendish, the former Adele Astaire. Lord Charles Arthur Cavendish, second son of the ninth Duke of Devonshire, had been smitten with Adele when she and her brother, Fred, brought *Funny Face* to London.

He followed her to New York. "I think I proposed to him," Adele recalled. "It was at Twenty-One, which in those days was a speakeasy. I'd had one drink . . . and I said, 'Do you know, we get along so well I think we ought to get married.' "

"Righty ho," replied Lord Charles.

As the Duke of Devonshire's son, Lord Charles received the use of Lismore Castle, which towered above the banks of the Blackwater River and had, according to Adele, two hundred rooms and one bathroom.

For several years Harry and Emily rented rooms in a wing of Lismore Castle, and Harry took great exception to Adele's habit of celebrating the Fourth of July by flying the Stars and Stripes from the castle's flagpole.

"It's damned well indecent!" he fumed.

"Oh come, Mr. Burroughes," Adele smiled. "Now, if I'd hung my panties from the flagpole, *that* might have been indecent." Harry, observers noted with delight, nearly died of apoplexy.

Adele may well have been the death of Harry, for in the end it was his blood pressure that carried him off. After Harry's death in 1939, Emily moved to a small house in Ardmore. She died there in 1944 "in some squalor," having been bedridden since Harry's death and quite deserted by her family. "On reflection, my parents really might have done a bit more to look after her," her great-nephew mused.

—

Of all Robert Dunsmuir's sons-in-law, none tried harder to pay his own way than Harry Croft. Mining, lumbering, real estate, land reclamation—Harry had tried them all and failed. A man who stumbled from one disaster to another could not hope to compete with the likes of Sam Matson, the man to whom his wife Mary had entrusted her mother's estate and for whom she had developed a deep attachment.

Matson seems to have been no more competent than Harry Croft, but where everything Harry touched turned to dust, everything Sam touched turned to gold. He arrived in Victoria in 1889 when he was twenty years old, opened his own insurance and real estate office, and never looked back.

When Mary Croft, impatient with the quiet incompetence of "poor Harry," first met Sam Matson, she could not help but be impressed. He was young—seven years her junior. He had broad shoulders, twinkling eyes and a shy smile. He was a man of character. As one friend put it, "He was the kind of a man to go tiger shooting with; determined, courageous and unflinching." His "boyish impulsiveness" combined with the "tender sensitiveness which he could never quite conceal" added to his appeal.

Mary badly needed advice. By default, she had become the chief custodian of her mother's affairs. Harry was of no use as an advisor. Sam Matson, the young up-and-coming real estate and insurance broker, was described to her as shrewd and possessed of a real talent for organization. And more than that, he was known to be scrupulously honest, and he enjoyed helping people. "What is the use of being able to help a lame man over a stile if you don't do it?" Sam liked to say. Mary sighed with relief at finding a champion, and fell in love.

Harry Croft knew that his wife was being swept away, but rather than compete for her affection, he beat a gentlemanly retreat. He went to England for a long, consoling visit with his sister and her husband. And there, Harry's bad luck held, for he spent most of their reunion flat on his back in considerable pain and watching his sprained ankle swell until it measured 13 inches around.

Harry's family was worried about him. "His business matter doesn't progress, and I am really afraid he is quite hard up," his brother-in-law mused. It was clear that they knew something about his troubles with Mary. "The Family Dunsmuir Lawsuit drags its long length along but it is hoped that when the ultimate verdict is given the daughters will all receive portions. So Mary will be in funds—but under the present circumstances I really don't know what would happen if we were unable to give Harry quarters."

In the end, Harry returned to Victoria where Sam, sometimes by inches, sometimes by leaps and bounds, was taking over Mary's life. From Joan Dunsmuir, Sam acquired a lot in the Mount Adelaide estate. By June 1906 his house was completed and the Matsons and the Crofts were neighbours. Everyone who lived in one of the little houses built on Harry's land, when it was still Harry's and when he still thought of himself as a real estate speculator, knew what was going on. "We all felt so sorry for Harry," one of them recalled. "He was such a nice man, such a 'gentle' man. A terribly decent chap."

The Dunsmuirs, mother and daughter, were under Matson's thrall. On 13 July 1906 Joan Dunsmuir allowed Matson to buy the shares she held in the Colonist Publishing Company, and Sam, who had never, ever, spoken of his love for newspapering, became the editor and publisher of Victoria's oldest daily. By 1908 all Joan's property had been transferred to Matson in trust. There is nothing to suggest that he did not intend to administer the estate to the benefit of Mary and her sisters. His reward would be the status he gained, coupled with the pure pleasure of manipulating large sums of money. If Matson had a fault, it was preening self-confidence, an unshakable belief that he could succeed at anything to which he turned his hand. And, on the surface at least, his faith seemed to be well founded. He purchased land at Cobble Hill north of Victoria, and, scorning "dude-farmers," he worked seriously at establishing a stock farm. He purchased the Victoria Transfer Company in 1906 in its horse and buggy days. Later, he would adapt with ease to the motor age, buying up small bus companies and combining their routes into a unified transportation system. In 1910 he bought newspapers in Vancouver and Nanaimo. The following year, he solved the contentious issue of the Songhees Reserve by convincing the Indians to relocate to Esquimalt. In 1915 he was appointed the British Columbia representative to the Dominion Hospital Commission and took personal charge of the establishment and management of veterans' hospitals in the province, recommending Craigdarroch as an ideal site for the facility planned for Victoria. All this and more—more than any one man, whatever his energy, could keep straight in his head.

Harry Croft stayed on at Mount Adelaide, trying to ignore the sympathy of his neighbours. "Well Ted," Harry wrote his brother in 1916, "I wish I was out of this and with you. Life would be a great deal brighter." In 1917 Harry died quite suddenly of a hemorrhage of the brain. He was sixty-one years old. The probate of his will revealed that he had nothing, not so much as one single dollar, that he could call his own.

A month after Harry's death, Mary was ensconced at Matson's "Hill Farm," writing to Harry's brother Ted. "I have not had the courage to face Victoria yet. I haven't gone through poor Harry's things yet, but I found the manuscript pertaining to the family history which I think you would like to have . . . Poor dear Harry's affairs are in a hopeless muddle and I am miserable about it."

Poor dear Harry. Family meant so much to him and he had died childless, with no one, save his brother, who might be at all interested in the family genealogy he had so painstakingly reconstructed. And as for Harry's affairs being in a muddle, Mary could only blame Sam Matson for that, for one way or another, Matson had inveigled himself into every aspect of Harry's life. Sam continued to tinker with Mary's estate—a little bit shifted over here, a little bit transferred there—and while there may have been a grand scheme to his dabbling, only Sam had the total picture.

Mary died on 15 August 1928 after a long, tortuous decline. "Bigheartedness was the distinguishing character of Mrs. Mary Croft," Sam Matson's newspaper editorialized. "To those whom she leaves in grief it will always be a comfort to remember that her faithfulness to high ideals and the part she played in inculcating them . . . represented spiritual treasure laid up while on earth."

Those she left in grief might have felt more comforted if she had also left her affairs in some kind of order. She had written a will shortly before her death—a will that was so short and contained so many corrections that one can only assume that it was an eleventh hour, ill-considered affair.

In it she left her estate to her nieces and nephews, the children of her older sisters Elizabeth and Agnes. Her personal estate she was free to dispose of however she wished; her share of the trust established by her mother would automatically revert to her sisters. Thanks to Sam Matson's manoeuvrings, it was difficult to separate what Mary owned in her own right from what she possessed as part of the trust. In 1907 Joan had given her title to Mount Adelaide. Did

Mount Adelaide now revert to her sisters, or was it Mary's to bequeath?

The first step to unlocking that puzzle was to unearth the document Joan Dunsmuir had signed in 1908, the agreement with her daughters that Matson had designed and that overrode her will. Matson could not find it. And then, while Mary's estate was still in limbo, Sam Matson collapsed and died, leaving the probate office with a problem of monumental proportions. What was Mary's? What was Sam's? What had he held in trust, and what had he held by right of purchase? And what about the documents that suggested Mary had sold him certain properties, including Mount Adelaide? Had the sale been completed, and if so, why had he not registered the title?

Busy with his farm, his newspaper, his bus line and his taxi service, Matson had allowed Mary's estate and his own affairs to tumble together in a confused clutter. When the mess was finally sorted out, Sam's widow got almost everything.

Ada Matson must have felt that justice had been served when she took up residence in Mount Adelaide. And she may have had a wish fulfilled when, after her death, the Salvation Army, to whom she left the house in her will, decided that its interests would best be served by flattening Mount Adelaide and by building a new structure, "Matson Lodge," in its place.

—

And so Alexander and James had guessed correctly. Entrusted to their sisters, the Dunsmuir fortune would have disappeared—gambled away, frittered away, or lost in a muddle of misplaced trust. By winning the will case, it seemed as if James had insured that the Dunsmuir millions would become a powerful economic force. Instead, he would prove to be the architect of its destruction. But there is a greater irony. The least likely candidate of all those who had competed for Alexander's estate later proved that the Dunsmuir millions might have become billions if placed in her hands.

Edna Wallace Hopper knew how to rebound from defeat. In 1908, two years after the Privy Council dismissed the final will case appeal, she married Albert Brown, a New York stockbroker. From him she received valuable insights into the workings of the New York exchange, information which she filed away for future use. She continued her Broadway career, but by 1920, as she entered her mid-forties, she was finding it more and more difficult to find suitable roles. Rather than accepting retirement, the redoubtable Edna found a surgeon who not only agreed to perform a face-lift on her but also allowed the entire procedure to be filmed. And then, with several reels of film tucked under her arm, she took her show on the road. At movie houses across Canada and throughout the United States, she showed the film of her operation and lectured on how to remain young and beautiful and, failing that, how to regain through surgery the youth and beauty one had lost.

The "wonderful apostle of perpetual youth" played to packed houses at Victoria's new Royal Theatre. "I resorted to plastic surgery, a lifting of the skin and a cutting away of the surface," she explained brightly as she introduced her film.

Edna trumped her ace by giving special women-only matinee performances in which she took an on-stage beauty bath on a set that harkened back to the days of Pompeii. Interest, needless to say, was intense. "For the occasion the doormen and the stagehands were girls, and women were installed throughout the theatre to keep eyes open, and see that there were no men present, though there are several reports that a few sneaked in dressed up as women," the *Colonist* blushed.

She managed to keep that performance going for more than a decade. Eventually, she decided that the time had come to give up the stage, dive into her savings and try her hand at playing the stock market. She proved to be so canny a Wall Street trader that in 1938 she was invited to join the venerable firm of L. F. Rothchild & Company. By 1953 she had quadrupled her capital. Conducting business from a desk in the firm's board room, the only woman among thirty-five men, seventy-nine-year-old Edna remained "addicted to girlish hats, high heels and frills."

"A lot of people believe that I've been dead and buried for ages," Edna exclaimed. "But just now, I feel as if life were only beginning. I can't imagine a time in the future when I shall not be working. I'll retire when I die."

And she was as good as her word. On Friday 11 December 1959 she was at her desk. The following day she contracted pneumonia. By Monday she was dead. She was eighty-five years old, a tiny 83-pound woman, less than 5 feet tall. She had outlived all the major players in the will case—James Dunsmuir, his mother and all his sisters. And what might she have accomplished with several million dollars if she had won Alexander's estate?

Twenty

———

In June 1905 a rumour that had been circulating in Victoria for several months appeared in Vancouver newspapers—James Dunsmuir would be appointed the next lieutenant-governor. His term as premier was recognized as having been "short and not particularly merry," and it was widely known that he had "neither a liking nor an adaptability for public life." Why, then, would he even consider accepting an office which was highly public and would require his attendance at countless social functions? Some commentators suggested that his sense of duty propelled him into office. But it seems more likely that he agreed to accept the appointment to please his wife.

Her position in society meant a great deal to Laura Dunsmuir. From the moment she arrived on Vancouver Island she took pains to let everyone know that she was a member of the distinguished Byrd family of Virginia—even though she had to peer back over eleven generations before she could establish a connection. It was tenuous, but for Laura, it was enough. She christened her first daughter Sarah Byrd and pointedly bestowed on her the diminutive "Byrdie." And when James purchased a Rockland area home and registered it in Laura's name, she was quick to rename the house "Westover," after the Byrd estate in Virginia.

In addition, Laura welcomed the assumption that her father was a member of North Carolina's planter aristocracy, possessed of thousands of acres and hundreds of slaves. But Laura's father, William Bright Surles, was not so grand as all that. Even before the Civil War sent Southern fortunes on a downward spiral, fewer than a dozen slaves worked Elm Grove, his 300-acre farm, and Surles was considered a middle-class farmer rather than a plantation aristocrat.

Laura had just passed her seventeenth birthday when she fell in love with Lunsford Richardson. A North Carolinian, born in 1854 on Parker Heights, his family's prosperous Johnston County farm, Richardson was just the type of man Surles might have welcomed as a son-in-law. But four years of war had left the Richardsons with little except for their land and "one carriage horse, one buggy horse and one chicken." Lunsford, who had hoped to become a lawyer and who had won medals for Greek and Latin and debating during his undergraduate years, was forced to abandon his studies and take a job as a schoolmaster. William Surles was sure that his daughter could do better, and Laura lived long enough to appreciate the irony of her father's decision, for Lunsford Richardson, despite the paucity of his prospects, did very well for himself indeed. In 1880 he deserted the schoolroom and used the $450 he had saved to purchase a drugstore. It soon became apparent to him that most of his customers were looking for cold remedies. It worried him that all he could offer were expensive and cumbersome vapour lamps, which wafted medication to the patient's lungs, or poultices and plasters which were intended to warm the chest but which all too often produced painful blisters and burns. He began to experiment with other cures, the most efficacious of which was a petroleum-based salve to which he added a healthy helping of menthol. Used as a chest rub and vapourized by body heat, Richardson's Croup and Pneumonia Cure Salve opened the air passages while it stimulated the flow of blood to the chest. The remedy proved instantly popular, only the ponderousness of its name standing in the way of nation-wide sales. Casting about for a marketable brand-name, Richardson decided to recognize his brother-in-law, Dr. Joshua Vick, in whose pharmacy he had trained. By 1919, when Lunsford Richardson died, Vick's VapoRub had become the largest selling cold remedy in North America with annual sales of more than $11 million dollars.

But in 1875 Richardson was a man without means, and William Bright Surles discouraged the courtship. He felt rather different about James Dunsmuir, who had become acquainted with Surles's son, Hannibal, when both were students at the Virginia Agricultural and Mechanical College in Blacksburg. Jim, who was studying mining engineering, boasted about his family's status. His father owned coal mines; he was his father's right-hand man. When it became apparent that Jim had become enamoured of Laura, William Surles found good reason to encourage his suit.

Eighteen-year-old Laura Miller Surles married James Dunsmuir on 5 July 1876 at the Old Sardis Church in Cumberland County. With one of her brothers to keep them company, they spent their honeymoon making their way to Vancouver Island.

Laura's first child, christened Robert William after his two grandfathers, was born at Wellington on 21 August 1877. Three months later, she received distressing news from North Carolina—her mother, Sarah, had died of consumption. As soon as she could, Laura packed her bags and headed south. A rumour quickly spread among Laura's Cumberland County friends that she had left her husband and had come home to stay. It was certainly true that she had been terribly homesick and that her absence from Wellington lasted for almost a year. But Laura had good reason for delaying her return. Soon after she arrived back at Elm Grove, she discovered she was pregnant. And, in the end, she remained away only until she and her baby—a little girl she named Sarah Byrd after her mother—were fit enough to travel.

She gave birth to her third child, a daughter named Joan Olive White, on 7 August 1880 while she and Jim were still residing in Wellington. Later that year, Laura's spirits lifted when his transfer to Departure Bay allowed her to escape the grim coal town. Robert Dunsmuir presented them with a fine new house built on the hillside above the wharves. Square and two storeys tall, with eleven rooms and 14-foot-high ceilings, the Departure Bay house was said to have cost as much as $13,000, an amount the colliery's highest-paid employee would have had to work ten years to earn. It was a residence of considerable charm, with eight fireplaces, each decorated with the latest thing in imitation marble, and with the most modern of conveniences—a large tank in the attic which delivered running water to the bathroom and made it necessary to carry only hot water up the stairs.

The eight years Laura spent at Departure Bay were marked by tragedy. In 1884, her three-year-old daughter Joan died of "brain fever." Three years later, the Departure Bay wharves were once again hung with black crepe when her sixth child, Alexander Lee, died before his first birthday. But later, when she was an old lady and living in a style befitting a duchess, Laura would recall her years at Departure Bay as the happiest time in her life.

In 1889, after his mother decreed that James would move to Victoria, Laura set up housekeeping in Fairview. By 1891, James had acquired 20 waterfront acres on the Gorge, and architect John Teague had prepared plans for a wonderfully excessive Queen Anne-style house. "While it cannot be classed as any particular style of ar-

A simple man, with little imagination and even less ambition, James Dunsmuir obediently assumed the burdens thrust upon him.

A distant descendant of the distinguished Byrd family of Virginia, James's wife, Laura, was often described as a "Southern belle." Socially ambitious, she became the province's most prominent hostess.

In 1891, James built Burleith, a rambling Queen Anne-style house surrounded by acres of woodland and gardens.

Burleith offered tennis courts, croquet lawns and a playhouse for James and Laura's daintily dressed children.

Like Joan Dunsmuir, Laura produced eight daughters and two sons. Missing here are her son, Robin, and her daughter, Dola (not yet born). Left to right: (back) Maye, Byrdie, Bessie; (middle) Muriel, Laura, Marion, Elinor; (front) "Boy," still being dressed as a girl, and Kathleen.

Miners at Extension had good reason to resent their employer. Because James was determined to build up the townsite of Ladysmith, they were forced to travel 12 long miles from their homes to the mine.

Built on the Clyde in 1908 at an estimated cost of $200,000, the Dolaura *was a magnificent craft, 218 feet long, built of steel and capable of 14 knots.*

Laura (smiling in the background) with Kaiser Wilhelm, who toured the Dolaura *during her shakedown cruise. This faded photograph, found a family album, was captioned "Mother and the Kaiser."*

With its medieval centre block and Tudor additions, Hatley (front view) was designed to appear as if it had been standing for centuries. B.C. ARCHIVES AND RECORDS SERVICE/HP79952

Sold in 1940 to the Department of Defence for a meagre $75,000, Hatley (rear view) is now the home of Royal Roads Military College. B.C. ARCHIVES AND RECORDS SERVICE/HP63863

James and Laura at Bisham Abbey in 1912. After selling his railway and his coal mines, James quite suddenly and as if by magic acquired a sense of style.

The Dunsmuir family around 1908. Left to right: (back) *Robin, Maude (Robin's wife), John Hope, unidentified man, Arthur Bromley, Maye, Guy Audain;* (middle) *Bessie, Laura, Boy, James, Byrdie;* (front) *Marion, Kathleen, Dola, Jimmy Audain, Elinor, Muriel.*

En route to Vancouver to take in a concert by Paderewski, a teenaged Robin found it easy to charm his mother, Laura (second from right) *and her friends.*

Robin's wife, Maude, was charming and stylish but rather plain. Robin, despite his expanding waistline, projects the dangerous energy that made his private life the favourite topic of Victoria gossips.

With trusted friends like "Dib" Little (far right), James (second from left) spent happy hours aboard the Dolaura *shooting and fishing. The bag for 14 December 1910 was at least ten geese and more than three dozen ducks.*

In this photograph, taken in 1911 when he was seventeen, Boy appears characteristically dour as he stands on the Dolaura's *deck displaying his share of the day's catch.*

A talented equestrian, Boy won many prizes on Kismet, his dappled grey. In 1915, en route to England to join a cavalry regiment, he booked passage on the Lusitania.

Byrdie and her family at Burleith when she married Guy Audain in 1901. Robin (far left) appears as if to the manor born. His father, James, strikes an "everyman" pose while holding Boy's hand.

Byrdie in India. She so detested living there that her father provided Guy Audain with a lifetime annuity, conditional on his bringing Byrdie home. PRIVATE COLLECTION

When he was not hunting or fishing with his father-in-law, Guy Audain developed the grounds of his home, Ellora, into one of the most admired gardens in Victoria.

B.C. ARCHIVES AND RECORDS SERVICE/HP100084

By 1921, when this photograph was taken, Elinor (left) had given up all pretence. She smoked cigars. She dressed like a man. And she had found friends who shared her tastes.

B.C. ARCHIVES AND RECORDS SERVICE/
HP99171

Accompanied by Victoria friends, Kathleen (centre), appeared in Vancouver at a benefit concert for the Belgian Relief Fund. Her performance of "The Boys in Navy Blue" received three encores.

B.C. ARCHIVES AND RECORDS SERVICE/
31199

Kathleen "went Hollywood" in 1931. She settled into a luxurious home near Rodeo Drive and set out to woo producers with her talent and, more importantly, her money.

Dola (second from right) felt ill at ease with her sisters' fast-set friends—in particular her brother-in-law, couturier Edward Molyneux (far right). PRIVATE COLLECTION

At her home, Windows, Tallulah Bankhead (right) is trying, unsuccessfully, to coax Dola into facing the camera. The two women were friends for more than forty years.

PRIVATE COLLECTION

chitecture, it may be said that a lesson has been taken from all the schools and the best points adopted," the *Colonist* ventured. Reached by a gently curving carriage drive and set amongst croquet lawns and tennis courts, the house, named "Burleith" after Robert Dunsmuir's Ayrshire birthplace, was deemed to be "one of the most attractive of Victoria's suburban residences." James's "Scotch caution" had suggested to him that it would be only prudent to substitute wood-frame and shingles for the brick and stone the architect had planned, but still Burleith cost as much as $50,000 to build. The ground floor boasted a drawing room, a dining room, a breakfast room, a billiard room and a smoking room. Wide stairs rose from the oak-panelled central hall to the bedrooms and the day and night nurseries on the second floor, and then on to the third floor and an observation tower that provided a view across the waters of the Gorge where Emily's home, Ashnola, could be glimpsed through the trees. And James had not stinted on providing his family with the best in creature comforts. "The house throughout will be lighted up by electricity, with electric bells, speaking tubes, and every modern convenience," the *Colonist* reported.

—

During the 1890s the Dunsmuirs found themselves at the very peak of Victoria society. Any reservations the city's first families might have had in 1883 when Robert Dunsmuir had first taken up residence in the city melted away. Their homes—Mount Adelaide, Ashnola, Burleith and especially Craigdarroch—set standards that none could match. Mary Croft was an avid hostess—"Japanese Teas," strawberry socials, fancy dress balls, tennis parties—the invitations poured forth from Mount Adelaide. At Ashnola, Emily responded by hosting even more gala events—fancy dress parties, luxurious picnics on Ashnola's seaside lawns and elegantly lazy afternoons of boating on the quiet waters of the Gorge. And who could resist an invitation to Craigdarroch, the most expensive private residence in the province, and the opportunity to waltz into morning in the castle's fourth-floor ballroom.

People like the O'Reillys, who counted themselves members of the city's *real* aristocracy and who put great store on taste and breeding and gentility, found they had little choice but to be openly friendly even while they remained quietly convinced that they were members of a better class. In 1891 the O'Reilly's daughter, Kathleen, had declined the pleasure of serving as one of Jessie Dunsmuir's bridesmaids, choosing instead to flit over to Vancouver to attend a performance by Sarah Bernhardt. But five years later, when Jessie and Sir Richard were returning to Ireland after Jessie's annual visit with her mother, she eagerly accepted the invitation to travel with them to London. And once they were there, she was provided with an intimate view of Jessie's life. Impressed in spite of herself, Kathleen struggled to find reasons to feel superior. Jessie, she decided, was "most extravagant . . . I never see any people so much dressed as the Dunsmuirs. I don't think it is considered good taste in England."

As far as the Dunsmuirs' social position was concerned, good taste had nothing to do with it. Money, mountains of money, had won them pride of place. Providing the refinements that came with culture and breeding, Laura saw as her responsibility. She introduced James to the arts and she succeeded in turning him into an "admirer of the drama, and an ardent lover of good music." In 1901 she took delivery of a Steinway parlour grand, the "most costly and beautiful piano ever imported to British Columbia," and began to hold recitals at Burleith. And every winter she insisted that the family travel south to spend a month at San Francisco's Palace Hotel for the city's opera season.

—

Laura enjoyed her husband's premiership much more than he did, not least of all because it provided her with the opportunity to rub shoulders with royalty. In the autumn of 1901 Victoria was preparing for the visit of the Duke of York, who would later become King George V. The Parliament Buildings were outlined with electric lights for the occasion. Once installed, the lights remained as a permanent fixture, and over the years as the number of postcards bearing the image of the illuminated buildings reflected in the dark waters of the Inner Harbour climbed into the millions, Victorians who made their money from tourism could be forgiven if they felt that this was the most important decision of the Dunsmuir administration.

The Duchess of York, the future Queen Mary, accompanied her husband, and while he was engaged with official duties, she slipped away with several members of her party to sail up the quiet waters of the Gorge for a visit to Burleith. Since her marriage in 1892, the duchess had made her home at Sandringham in York Cottage, "a glum little villa" with primitive plumbing and "bedrooms like cubicles." The duchess, Laura discovered, was intensely interested in how other people lived. As Laura's daughter Bessie recalled, "The

Duchess looked over the whole house, from top to toe, and much embarrassed my mother when she insisted on going upstairs. Mother was so worried it wouldn't be all tidy, because everybody had been so busy all morning tidying up the downstairs."

—

James Dunsmuir was eager to leave the premier's office, but Laura was equally eager that he stay on—especially after 22 January 1901 when Queen Victoria died. As the premier and his wife, the Dunsmuirs would be invited to attend the coronation of Edward VII.

The ceremony was not scheduled to take place until 26 June 1902, but with dressmakers to visit and invitations to sort out, Laura made sure she was in London well in advance. The premier dallied until the last moment, and when he did leave for London, he quite deliberately booked passage on the ship that was carrying the Prime Minster and Lady Laurier to England. Dunsmuir had hoped to seize the opportunity to discuss a new deal for British Columbia, but Laurier and his wife both suffered from seasickness and spent most of the voyage confined to their cabin, and he had to content himself with whiling away the time playing poker with the premier of Ontario.

Meanwhile, Laura and her twenty-year-old daughter, Bessie, made the most of the special coronation season. Both were presented at court—Laura wearing an "exquisite gown" of ivory satin, adorned with jewelled chiffon roses and with gold and diamond-embroidered *point de gaze*, and Bessie clad in "a charming gown" of cream chiffon embroidered with silver and white lilies of the valley. Invitations poured in—luncheon with the Duchess of Malmesbury; a garden party with the Countess of Jersey; evening receptions hosted by Lady Sassoon, the Duchess of Somerset, Sir Henry Irving—on and on—at homes, teas, dinners, country weekends.

The premier of British Columbia and his family were "the most honoured of all the colonials," a society paper reported.

—

Less than two months later, on 21 November 1902, James Dunsmuir resigned the premiership. He was determined to simplify his life, not only by turning his back on politics but also by selling his railway. A few months earlier he had come close to signing a deal with "some very rich Dutch people." But negotiations had broken down when the potential purchasers, who were interested in acquiring the coal mines as well as the rail line, sent a representative to California to investigate the booming new oil industry. "The outlook frightened them off," James noted ruefully. "I anticipated that oil was cutting seriously into the coal market in California . . . still I did not expect that the conditions of the market as it is now, would come so soon. We are certainly unable to compete with oil on steam business, and I look to see almost every industry in California using oil before the end of the present year."

His American partners, aware that other New York investors were preparing to pour money into the burgeoning oil business, decided that the time had come to disentangle themselves from a poorly managed railway and its declining mines. On 17 October 1902 Jim Dunsmuir bought out his partners. For one million dollars, he became sole owner of the E & N.

He was now free to negotiate a sale without referring to others, but almost three years passed before he found a buyer. The Canadian Pacific Railway, after snubbing its nose at Victoria twenty years earlier, was now showing a lively interest. The city was an important port of call for its ocean-going *Empress* steamers; its coastal *Princess* boats had established regular connections between Victoria and Vancouver and Seattle; and in September 1903 the company had confirmed its plans to build a tourist hotel on the land reclaimed from the James Bay mudflats. The prospect of the CPR acquiring Dunsmuir's railway was a welcome one to most Victorians, and particularly so to the city's mayor. "The road would be better in the hands of any one other than Mr. James Dunsmuir," he said. "He will do nothing for any one but himself."

On 5 June 1905 the final agreement was signed. For $2,330,000 Dunsmuir conveyed to the CPR all of the Esquimalt & Nanaimo Railway's 25,000 shares. On its part, the CPR agreed to convey to the Wellington Colliery Company all the lands and rights-of-way required for the operation of the mines at Alexandra, Extension and Cumberland. And, in addition, the coal company was granted the rights to all coal under the land within the railway belt.

Dunsmuir would receive $1,075,000 once the share transfer was complete. The remaining $1,255,000, the CPR had the option of paying in the form of four per cent debentures with a twenty-five year maturity. At first glance, it seemed as though Dunsmuir had pulled off quite a coup, but the cash payment he received did little more than cover the sales commission and the amount he had already paid to acquire the shares of the Pacific Improvements Company. And the CPR debentures would provide him with an interest income of only $50,000 a year, a handsome amount in turn-of-the-century dollars but not the vast riches that his enemies fantasized. Still, he had managed to relieve himself of the pressures of running the railway, and at the same time he had retained his coal mines.

—

In March 1906 the *Toronto Globe* identified James Dunsmuir as "one of the most prominently mentioned" candidates for the lieutenant-governor's office, and gave two reasons for predicting his appointment. "First, that the British Columbia people want a Lieut-Governor of their own province; and second, that few prominent British Columbians can make the financial sacrifices required of the Lieut-Governor."

Those reasons apparently being as good as any for making the final selection, on 11 May it was made official. And the man who shrank from public appearances and who was ambitious for nothing more than the comforts of his fireside and the pleasures of hunting and fishing with a few hearty male friends prepared to accept one of the highest appointed positions his country had to offer.

On 26 May, James Dunsmuir was sworn into office and became the province's eighth lieutenant-governor. Even left-leaning newspapers found his appointment "generally acceptable," for while he might be perceived as an arch conservative, he had been recommended for office by a Liberal prime minister. Praise for Laura was more wholehearted. "Mrs. Dunsmuir is in every sense a helpmeet to her husband," James's old enemy, the *Victoria Times*, purred. "She will perform her part as hostess of Government House with grace and tact, and we predict that the new regime will be highly successful from every point of view."

And highly successful it did indeed seem to be—at least in the first year of Dunsmuir's tenure. Perhaps he surprised even himself with his ability to bring a common touch to the vice-regal office. At his first official function, the opening of the new YWCA home in Vancouver, his ruddy outdoorsy appearance and his obvious nervousness endeared him to the mostly female audience. "There was a notable faltering in this little speech, indicating an attack of nerves," the *Province* sympathized. He did much better a week later at the annual meeting of the provincial Rifle Association held in Richmond. Invited to open the competition, he was handed a loaded rifle, and to the delight of the spectators, he threw himself down at the 300-yard line, "took careful deliberate aim," and "pumped a dead centre shot in the bull."

He won the hearts of golfers when he offered a $1,000 prize to the Pacific Northwest Golf Association. Yachtsmen were equally pleased when he donated a silver trophy, to be known as the Alexandra Cup, to the Northwest International Yacht Racing Association. And Victoria city fathers were described as elated when he purchased an entire issue of local improvement debentures at their full $55,726 value.

He had been in office for over a year before running into serious trouble. The federal government, while it had continued to disallow anti-Oriental legislation passed by the province, sought to placate British Columbians by instituting a $500 head tax. Since coming into effect in 1904, the tax had succeeded in slowing Chinese immigration to a trickle. But workingmen's associations and their Socialist party allies had found a new threat in the rising number of Japanese being imported to the province by railway contractors and other employers who insisted that they could not operate without a large pool of cheap labour.

During the session of 1907, the provincial government passed "An Act to Regulate Immigration into British Columbia" designed to exclude the Japanese. Dunsmuir sent a personal note to the premier, serving notice that he, as lieutenant-governor, would refuse to give his assent to the bill. To the Secretary of State in Ottawa, he confided his reasons: all similar legislation had been disallowed and, in addition, the federal government had recently concluded a trade agreement with Japan, so the passage of a discriminatory bill "might seriously interfere with our international relations and Federal interests."

At first his action was debated only as an interesting constitutional question. "It would be an unthinkable thing in Canadian politics that a lieutenant-governor can on his own responsibility prevent legislation from coming into effect," the *Toronto Globe* editorialized. But constitutional questions and diplomatic niceties were of little interest to the members of the Vancouver Trades and Labour Council. The city was full of wild rumours: a railway company was importing 5,000 Japanese labourers; several thousand were on their way from Hawaii; the Japanese would soon form one-third of the province's population. On 24 June 1907 the *Kumeric* disembarked almost 2,000 Japanese in Vancouver. That evening the Labour Council met to form the Asiatic Exclusion League.

On 7 September, the league staged a parade and rally "to awaken slumbering Vancouver to the seriousness of the Japanese question." Led by a band playing "Rule Britannia" and "The Maple Leaf Forever," seven thousand people, including the representatives of fifty-eight labour organizations, marched to City Hall, singing patriotic songs and carrying placards—STAND FOR A WHITE CANADA, A WHITE CANADA FOR US, STEAMER *WOOLICH* WILL ARRIVE IN A FEW DAYS WITH 500 JAPS. At City Hall, a crowd 24,000 strong cheered and howled as Lieutenant-Governor Dunsmuir was burned in effigy. After "some youngster" threw a brick through a window, releasing the "pent-up hatred of invading Orientalism," the rally turned into a riot, and a mob surged through Chinatown and on to the Japanese district, smashing every window in sight.

Concerned by the diplomatic implications of the Vancouver riot, the prime minister dispatched Mackenzie King to investigate the cause of the disturbance and to assess Japanese property losses and arrange for compensation. As part of his investigation, King marched into the office of the Canadian Nippon Supply Company, a Vancouver-based firm that acted as a contractor arranging for the recruitment of labour in Japan, and demanded to see its records. Among them, he made an interesting discovery. In June 1907, only weeks after he had refused to sign the immigration bill, James Dunsmuir, as colliery president, had been negotiating a contract for the importation of five hundred Japanese coal miners.

"The people of British Columbia seem determined to press for the retirement of Lieutenant-Governor Dunsmuir," the *Globe* reported soon after the news broke. But pressing for his retirement was putting it mildly. The Asiatic League and their Socialist allies in the legislature wanted his scalp. At a league meeting held on 5 January 1908 in Vancouver, Parker Williams, the "Socialist orator," planted his tongue firmly in his cheek to state, "This is a commercial age, and the Lieutenant-Governor should be permitted to enjoy the full benefit of what he has bought and paid for. In his enmity to labor, the Lieutenant-Governor is at least consistent, and he is no worse now than when he got his present job." In Nanaimo, the Socialist leader James Hawthornthwaite announced that the impeachment of the lieutenant-governor was essential.

On 16 January, an agitated James Dunsmuir, resplendent in his official regalia, attended the legislature to open the session with the Speech from the Throne. In anticipation of planned demonstrations, he was accompanied by a bevy of plainclothes policemen. He was "expecting a bomb," Hawthornthwaite chortled. "He stuttered and stammered through his speech his knees knocking together."

"A measure will be laid before you with a view to the restriction of the immigration of undesirable persons," Dunsmuir read. The government would re-enact its Immigration Bill; and this time he would have little choice but to sign it. As the *Province* pointed out, "In the light of the contract revelations it is generally expected that assent will readily be granted."

But the Liberal and Socialist members of the house were after more than the bill; they were determined to bring down the lieutenant-governor. Liberal member John Oliver plunged into the depths of sessional papers and parliamentary textbooks, searching for a precedent. "The British House of Commons not only impeached, but executed Charles I," he noted wistfully, but otherwise he came up empty. Meanwhile, Hawthornthwaite was doing his best to rally the troops. In an inflammatory speech delivered in Vancouver on 2 February, amid "howls of applause" from the audience, he described the lieutenant-governor as "a brute," "an inhuman monster," "a champion union-smasher," "an honorable scallawag" and "a human hyena."

—

James Dunsmuir easily survived the opposition's motion of censure, but he had no intention of clinging to office. Ordinarily, a lieutenant-governor was expected to hold office for five years. In Dunsmuir's case, his tenure would have continued until the summer of 1911, but as early as 1907 he had begun to prepare to leave Government House. That November, Sam Maclure, Victoria's pre-eminent residential architect, unveiled plans to practically rebuild Burleith, the Dunsmuirs' Gorge-side house. The work would cost $60,000 and was expected to be completed by the following spring. But then, a piece of land that fitted much better into Dunsmuir's retirement plans became available; Roland Stuart had decided to sell Hatley Park.

Gilzean Roland Whately Stuart had moved to Vancouver Island after twice failing to qualify for a crack English regiment. In 1892 he acquired title to 250 beautiful acres on the Esquimalt Lagoon, immediately west of the deep bay that was home to the naval station, and facing south across the Strait of Juan de Fuca for a breathtakingly unrestricted view of the Olympic mountains. There, in a picturesque Tudor-style house with curtains of Battenberg lace, and with a series of young men to keep him company, Stuart lived a gracious life. In 1902 his mother died, and after erecting a towering obelisk in her "dear and most gracious memory," he built a new wing on the house to accommodate his inheritance. In August 1905 his house burned down. Gone were the rich oil paintings valued at $5,000; reduced to ashes were his mother's antiques; and lost, too, was his library, which had contained manuscripts and a lengthy correspondence belonging to his mother's friend, Mary Ann Evans, the novelist George Eliot.

In 1907, Stuart having announced that he intended to leave the island for good, James Dunsmuir plunked down $50,000, took possession of Hatley Park and announced that he planned to lay out a model estate. Maclure shelved his Burleith sketches and began working on the most important commission of his life.

Following Dunsmuir's instructions, Maclure designed a huge stone house—200 feet long, 86 feet deep and with a turret 82 feet high. But more than its size set Hatley apart. It was designed to appear as if it had been settled on the site for a thousand years. To a castlelike medieval centre block built of rough stone and replete with battlements, arrow-slit windows and tortuously winding stairs leading up to the turret room, Maclure added two Tudor half-timbered wings. The message was clear; the Dunsmuirs had been landed aristocrats for centuries.

In 1908 James added a second 250 acres, and after a third acquisition two years later, Hatley encompassed almost 800 acres. He spent $134,000 for the land. What the rest of it cost can only be imagined. The house alone may have run as high as $300,000. But James was planning much more that just a fine house in the country. He saw himself as the lord of the manor, at the centre of a self-contained feudal village. There would be a model dairy and stable, both floored with rubberized bricks; a glass conservatory, capable of growing vegetables and fruits, including bananas, as well as Laura's favoured white orchids; and Hatley would have its own slaughterhouse, smokehouse and refrigeration plant. Hidden in the trees, a discreet remove from the main house, would be a Chinatown large enough to accommodate the labourers required to weed the gardens, thresh the grain, collect the eggs, milk the cows, harvest the crops and to turn Hatley into a working farm and a paying proposition. Meanwhile, the master of the house would stock Hatley's wooded acres with game and invite his friends to come for country-house weekends of shooting and hunting.

And then there was fishing. James Dunsmuir's love of fishing bordered on obsession. He was afraid of the sea. Whenever he was required to go San Francisco, he preferred to travel by rail. But it was only by ship that he could reach his favourite fishing haunts— Knight Inlet 150 miles north of Vancouver, and the inlets and bays of the Queen Charlotte Islands. Whenever he could, he scrambled aboard the *Thistle*, sailed away from his troubles and, with undemanding friends like his mine manager, Dib Little, did his best to shoot every bird out of the sky and fish every last fish out of the sea.

That was just what he was doing in May 1907—escaping aboard the *Thistle* from the unpleasantness swirling around him in Victoria and Vancouver—when he came within a whisker of losing his life.

Dunsmuir and three companions had decided to divert themselves from the pleasures of fishing with a little blood sport. The *Thistle* anchored at Gardiner's Inlet, and the vice-regal party enjoyed a satisfying morning ashore, returning with a bag of twelve bears including four grizzlies. The *Thistle* was steaming through a quiet sea in Queen Charlotte Sound and the happy hunters were sitting down to lunch when the engine-room crew came running up from below, screaming "FIRE!"

The entire ship's party—the four excursionists together with Captain Bissett and his twelve-member crew—made the safety of the lifeboats, only to spend a few anxious moments as the helmless *Thistle* circled wildly and seemed about to bear down on them.

Asked to speculate about the cause of the fire, Captain Bissett guessed that the coal dust in the ship's hold might have spontaneously combusted—the agent of death for so many miners had very nearly carried off their employer.

Interviewed after his narrow escape, Dunsmuir said that his "greatest regret" was losing the twelve bearskins. He was insured against the *Thistle*'s $50,000 loss, and besides, he had already decided to replace her.

After months of planning, the contract for the *Dolaura* was let in August 1907. Named after James's wife and his youngest daughter, and built on the Clyde at an estimated cost of $200,000, she was a magnificent craft—built of steel, 218 feet long, with a 32-foot beam and capable of 14 knots, "the finest and most completely equipped vessel of its class on the coast."

The drawing room, measuring 24 by 18 feet, was panelled in Spanish mahogany, furnished with comfortable chairs covered in pale blue silk brocade, and warmed by a huge fireplace. In the oak-panelled dining room, twenty-four people could sit down to dinner without feeling crowded. The Dunsmuirs' private suite included a large sitting room, a bedroom, a clothesroom, and a white-tiled bathroom with a Doulton tub and washbasins of Venetian marble with silver fittings. There was a library, a smoking room, and a special room for guns and fishing tackle with an adjacent drying room for wet clothes.

In March 1908, a month after surviving the motion of censure, James and his family left for Scotland to collect the *Dolaura* and to take her on a shakedown cruise to North Sea ports. After passing through the locks of the Kiel Canal, which connected the North Sea and the Baltic, the *Dolaura* found herself beside the *Hohenzollern*, the slightly larger but rather less up-to-date yacht belonging to the German emperor. The kaiser's curiosity was piqued. He sent a note to the *Dolaura*, inviting the lieutenant-governor to come aboard the *Hohenzollern*. Dunsmuir enjoyed his tour of the kaiser's yacht and reciprocated with an invitation to tour his own. Wilhelm was deeply interested in the fine new ship, inspecting every part of it from stem to stern. Laura found the kaiser very charming. "Yes," James agreed. "The Emperor is a nice fellow."

It was a mellow lieutenant-governor who returned to British Columbia in August 1908. He had "banished thoughts of business" from his mind and had "given himself up to enjoying himself." He felt rejuvenated. And more determined than ever to put his days as lieutenant-governor behind him. He remained in office only until his new house was ready for him, resigning from the governorship in June 1909, a full two years short of his expected term. And in December, under "secrecy of the most extraordinary sort," he entered into negotiations to sell his coal mines.

In 1902 William Mackenzie had failed to win federal support for the Canadian Northern Railway. But by 1909 times had changed. The government had come to regard as highly desirable the construction of a transcontinental line that would compete with the CPR and drive down freight rates. When Mackenzie arrived in Victoria to seek provincial approval and support, he already had federal subsidies in hand. In January 1910 he signed a contract with the province. Construction of the B.C. section of the line would begin in July of that year, with full transcontinental service promised by July 1914.

Unfortunately for Mackenzie, the E & N was no longer for sale. Since 1905 it had been the property of the CPR. But the Canadian Northern president made an interesting discovery. His chief rival had failed to exercise its option to purchase the Dunsmuir coal lands. Responding to Mackenzie's overtures, Dunsmuir decided that it might be prudent to establish an arm's-length position before the deal was concluded. He was, after all, serving a term as one of the CPR's directors, and he was receiving four per cent interest on the million dollars in CPR debentures he had accepted as part payment for the E & N. On 3 January 1910 he transferred to solicitor Richard Elliot all his shares in the Wellington Colliery. Nine days later, Elliot assigned those shares to William Mackenzie, who in turn conveyed them to a newly chartered company, Canadian Collieries (Dunsmuir) Ltd.

Dunsmuir had made a spectacularly good deal. In 1902 he would have happily accepted $8 million for both the railway and the mines. Now, for the mines alone, he had been offered $11 million—a handsome sum, even if the bulk was in the form of railway-issued debentures.

The contract signed in January was, in effect, an agreement to purchase. Transition to Canadian collieries would not be completed until June, but meanwhile, rumours of the sale began to drift around Victoria. It was not until May that the *Victoria Times* felt confident enough to go to press with the story. "The passing of these large holdings from the family whose name is so interwoven with the history of the development and progress of this province is a business transaction of the greatest moment to the people of Vancouver Island," the *Times* reported. "It is the popular belief that with the passing of these properties into the hands of new owners there will be developments of the most important character."

But any developments Mackenzie might have been planning were put on hold while he tried to figure out just what exactly he had bought. The bill of sale he had signed was breathtakingly nonspecific. For his $11 million he had received "all his [Dunsmuir's] properties in British Columbia and in California in anywise relating to coal or coal mines and fire clay and all machinery, articles or things used, or which may be used in connection herewith." No inventory; no list of assets; no legal descriptions of lands.

William Mackenzie, who had every reason to believe that the colliery had been operated on a businesslike basis, found himself the victim of James Dunsmuir's difficulty in keeping separate, in his own mind and in the company's books, what he owned as an individual from what he owned as a corporate head. What about the coal-carriers, the ships that transported the coal to Vancouver and San Francisco? Weren't they included in the deal? Not according to Dunsmuir. And what about the large farm located near the original Wellington mine, the proceeds from which were entered in the collieries' books? That was his personal property, Dunsmuir declared. What about the 80-acre holding on Hornby Island? "They can have it if they want it, although it does not really belong to the mines," he retorted.

Also hindering Mackenzie's development plans was his discovery that he had taken over a company that possessed no operating capital. Two weeks before the sale was completed and the shares conveyed, James Dunsmuir, the sole shareholder in the Wellington Colliery, had called a shareholders' meeting, declared a dividend and paid himself $700,000. "I used the colliery books as my private account," Dunsmuir shrugged. "When I felt like it, I would declare a dividend to balance it. I owned all the shares."

—

Leaving Mackenzie contemplating legal action, Dunsmuir put corporate considerations firmly behind him. On 24 November 1911 he and Laura sailed out of Victoria to begin a year-long sojourn abroad. They spent Christmas at Caux in Switzerland with their family gathered around them. Then it was off to Egypt and a cruise up the Nile. After six weeks in Egypt, they moved on to England where they took over Bisham Abbey, a stately house on the banks of the Thames near Henley, for the spring and summer.

The effect on James Dunsmuir was magical. Somehow, during his months away, he acquired a sense of style. He became positively dapper, and he appeared to relish his new-found rakishness. Gone were the ill-fitting suits and the heavy tweeds. In their place were cream-coloured trousers, spats, wide-brimmed hats worn at a jaunty angle. And suddenly there were glints of humour, a twinkling enjoyment of life. He was a man transformed.

He was sixty-one years old in the autumn of 1912 when he returned to Victoria. He had shed his responsibilities with astonishing ease. He looked forward to a carefree retirement—hunting in Hatley's woods, fishing from the *Dolaura*'s launches. He had all the money a man could ever need, and he was confident that soon he would be able to entrust his fortune to the cautious management of his sober, serious son.

Twenty-one

—

Of Robert and Joan Dunsmuir's eleven children, ten survived infancy—eight daughters and two sons. Of James and Laura's twelve children, ten lived to adulthood—eight daughters and two sons. And in each generation, the two brothers were as different as chalk to cheese.

Born in 1877 and christened Robert William, but always known as Robin, James and Laura's first son grew into a handsome man with dark hair and eyes and olive-hued skin that tanned to a healthy brown. Imbued with the self-possession and arrogance of a rich man's son, he carried himself with a haughty bearing. And he crackled with dangerous energy. In even the most faded photographs, he projects an electric vitality. He was a man with a lusty appetite for life.

Robin had been educated to play a role in the family business. He was sent to England, to a good public school at which he "earned no very great credits," and then spent two years studying at a German university. By the summer of 1899, he was back in Victoria, twenty-two years old, bursting with energy and eager to go to work.

His father appointed him the collieries' treasurer and kept an eye on his progress. "I wish you would look over the pay book," James grumbled on 11 May 1900. "You will notice a number of the employees have overtime, this is a very bad practice."

Ready or not, Robin was given wider responsibilities when his father assumed the premiership. On 15 February 1901, when the Cumberland mine blew, he was acting as his father's spokesman. He did not handle things well. When he learned of the accident, he ordered a special train to carry him and his office manager, James

Lindsay, to Nanaimo where the company's steamship *Joan* would be standing by to take them on to Union Bay. Victoria newspapermen, clamouring to get to Cumberland, were "peremptorily refused permission" to board the train. And when Robin reached Nanaimo, reporters from three Vancouver papers were "summarily" ordered to climb off the *Joan*. It was not an approach calculated to win sympathetic coverage for the company.

When James Dunsmuir reached Vancouver, he was forced to make amends for his son's behaviour, expressing deep regret that the incident should have occurred and extending an invitation to all newspapermen to join him as he made his own way to Cumberland.

Robin had already proven himself to be impatient with details and possessed of an imperious nature. A month later, he demonstrated that these were not the only character traits that militated against a satisfactory future as son and heir and successor. On 15 March 1901 the collier *Willamette*, outbound from Union Bay with 1,000 tons of coal, ran into heavy fog and went aground near Denman Island. James sent Robin to the scene with enough cash to pay for the salvage operation. "Robin met up with the boys in Nanaimo and squandered the whole payroll overnight," one of the merrymakers recalled.

James ordered Robin to stay put in Nanaimo and sent word to all points on the line that his son was to be kept off the train. Robin responded by grabbing a hammer, marching up to the train and breaking all the engine gauges.

The company's employees came to regard Robin as quite a rogue. In January 1905 when a company payroll of almost $10,000 went missing, the suspicion soon arose that Robin might have had something to do with its disappearance. And perhaps Dunsmuir thought so too. To solve the case, he relied on Pinkerton's National Detective Agency rather than the local police, and he made it clear that he wanted the matter handled quietly.

Robin was ambitious to assume his uncle Alexander's role as president of the E & N. He regarded the railway as an important part of his legacy; he was frustrated and angered by his father's determination to sell. Unable to convince him to change his mind, Robin decided that his only recourse was to buy the line himself. On 30 March 1905 he wrote a letter, carefully marked "Confidential," to James J. Hill, president of the Great Northern Railway.

I am James Dunsmuir's eldest son and he is owner of the Railway + land and I, naturally, am bitterly opposed to the sale because I consider he is *giving* it away therefore I am trying to raise $2,000,000 to buy the road and land for myself. My idea is to borrow $2,000,000 from someone for six months giving the entire stock of the Railway Co. as security and immediately issue $2,500,000 of Bonds with which to pay back the $2,000,000 I borrow.

Mr. Hill you can't loose [sic] one dime and I promise you will make money on the deal . . . My father wants $2,250,000 for Road + Land but I have $250,000 of my own therefore I need only the $2,000,000. Will you please help me? Remember in six months you will have your money back. I swear it. If you will consider it will you please telegraph me and I will come over immediately to see you about it. You will never regret it Mr. Hill. Trusting this meets with your approval and satisfaction.

Hill found Robin's offer easy to resist. But could Robin have made something of himself if he had managed to acquire his father's railroad? Perhaps. But perhaps not, for he shared his uncle Alexander's love of the bottle, and that, combined with his devotion to gambling, did not bode well.

Marriage certainly did nothing to settle him down. In November 1901 he married Maude Allingham Shoobert, "a beautiful and accomplished girl" and a member of a prominent Sausalito family. The week before the ceremony, while staying at the Palace Hotel in San Francisco, Robin followed his inclination to find his evening entertainment in "billiard saloons and even less salubrious spots." He rambled into the Cafe Royal, an infamous Market Street gambling den. He woke up the next morning to the horrible realization that he had dropped $1,000 in gold and covered further losses by writing $8,000 worth of cheques. Learning nothing from that experience, he went on a similar bender while he and Maude were honeymooning in Southern California, vanishing for several days and leaving his bride to entertain herself.

Maude fitted in well in Victoria. "Very warm" and "very nice," she quickly established herself as a favourite, Laura Dunsmuir in particular becoming "terribly fond" of her American daughter-in-law. But soon Maude found it desirable to spend less and less time in the city and more and more time away from her husband.

She spent Christmas of 1904 with friends in Baltimore and dallied there until March, returning to Victoria only after Robin had crossed the continent to persuade her to come home. Five months later she sailed for England. Early in 1906 Robin crossed the Atlantic in an attempt to win her back, but this time he returned to Victoria alone.

She prolonged her holiday until May, eventually wooed home not by Robin but by her father-in-law's appointment as lieutenant-governor and the opportunity to take her place beside Laura at society's peak.

Robin seems to have held his ladylike wife in some esteem. Or at least he evidenced a desire to keep up appearances, for, from time to time, he made attempts to settle down. During the first years of their marriage, he and Maude had lived in rented houses or at Burleith. Early in 1905 Robin began to acquire property on the Esquimalt waterfront, and the next year he commissioned Sam Maclure to design a home, an impressive two-storey shingled house costing $20,000 and carefully sited to take full advantage of the view. By January 1907 the house, named "Allingham" in Maude's honour, was completed. But although the architect had incorporated heart motifs wherever the opportunity arose—hearts inlaid with mother-of-pearl in the newel posts, cut-out hearts in the balcony balustrade, inlaid hearts in the mantlepiece—Maude's tenancy at Allingham was brief.

"He was a terrible womanizer," her Victoria friends said of Robin, shaking their heads in disapproval. And that he may well have been. Rich, handsome, compelling—he cannot have lacked for opportunity. Such was his reputation that no rumours seemed too wild. When Roland Stuart sold Hatley Park to James Dunsmuir and left Victoria never to return, some of his friends suggested that, as part of the deal, he had agreed to marry a woman who was pregnant with Robin's child.

Whatever the case, Maude decided to leave her husband for good. In June 1909 she was living quietly in her mother's house in Sausalito when the *San Francisco Chronicle* went to press with a scandalous story: Maude had obtained a divorce and was "trying to forget her brief and tempestuous marital career."

It is stated that the Lieutenant-Governor of British Columbia paid $100,000 to his daughter-in-law rather than have her tell in court the miseries of her married life . . . Report says Dunsmuir was guilty of personal cruelty and humiliation of his wife during their married life together.

And although he was largely to blame it is likewise asserted that the wife on her part was responsible for no little agitation. Dunsmuir's family took particular offense at her conduct and costume at a fashionable ball given at the Empress Hotel. The costume excited talk by its close adherence to all lines of the body.

The wife of the Lieutenant-Governor is said to have protested at her daughter-in-law's conduct generally, threatening to strike the younger Mrs. Dunsmuir from the Government House calling list.

Robin was quick to deny the story. "My wife's conduct and costume at the Empress ball or any other time or place has never been the cause of the slightest offense," he informed the *Chronicle*. That part of the story did indeed appear to be baseless. Maude was nothing if not stylish and stately, and the warm relationship she and Laura enjoyed would continue to the end of her mother-in-law's life. But Robin added, "There has been no divorce at all, nor is one contemplated. My father has not given my wife $100,000 or any other sum for any purpose whatever. The report of my cruelty and humiliation is absurd."

It was true enough that there had been no divorce. But Maude had certainly left her husband, and while she may not have received an outright cash payment, Robin's parents had agreed to pay her a lifetime annuity of $1,800.

Less than a year later, in May 1910, Robin Dunsmuir was once again the talk of San Francisco. Enroute to South America, where he hoped to make his own mark as a railroad builder, he stopped off at the Palace Hotel, and during his sojourn there, became enamoured of Lillian Russell's daughter, Dorothy.

Twenty-six-year-old Dorothy had hoped to follow in her mother's footsteps. But while Lillian Russell reigned as the "Queen of Broadway," showered with diamonds and furs by millionaire admirers like Diamond Jim Brady, Dorothy's plans for a stage career had met with only indifferent success, and by 1910 she had sunk to performing exotic dances in the notorious dives of San Francisco's Tenderloin district.

Robin saw her undulating through a Turkish number and was charmed. Soon Dorothy was excitedly telling her other admirers that the Canadian millionaire was pressing her to come away with him. When he sailed for Peru without her, there was "great rejoicing" in the city's "lidless" district. "The revelling throngs celebrated in truly Bacchanalian fashion," the *Chronicle* reported. But Robin and Dorothy were simply being discreet. While Robin sailed away on a the German steamer *Itauri* bound for South America, Dorothy hopped on a train for Mazatlan and there, the *Chronicle* discovered, she "joined forces with her admirer."

At one Central American port, the *Itauri* tied up beside the U.S. navy's cruiser *Princeton*. Robin invited the ship's officers to join him for "an elaborate repast" aboard the *Itauri*. "Wine bottles were opened as fast as the stewards could extract the corks," the *Chronicle* gasped. It was not long before Dorothy was invited to demonstrate her "talents as a dancer." The *Princeton*'s officers responded by hosting a "highly unrestrained" dinner of their own. And then the *Itauri* sailed away, amid rumours that Robin and Dorothy were secretly wed.

But soon after they arrived in Peru, Dorothy floated away, and Robin moved on to Buenos Aires, where he found a new companion. She was Florence Swindon, a twenty-three-year-old Londoner whose father was working in Argentina. Florence was a good sort, a "total extrovert" who "smoked like a chimney" and who enjoyed a drink and a good time. In November 1912, she gave birth to Robin's son, and she was pregnant with a second child before Maude finally agreed to a divorce. On 25 January 1915, with Robin pleading guilty to adultery, the divorce was granted; on 1 April, Robin and Florence were married; and four months later she gave birth to a daughter. Years later, when Robin had settled her in Victoria, his mother's society friends would stand agape at Florence's habit of enlivening dull parties by turning somersaults. "Oh, it sounds terribly snobbish, but she just wasn't of the same class."

—

In 1922 when he was forty-six years old and had spent a dozen years in South America, Robin succeeded in convincing the Peruvian government that he was just the man to provide the country with a unified transportation system. He would lay 2,400 miles of track, linking a number of small mountain lines with the coastal belt, and guaranteeing, as the Peruvian president confidently assured his Congress, the country's future and its "definitive aggrandisement." Robin would receive a land grant of 24 million acres together with oil and mineral rights. The undertaking would require an enormous investment, as high as $120 million according to some estimates. To raise the required start-up capital, Robin planned to float a bond issue in New York and London. And that bond issue seemed destined to succeed, for he had negotiated a most unusual deal with the eager Peruvians. His syndicate would pay $5 million and take over the tobacco monopoly. Given that the tobacco monopoly was capable of producing revenues in excess of $7 million a year, he could promise bond buyers security as well as an attractive rate of interest.

Robin's life was governed by two powerful and contradictory urges: the desire to pursue pleasure whatever the cost, and the ambition to prove himself the equal of his father and grandfather. Now, just as he was on the verge of completing a deal calculated to make his grandfather's achievements pale into insignificance, he was undone by his lack of discipline and his love of alcohol. Robin was aboard the *Mauretania* on his way to London accompanied by a clutch of committed New York investors when he went on a "prodigious bender," which ended with his running wildly about the ship. Considerably shaken, his investors convened a meeting and decided to offer him a million dollars if he would agree to bow out and hand over all the plans and contracts. Robin went to his cabin, collected all the documents and hurled them into the sea.

His wife and children long since sent to Victoria to be supported by his mother, Robin spent the next few years wandering the globe, drinking heavily and playing the races. In January 1929, he died in a second-rate Singapore hotel. He was fifty-one years old.

———

Laura Dunsmuir's eleventh child, christened James after his father but always, perhaps unfortunately, known as "Boy," was born in 1894, soon after the family moved to Burleith. Pale and sallow, he was a serious young man who seldom smiled. He peers out from photographs—a tiny little fellow standing in front of the verandah at Burleith, clad in a perfect riding outfit and appearing exceedingly dapper and equally glum. A dour twelve-year-old, staring sorrowfully at the camera, he stands on the imposing steps of Loretto, the rigorous public school in Scotland to which he was sent. Slightly older, looking doleful rather than triumphant, he stands on the *Dolaura*'s deck dutifully displaying his share of the day's catch. Then a humourless young man, clinging grimly to a sled during a winter holiday at St. Moritz while everyone around him glows with pleasure.

If Boy had a passion in life, it was horses. The only time he ever held his head high was when he was astride a show jumper. He became a skilled equestrian, earning a cupboardful of trophies with his coal black mare, and Kismet, his dappled grey.

He was his father's favourite son, his golden-haired boy. Unlike his older brother, Boy was obedient and unambitious; and like his father, he took his inherited responsibilities seriously, and he accepted, without question, the role that had been assigned to him. James Dunsmuir would sell the railway and the mines; Boy would stand guard over the capital, acting as the family's junior trustee by directing it to worthwhile, but safe, investments. In 1912, after joining his parents for their tour of Egypt, he was left behind with a tutor in Versailles to polish his French, and then it was on to Montreal where he went to work in the offices of Sir Thomas Shaughnessy and the Bank of Montreal.

He was enjoying a summer holiday at Hatley when war broke out. Boy immediately volunteered, offering his services to the B.C. Horse, a crack unit of mounted militia formed in Vernon by former cavalry officers who had taken up ranching in the province's interior. He was sent to Winnipeg for officer training and returned to Victoria, a lieutenant in the 2nd Canadian Mounted Regiment.

The CMRs trained hard in anticipation of the day they would be ordered to France. But weeks passed, and it began to seem as though they would never leave Victoria, their only contribution limited to serving as a mounted escort for infantry units as they paraded through the city to the docks where patriotic crowds gathered to wave them off to war. "The CMRs should be renamed the See-Em-Offs," Victorians joked. Boy became impatient with the inactivity. He asked leave to resign his commission so that he might enlist in the Royal Scots Greys, a British cavalry regiment that was bound to see action. Permission granted, he sailed out of Victoria in April 1915.

Once in New York, he could have chosen to sail on a ship that flew the neutral American flag—a sensible precaution given that German submarines were operating off the Irish coast. But that would have seemed an act of cowardice for a twenty-one-year-old officer who was on his way to join one of His Majesty's most prestigious cavalry regiments. And so he booked passage on the *Lusitania*, the pride of the Cunard fleet.

—

On 1 May 1915, as the *Lusitania* cast off from Pier 54, her passengers were abuzz with talk of the notice from the German Embassy that had appeared on the front page of that morning's *New York Tribune*.

NOTICE!

TRAVELLERS intending to embark on the Atlantic voyage are reminded that a state of war exists between Germany and her allies and Great Britain and her allies; that the zone of war includes the waters adjacent to the British Isles; that, in accordance with the formal notice given by the

Imperial German Government, vessels flying the flag of Great Britain, or of any of
her allies, are liable to destruction in those
waters and that travellers sailing in the war
zone on ships of Great Britain or her allies
do so at their own risk.

IMPERIAL GERMAN EMBASSY

Worried passengers were given reassurance. The *Lusitania* was
fast; capable of 24 knots, she could outrun any submarine. But on 7
May, as they caught their first glimpse of the Irish coast, many of
the passengers noticed that the ship had slowed. Belle Naish was
leaning on the rail, relishing the sight of land after seven days at
sea, when she looked down at the water. "I could run faster than we
are moving," she thought.

Lying in wait off the Old Head of Kinsale, Kapitan-Leutnant
Walter Sweiger of the U-20 watched a distant smudge of smoke with
mounting excitement. He ordered the U-20 down and manoeuvred
her into position.

Aboard the *Lusitania*, Boy Dunsmuir, together with the other
saloon passengers, had just finished lunch in the first-class dining
salon. Some had drifted off to the smoking room for a quiet cigar;
others were strolling the decks, chatting and enjoying the air.

Sweiger took careful aim. As the *Lusitania*'s bow appeared in the
crossed wire of his sights, he fired.

Eighteen minutes later, it was all over. The *Lusitania* shuddered
and slipped below the surface, carrying over a thousand men,
women and children to their deaths. Boy Dunsmuir's body was
never found. He had been impatient to go to war and he had died
without firing a shot. Only twenty-four days later, the Canadian
Mounted Regiment received orders to proceed to France. If only he
had waited.

When news of the *Lusitania*'s sinking reached Victoria, the city
collapsed into mourning. Fifteen Victorians had been aboard, but the
only name everyone knew was young James Dunsmuir's. "There are
Victorians who will remember the fair-haired lad who used to ride
his pony through the streets of the city's suburbs," the *Colonist*
mourned. "Lieutenant Dunsmuir was exceedingly popular with his
brother officers and with the men under his command."

A rumour rapidly spread throughout the city that local Germans
had celebrated the sinking of the *Lusitania*. Patrons of the city's saloons gathered to rail against the Kaiser. "On to the German Club,"

came the cry, and three hundred men, shouting and singing, marched down Government Street. "Everything was stripped from the place," an observer reported. "Furniture too large to be conveniently shoved through windows was smashed and the parts cast into the streets." Led by men carrying two large portraits of the king, a mob, three thousand strong, paraded through town, shouting and singing and smashing the windows of any business they suspected of having a connection with Germans or Germany. On 10 May 1915 the mayor found it necessary to read a polite version of the riot act, requesting "all residents of Victoria to remain in their homes or places of business tonight and on subsequent nights until the popular excitement has abated."

Out at Hatley, James and Laura were in anguish. The family's future had depended on their trustworthy, dependable younger son. He had been their favourite, the apple of his father's eye. James withdrew to his study, firmly shut the door, cranked up the gramophone and played, over and over again until it wore thin, a recording of "Where, Oh Where, Is My Wandering Boy Tonight." Laura began to have nightmares. She would wake from sleep, sure that she had heard the sound of a hand pounding on glass. The image of her son—trapped in the sinking liner, pleading with someone to release him—would stay with Laura for the rest of her days.

James threw money at his grief—$7,000 to equip an operating theatre in a Paris hospital; $3,000 dollars to the YMCA; $500 to the Red Cross for every month that the war continued; $500,000 in Victory Bonds. But he was a broken man. "He never fully recovered," his friends agreed.

After the war, he sold the *Dolaura* and never went to sea again. He acquired a Cowichan River summer cottage and added some improvements to the simple log cabin—extra bedrooms and a wide verandah—but still it was spartan. James Dunsmuir preferred it that way. He felt at home in his Cowichan cabin.

James Dunsmuir died at Cowichan on 6 June 1920, a month away from his sixty-ninth birthday. None of his family was there, but otherwise he would have been hard-pressed to think of a better time and a better place to die. James had spent the previous day fishing and then passed the evening playing bridge with a few male friends. He went to bed early, feeling vaguely unwell and suspecting that he had taken a chill. During the night he suffered a stroke and died of a massive cerebral hemorrhage, shortly before seven o'clock in the morning.

After Boy's death, James had begun to share part of his estate with his daughters. They were given land within the Hatley estate, and on their behalf, he established a trust, funded by the income from the Canadian Northern debentures he had received in part payment for his coal mines. Other than that, his estate, or at least that part of his estate that failed to escape succession duties, was surprisingly small—and very revealing of his lack of expertise in manipulating large sums of money.

He owned Hatley Park, valued at $250,000. He owned 369 shares in the Canadian Pacific Railway valued at $126 apiece. He had shares in the Noble Fives Mines, a collection of Kootenay District mineral claims that had come his way when, in 1902, he foreclosed on a $182,792 mortgage and which, at the time of his death, had an estimated value of only $100,000. He had $394,000 invested in mortgages on Vancouver properties, but on some of those mortgages he had received no interest since 1916. In Victoria, he had provided the Esquimalt Water Works Company with a mortgage of $625,000, but because of its meagre 4 1/2 per cent interest and because the loan would not reach maturity until 1934, the market value of the mortgage had sunk to $464,125. And then there were the Victory Loans that would not come to maturity until 1933, and Victoria City Debentures that would not mature until 1957. He had $2,250,000 in Dominion of Canada bonds that had a market value of only 60 per cent of their face value. He had more than $150,000 in the bank and almost $800 in cash lying about the house. The estate totalled $3,332,000—much less than most British Columbians would have predicted, and most of it invested in an ad hoc manner with no evidence of a careful long-term plan.

Still, $3,332,000 in 1920 dollars was a considerable amount—more than enough to become an important economic force, especially if directed by a firm hand. But James, like his father before him, left his entire estate to his wife. It was odd, really. Robert Dunsmuir and his son James were the richest, most powerful men in British Columbia. And yet, when they contemplated their deaths and wrote their wills, neither of them could bring himself to make a decision or to divide his estate. Both of them, father and son, left everything up to their wives.

Twenty-two

Not for a moment had James Dunsmuir looked to his daughters for a possible heir-apparent. He expected them to be decorative rather than competent and business-wise; and he expected them to marry men who were attractive, high-born and relatively useless. For the most part, they lived up to his expectations.

The eldest daughter, Byrdie, born in North Carolina in 1878, bloomed into an appealing young woman. Refined at an English boarding school and with her musical talents improved by studies in Leipzig, Byrdie, at twenty-two, was sweet and plumply pretty. She had her share of suitors, but she remained unmovable until Capt. Guy Mortimer Audain arrived on the scene.

Tall and straight with an impressive moustache and more than a hint of Irish charm, Guy Audain was thirty-seven years old and a captain in the Indian Army when first he hove into Byrdie's view. Born in Belfast in 1864, he was the son and grandson of army officers. After leaving the Royal Military College, Sandhurst, he joined the Suffolk Regiment, which was then stationed in Cork. "The Cork girls are the prettiest in the world," he fondly recalled. But when his regiment was sent to India, he found that life on the subcontinent suited him even better.

When his regiment returned to England, Guy chose to stay on. He enlisted in the Hyderabad Contingent of the Indian Army, and as a British officer in an Indian regiment, he was treated to a gentlemanly existence with little hard work and plenty of free time to indulge in polo and *shikar*. It was *shikar*, the joy of the hunt, that imbued Guy with a love of India.

By 1901 Guy had been in India for more than ten years and was due for a long leave. Pausing in Victoria on his roundabout journey home, he looked up an Irish cousin, Robert Cassidy. Cassidy encouraged him to visit Burleith, saying, "Come along Guy, there is a family here blessed with many beautiful daughters, fairer than the girls in Cork! What's more, their father is the richest man in America."

That proved more than enough to pique Audain's interest. He called at Burleith, was introduced to Byrdie and let little time pass before he proposed. Guy Audain and Byrdie Dunsmuir were married on 30 October 1901, with the bride seeing nothing of an omen in the fact that her wedding dress, specially ordered from a London dressmaker, failed to arrive in time.

CAPTAIN AUDAIN AND MISS DUNSMUIR MADE HAPPY FOR LIFE," the *Colonist* headlined its account of their wedding. And if their happiness had depended on the extravagance of their sendoff, they would have been happy indeed. After being feted at Burleith, they were whisked away to the E & N wharf, where the Dunsmuir-owned ship the *Lorne* waited, bedecked with flags from bow to stern. In a haze of rice and good wishes, the *Lorne* pulled away from the company's docks to carry Byrdie and Guy off on the first step of their around-the-world honeymoon.

They had toured Japan, sailed up the Yang-tse and were hovering in Hong Kong when Byrdie discovered she was pregnant. While Guy sailed for India to rejoin his regiment, Byrdie went to England for her confinement. Her baby, a boy named James after his grandfather, was born at Bournemouth on 8 July 1903. Six months later, Byrdie sailed for India to join her husband at Aurungabad. Once there, she made an appalling discovery.

She loathed India with a passion matched only by her husband's love of the country. She hated the climate. She melted in the shimmering heat of the Hot Weather Season when daily temperatures seldom dipped below 100 degrees. She wilted with the humidity of the Cold Weather Season, despite the support of her Twilfit corsets, "famous throughout the Empire" and "specially designed to suit the Indian climate, being rustproof throughout." She hated having to stand the legs of her piano in saucers of water to drown the white ants intent on devouring it. She hated having to worry about sand-fly fever, malaria and "dhobi itch." But, perhaps most of all, she hated the loneliness. Guy had the camaraderie of the officers' mess; Byrdie had long empty days with only her little boy and her Indian servants to provide diversions.

Byrdie found the advice of old India hands easy to ignore. "Don't give in to the heat, and it will give in to you," Flora Steel scolded in *The Complete Indian Housekeeper and Cook.* To Flora and her ilk, exercise was all-important. "A languid stroll from your drawing room to your carriage and back again is *not* sufficient to keep your organism going," Flora insisted. Byrdie, who was convinced that she had already compromised her health by strenuous bicycle-riding when she was a girl, kept her organism going with as little exertion as possible.

For a time Byrdie tried to be a good army wife. She accompanied Guy on a tiger hunt. But she could not bring herself to share Guy's enthusiasm for hunting; she did not like living in a tent, and she made no secret of the fact that she felt hot, uncomfortable and unhappy.

She began to write pathetic letters home. She wanted to come back to Victoria—was there not *something* her father could *do*? And yes, there was. James Dunsmuir offered his son-in-law a handsome annuity—conditional on his resigning his commission and returning to Victoria.

Guy Audain needed little time to ponder his decision. He could live very well on the promised income. And he was more than prepared to pay for his keep by becoming the constant fishing companion of so well-known a sportsman as James Dunsmuir. Content that he was being offered the best of all possible worlds, Guy quit the army and, in May 1906, he brought Byrdie home.

James Dunsmuir had taken the measure of his son-in-law—good fellow, excellent fisherman, no head for business. He would, however, make an admirable *aide-de-camp*, and Guy happily assumed that role after James was sworn in as lieutenant-governor.

For a time Guy thought that he might fancy the life of a gentleman farmer. In March 1907, acting as James's agent, he arranged for the purchase of a 1,000-acre ranch on the shore of Okanagan Lake. It was a beautiful property with magnificent views of the lake, a fine bathing beach and an 80-acre orchard. But by 1909 when James tendered his resignation as lieutenant-governor, Guy and Byrdie had changed their minds. Byrdie sold the ranch and purchased land in Victoria, an acre of the Pemberton Woods on Foul Bay Road that came complete with a half-finished Maclure-designed house. And, with the exception of the war years, Guy never worked another day for the rest of his life.

The house, named "Ellora" after the fabulous Caves of Ellora in India, was one of Maclure's most inspired designs. Its interior bathed in light from two-storey-tall stained-glass windows, Ellora nestled snugly into its gently sloping site. Byrdie added three more acres to her original purchase, and Guy burned off energy by throwing himself into gardening. With his English gardener who lived above Ellora's stables, he plotted the design of one of the most beautiful landscapes in the city.

Life at Ellora should have been idyllic—a beautiful house filled with light and the scent of flowers; a stable for Jimmy's pony, and tucked away in a secluded glen, a playhouse for Laura, Byrdie's second child, born in 1909. And yet the Audains spent very little time in Victoria. Guy was plagued by restlessness. For the next few years, he and his family were always on the move—to the south of France in the spring, to a hunting lodge in Ireland in the summer, to Switzerland for winter sports, and then back to Ellora for a few brief months before the progress began once again.

The Audains travelled in style—touring in chauffeur-driven automobiles hired from Harrod's and staying at the best hotels. It was an exceedingly pleasant existence, but in 1914 when war broke out, Guy welcomed the opportunity to return to soldiering. While Byrdie remained in Victoria, writing anxious letters to her son, Jimmy, who spent the duration of the war at his English public school, Guy sailed for London, presented himself at the War Office and offered his services. He was given the rank of major and sent to Milford-on-Sea where Indian troops were collected before being sent to France.

When the *Lusitania* was lost, it fell to Guy Audain to travel to Ireland to search for the body of Boy Dunsmuir. In Queenstown, he walked through makeshift morgues peering at hundreds of bodies laid out in their sodden clothes. He found no familiar figure among victims collected in a shed at the Cunard wharf. Neither did he find Boy among the dead lying on the sawdust-covered floor of the Town Hall. He lingered in Queenstown while rescue boats collected more bodies and others washed ashore. And then he gave up. Victims recovered during the first week after the sinking were capable of being identified, but after that the sea was giving up only faceless corpses. Bodies continued to wash ashore all during June and into July, and perhaps Boy's was one of those recorded by policemen in towns along the coast.

Male body, washed ashore, 20 July. Very decomposed, head and hands missing . . .

Male body, recovered on 23 July. Unrecognizable, skull and bones of face bare . . .

Male body, 23 July. Portion only from hip to feet . . .

But if one of them was Boy, neither Audain nor anyone else would ever be able to tell.

Guy remained in England throughout the war, and then returned to Victoria and to the pleasures of extended hunting and fishing trips. But Byrdie was in a delicate state of health. She was suffering from kidney disease, and nothing Victoria doctors suggested seemed to bring her any relief. In 1920 after her father died, they decided to rent out Ellora and settle Byrdie in a European spa. They tried Dinard, a popular society watering place on the north coast of France, famous for its casino and its summer tennis tournament. But Dinard did nothing for Byrdie. In 1923, after she recovered from the effects of a slight stroke, Guy moved her to a villa in Pau in the Pyrenees, where the resident doctor had made a reputation for himself as a kidney specialist. She died there in January 1925 after having spent several years as an invalid. She was only forty-six years old.

Guy was sixty and brimming with health. He set off on a relentless pursuit of pleasure. "My father was a constant wanderer," his son Jimmy recalled. When he was approaching his seventies, Guy established his headquarters at a hotel at Dinard. Now, when he went to the casino, it was with a pretty young actress whom he had "palled up with" hanging on his arm. "My father was enjoying himself when he wasn't with me," Jimmy said.

Guy Audain died of a heart attack in November 1940. He was seventy-six years old, and it seems only fitting that he died in Hollywood, in the Beverly Hills Hotel, and that he had been driven down to California by an attractive young woman who doubled as his chauffeur and nurse.

—

On 24 June 1904 a "popular young naval officer" married "one of Victoria's fairest daughters." He was twenty-eight-year-old Lieut. Arthur Bromley, younger son of Sir Henry and Lady Bromley; she was twenty-year-old Laura Mary, James and Laura's fourth daughter. Their wedding was magical. "The grounds of Burleith presented a scene like Fairyland with colored electric lights and Japanese lanterns strung everywhere across the paths and drives and through the woodland portions of the estate." Five hundred guests wandered through the grounds and danced into morning.

"Maye" Dunsmuir had made a brilliant match. Not only was her husband high born and good looking, but also he radiated good humour, and, as a career naval officer, he was blessed with the satisfaction of having a definite purpose in life. Maye's marriage proved to be the most successful, or at least the longest lasting, of all the Dunsmuir sisters. And her husband's status catapulted her into the social stratosphere.

Twice decorated by the Royal Humane Society for saving life, Bromley served on the navy's active list from 1892 until 1922. Shortly after he retired in 1926 with the rank of vice-admiral, he was appointed Gentleman Usher to King George V, a position he held through the reigns of Edward VIII and George VI, and in which he continued to serve Elizabeth II until his death in 1961.

Maye led a charmed life. In England, she divided her time between a London townhouse and Stoke Hall, the Bromley's stately country home, set amongst ancient trees and with broad lawns sweeping down to the banks of the river Trent. And she spent easy west coast summers visiting her family at Hatley Park and the Cowichan River fishing retreat.

She died in London in 1959 at the age of seventy-five. And because her husband's older brother had died childless, she went to her grave as *Lady* Bromley, the only one of James and Laura Dunsmuir's daughters to have achieved that longed-for status.

—

For the Dunsmuirs' third daughter, Elizabeth Maud, life was not nearly so settled. In April 1908 twenty-three-year-old "Bessie" made a brilliant marriage when she was escorted down the aisle by the prime minister, Sir Wilfrid Laurier, to become the bride of John Hope, a member of the aristocratic Linlithgow family. Bessie shared with her younger sisters a love of the theatre and longed to be a performer. But she was short and stout and did not look well on stage, and so Bessie, a born organizer, contented herself with the role of producer. During the war, while her husband was serving as a major in the Canadian Scottish regiment, Bessie helped the cause by organizing benefit performances in London, her most spectacular success being the Canadian Matinee, staged at His Majesty's Theatre on 11 May 1917. Her younger sister, Muriel, was one of the star performers and the list of patrons included King George and Queen Mary, Queen Alexandra, and the Canadian prime minister, Sir Robert Borden.

Her marriage ended in divorce in 1923. By then, Bessie had produced two children and developed a wanderlust. "She was constantly here, there and everywhere from British Columbia to England and Scotland, and then Cannes, Monte Carlo and back to Canada, each time with a new house on her hands," her nephew, Jimmy Audain, recalled.

To the end of her days, Bessie was a frequent visitor to Victoria, staying at Hatley, and after Hatley was sold, booking herself into a suite of rooms at the Empress Hotel. And always, she looked for opportunities to order people around and to prove that she was needed. Learning that a friend's daughter was in hospital recuperating from the birth of her child, Bessie decided to visit her. She was marching purposefully down the corridor when she was stopped by a nurse who told her that only family members were allowed. Bessie stared at her through her thick glasses. "Never heard anything so ridiculous in my life!" she exclaimed and elbowed her way past. That was Bessie, bustling into other people's lives, goodhearted and brusque, and at a loss to find an enduringly useful purpose in life.

For a time she thought she might find happiness with Robert Droste, who was heir to the Dutch chocolate fortune and considerably younger than Bessie. About the same time that she acquired Droste as her second husband, she purchased a home at Praria da Rocha in Portugal which was, Bessie said, "a perfectly beautiful spot with acres of golden sands and beautifully colored rocks, inhabited by a clean and industrious people." The house, Bessie found more enduringly appealing than her new husband. The marriage did not last long, but Bessie was still in Portugal and had resumed the name "Mrs. John Hope" when she died in 1962 in her eighty-first year.

—

Their birth order divided the Dunsmuir daughters into two groups: the older girls, Byrdie, Bessie and Maye; and their younger sisters— Elinor Emily, Joan Marion, Jessie Muriel and Kathleen Euphemia— born over a span of only four years and known collectively as the "Dunsmuir Kids." The Kids came of age during the years their father was lieutenant-governor, and they were already at society's peak when they made their debuts. They had money, advantage and social position. Not one of them would find that that was enough to guarantee contentment much less happiness.

Perhaps the saddest of all was Elinor. For a time Elinor tried to force herself into the mould into which her sisters slipped so easily. In her early teens, dressed in prim white blouses and with a straw boater fixed to her dark hair, she gave promise of becoming a beauty. With her sisters, she studied music at Dresden, and of all the girls she became the most accomplished musician. She tried to blend in with Marion and Muriel and Kathleen, but, as she approached her twenties, it became apparent that she was cut from a different cloth.

Elinor was nineteen when she made her debut with her sister Marion in 1906, at the first Government House ball of the Dunsmuir regime. Society columnists described the event in detail, paying particular attention to the costumes of the Dunsmuir women. Laura, wearing a tiara, necklace and earrings, "magnificent diamonds of the first water," was regal in a dress of black silk-embroidered net over cloth of gold, "the handsomest ever worn in Victoria." Byrdie Audain "looked extremely handsome" in rich white silk with gold and pearl embroidery, and Maye Bromley was elegant in a grey empire gown trimmed with pearls. Robin's wife, Maude, wore "a dazzling gown of goblin green net over silk of the same hue with a jaunty feather in her hair" and was deemed to have shared the honours of the evening only with eighteen-year-old Marion, who was radiant in "a pretty white net empire French gown with seed pearl trimmings" and looked "the typical French belle." And as for Elinor, who did after all deserve some attention since she too was making her debut, she "looked well in white net with a satin ribbon," the *Colonist* struggled. To even the most enthusiastic of society columnists, it was obvious that Elinor's heart just was not in it.

By the time she was twenty-one, Elinor had decided to go her own way. She gave up the battle to control her weight, with the unfortunate result that she earned the nickname "Elk"; and she began to wear masculine clothes, a skirt still, but an unadorned dark skirt topped by a man-tailored jacket and worn with a shirt and tie. In a family photograph taken in 1908, she demands attention as she sits, a challengingly masculine presence among her lacy, feminine sisters. She took to smoking strong French cigarettes and gradually acquired a liking for cigars. She found female friends who shared her preferences, women who favoured stout tweed jackets and jodhpurs, and who, like Elinor, wore their hair cut short and blunt.

Everyone who knew her recognized she had a brilliant mind, and Elinor put that mind to work. Unlike her parents and sisters, who regarded books as decoration to be selected for their attractive binding rather than their content, she accumulated an eclectic collection of prose, poetry and philosophy. One slim volume of poetry, inscribed in a childish hand "To Elinor From Elinor. Wishing her a Merry Christmas," suggests that she recognized early that she was the only intellectual in the family. She developed a taste for the offbeat, becoming particularly interested in Eastern religions and Russian revolutionary philosophy. Books such as *The Modern Zoroastrian*, *Early Buddhist Monachism* and Kropotkin's *Memoirs of a Revolutionist* were not only collected but also well read. She pored over *George Sand and Her Lovers*, finding in the life of the French novelist a model for flouting convention by adopting masculine attire and smoking cigars. And she searched through the works of Havelock Ellis for an explanation of her own sexual identity. Finding no answers that gave her any comfort, she succumbed to self-loathing, on one occasion going through a family photograph album and defacing every image of herself that appeared on its pages.

During the 1920s she found escape in the casinos of Monte Carlo, Nice and Cannes. Clad in a velvet smoking jacket and chain-smoking cigarettes in a long holder, Elinor was treated with deference by waiters and croupiers to whom she flung huge tips when she was on a winning streak. She became known as *la riche canadienne*, an inveterate gambler who won fame for breaking the bank at Monte Carlo one night and then returning the following evening to gamble her winnings away.

Even when she found herself down to only a handful of francs, Elinor was unable to tear herself away. She sent cables begging her mother for money; the "money poured in" and Elinor gambled it all away. She became desperate. "Some of the cables threatened suicide and other dire consequences if her pleadings were not answered," her nephew recalled. Maye's husband, Arthur Bromley, was sent to the rescue. He marched down to Monte Carlo, dragged her away from the gaming tables and shipped her home.

In 1930 Elinor retired to a more peaceful life at Hatley, where she whiled away the days reading, golfing, playing endless games of patience and holding herself ready for the times her mother needed a fourth for a game of Five Hundred.

In 1938 Elinor suffered the last of a series of strokes and died in hospital in Victoria in her fifty-second year. "Gifted in many ways, music and art were her chief interests, and she was a keen student of literature," the *Colonist* intoned. "Of a quiet and unassuming character, few except her most intimate friends knew of her talents and accomplishments."

—

Like Elinor, most of the Dunsmuir girls inherited their mother's big-boned stocky frame. But both Muriel and Marion, the two sisters closest in age to Elinor, were petite and fine-boned, and both found that their willowy elegance was a decided asset in lives that were devoted exclusively to "a dizzy search for pleasure."

Muriel, or "Moulie" as she was known, went to the altar three times, displaying an unerring instinct for selecting quite the most unsuitable husbands. In 1921, when she was thirty-one, she married Capt. Edward Molyneux a tall, handsome, grey-eyed Anglo-Irishman who was artistic, hard-working, ineffably sophisticated, "terribly charming," and openly homosexual.

Born in London in 1891, Molyneux had set his heart on becoming an artist. At nineteen he entered a newspaper competition to design an evening dress, and walked off with first prize—a job at Lucile's, Lady Duff Gordon's London fashion house. When war broke out in 1914, Molyneux joined the Duke of Wellington's regiment and was quickly raised to a captaincy. Serving in France, he was twice mentioned in dispatches and received the Military Cross for bravery. He was wounded three times, eventually losing the sight of his left eye when a shifting piece of shrapnel disrupted his optic nerve.

After the war, Molyneux moved to Paris and opened his own fashion house on the Rue Royale with a staff of twenty and a shoe-string budget. He was an overnight success. He regarded *haute couture* as a serious form of applied art. "I detest the blatant and the bizarre," Molyneux maintained. And with a combination of English restraint and Parisian flair, he specialized in the creation of "exquisitely simple" designs. He liked to say that he "abhorred self-advertisement," and yet he was canny enough to realize that the image he projected would set the style of his salon. With his friends, he continued to use the English pronunciation of his name. But while he might be "Mollynooks" in London, he was definitely "Mollynew" in Paris.

However he chose to pronounce his name, he still made little attempt to disguise his sexual preference. In 1919, Harold Nicolson, a member of the British diplomatic corps who was in Paris for talks that would lead to the establishment of the League of Nations, and who found pleasure with men as well as women, had no trouble in identifying Molyneux as a likely companion. On 15 September, he wrote a teasing letter to his wife, Vita Sackville-West, who was about to set out on a tour of Greece with her lover, Violet Trefusis. "I have got such a funny new friend, a dressmaker, with a large shop in the Rue Royale, a charming flat at the Rond Point (where I spent the whole of Saturday night, sleeping on the balcony) and about ten mannequins of surpassing beauty. I am lunching at the shop today. My dressmaker is only 27 . . . very attractive."

Molyneux's acquaintances were somewhat puzzled by his decision to marry. But perhaps it was not so surprising. Moulie was "beautifully made"; as his wife, she would become a walking advertisement for his salon as she wound her way through the social life of the idle rich. And she was prepared to invest in his business. As for Moulie, marriage to Molyneux would plunge her into an artistic, fashionable world, inhabited by Cecil Beaton, Noel Coward and Gertrude Lawrence, and would allow her to glide through Paris on the arm of a handsome, elegant man who was "charming to be with."

They were married on 22 October 1921 at the British Consulate in Paris, with Moulie wearing a wedding gown of brown crepe designed by the groom. "Brown in every shade runs through his winter collection," readers of *Vogue* were informed.

The marriage was soon over. They discovered they were "temperamentally unsuited," Moulie's family explained. But both Moulie and Molyneux had benefited from the experience. Thanks to the backing of Dunsmuir dollars, he had been able to expand his establishment, moving to a larger shop on the Rue Royale and employing as many as 250 people at his Paris headquarters and in the smaller shop he had opened in Monte Carlo in 1925. During the 1930s, "Molyneux" was acknowledged to be "one of the world's greatest dress making houses" and the equal of Chanel, Mainbocher and Schiaparelli. Both the Princess Royal and Princess Marina of Greece went down the aisle in Molyneux-designed wedding dresses. And in 1938, when Joseph Kennedy was appointed American ambassador to the Court of St. James, his wife, Rose, turned to Molyneux to design the dress in which she would be presented to the king. "Clothes," Molyneux often said, "must avoid the overdressed, the obvious, the showy; they must also wear well." And with Rose Kennedy's gown, he set a standard for timeless elegance. In 1961, when her son, John Fitzgerald Kennedy, was sworn in as president of the United States, Rose attended his Inauguration Ball in the same Molyneux-designed dress she had worn twenty-three years earlier.

Moulie remained on good terms with her former husband. But then, why not? She was a woman who seems to have expected very little of the men she married. In 1928 she married Maurice "Tolly" Wingfield, a bon viveur who worked for a London bookmaker and who "when intelligible" was an excellent raconteur. Asked what had possessed her to marry him, Moulie answered airily, "Well, I guess I just had to have someone to walk into a restaurant behind me when I wanted to go out to dinner!"

In 1932 Moulie and Tolly decided to build a house on the Hatley estate. Moulie christened the house "Journey's End"—but of course it was not. Hatley was far too quiet a backwater after the glittering nightlife of Paris and Monte Carlo. After Tolly drank himself to death, Moulie married again, choosing as her third husband a man described as "a sissified idiot" by her Victoria acquaintances. She had acquired a divorce, sold Journey's End, gone back to using her maiden name and was living in Paris when her particular journey ended with her death in 1959 in her seventieth year.

———

Marion Dunsmuir made only one trip to the altar. In England in the winter of 1913, she married Percy Stevenson, "an extensive traveller, an ardent sportsman, and a man of unusually high literary tastes," who came equipped with a former wife and two young sons. The Stevensons' search for the good life was interrupted only by the outbreak of war. Stevenson served his king, winning a Distinguished Service Order in 1917 and retiring from the army a colonel. He died in Paris in 1922, so suddenly and unexpectedly that many of his friends suspected that he may have committed suicide.

Marion and Moulie, accompanied sometimes by Elinor and sometimes by Bessie, swirled through the Paris of the 1920s in a champagne haze, surrounded by recklessly high-living, smart-set friends, pursued by Russian "counts" of dubious lineage and flattered by the oozing charm of sycophantic *maîtres d'* and waiters. To detached observers, they appeared as pathetic characters, whose company was valued only because it was they who reached into their pocketbooks and settled the accounts after a night of revelry. But Moulie and Marion seem to have loved every moment. They adored the gay carefree life of restaurants and nightclubs of Montmarte and Montparnasse. Others might recognize their companions as hangers-on and sharpies, but for both Marion and Moulie, their Paris years were the best years of their lives. For them, fun was the only thing that mattered.

Twenty-three

—

Kathleen, the youngest of the four "Dunsmuir Kids," was Laura's eleventh child, born on 22 December 1891 while the family was living at Fairview. The prettiest of all the daughters, she was a golden girl with thick wavy blond hair, flawless fair skin and deep, wide-set eyes. She was twenty-three when war broke out, and for a time she was content to support the cause by performing in benefit concerts in Victoria, Seattle and Vancouver. She won local fame as a talented amateur artiste. In November 1914, the *Vancouver Province* breathlessly reported that the Women's Employment League was staging a French cabaret at the Avenue Theatre and that one of the highlights of the evening would be a "futuristic song and dance" performed by "Miss Kathleen Dunsmuir of Victoria," supported by her sister Muriel.

By Christmas, Kat and Moulie were in London, staying with their sister Bessie and looking to her to organize them into worthy causes. Moulie chose to do her bit by gliding across the stage in a tasteful *gavotte*; Kat yearned to do more.

By February 1915, while her older sisters remained behind in London and her brother Boy languished impatiently in Victoria, Kat had crossed the channel and was working twelve hours a day at a soldiers' canteen that she and a Victoria friend, Kay Scott, chaperoned by Kay's mother, had established on the quay at Le Havre. She peppered her family and her Victoria friends with cables and letters—cables in which she begged for money and letters in which she revealed herself as a young woman who was often exhausted but always excited and revelling in the unusual sensation of feeling truly useful and acutely alive.

"We love the work," Kathleen wrote in April 1915. "I am cabling to see if you can possibly get $2500. We still have some money left, but we give so much . . . we give two big buns for a penny, instead of one. Even then we might do all right, but we feed all the men who have nothing free, as well as trains of wounded . . . We also give everything free to the guards who bring in the German prisoners, so you see we do need a lot. How they do love on a cold morning at 5 or 6 o'clock to have hot chocolate and buns!"

Kathleen's days began at the Hotel Continental at five in the morning, when Kay's mother crept into her room with a cup of tea. By six she was at the canteen, a specially fitted-out van parked at the end of the quay. Every day she sliced 300 loaves of bread, sweated over the boilers brewing 60 large vats of tea and boiling 200 dozen eggs, and put her finishing-school French to use shopping in Le Havre for jam rolls, buns and cakes. "We seldom get back before 7 o'clock, so we have no time for much writing. We are all so tired that we just flop into bed."

Later that month, Lieut. Col. Marescaux wrote to his sister in Victoria to tell her that he had encountered Kathleen. "I meet her every day at the quay at 7 am with her van, just the two girls, and they have been up since 5 a.m. getting water boiled, bread and butter cut etc. I admire her pluck and endurance; and she has a kind heart . . . When I tell you that they are there with their van, and 4000 men have landed after a night's crossing, they have their work cut out. They serve about 200 an hour, hard at it, and it is hard work standing on their feet for long hours. She says that she is at times so fagged and, what with the smell of food, she has no appetite."

By an eerie coincidence, the *Colonist* chose 7 May 1915 as the day to publicize Kathleen's activities. Within hours of going to press with the news that she was not far from the front line, operating the first soup kitchen to be sent from England to the Continent, the paper would be selecting its largest type to announce the *Lusitania*'s sinking.

Boy's regiment reached the Continent six months later. "Who do you think we met almost immediately on arriving in France?" an officer in the Canadian Mounted Regiment wrote. "Why, Kathleen Dunsmuir, of course."

After the men had all had their tea in big generous mugs, we formed up again and Miss Dunsmuir sent over about 5000 cigarettes as a present to the men . . . [They] gave three hearty cheers for Jimmie's brave sister as we moved away.

It is not so much what she gives, though that must be considerable, but rather the fact of her giving up all the pleasures and luxuries, living in that hole and getting up at all the most unearthly hours to meet the incessant flow as it arrives.

Kathleen had never been happier. Not only had she amazed herself by her capacity for hard work, but also she had fallen in love. Arthur Selden Humphreys was a major with the Army Service Corps, assigned to the post of assistant quartermaster general at Le Havre. A "dapper little man" with a well-trimmed mustache and kindly grey eyes, he must have thought that he was in for a singularly enjoyable war when Kathleen fetched up on the quay at Le Havre, needing his assistance and relying on his co-operation. They were married in London on 20 October 1915 and, because of the rule that no wives of officers serving in France were permitted across the channel, Kathleen was forced to give up her canteen work and remain in England.

After the war, Selden and Kat settled in Victoria. Humphreys was contemplating a life of leisure. "Well, my dear, he wasn't *expected* to *do* anything," one of Kat's friends explained. However he did allow himself to be tempted into activity when he was asked to serve as *aide-de-camp* to the lieutenant-governor, Walter Nichol. He and Kathleen moved to Westover, the Rockland area mansion that Laura had acquired as a Victoria *pied-à-terre* and that was conveniently close to Government House. And Kathleen, who often exclaimed, "You know how I hate sluggards!" threw herself into entertaining with relentless energy.

The parties at Westover became legendary for their abandonment. On one occasion, Kat greeted her guests wearing a bright green wig. "It made quite an impression on me," one of the company remembered. Her house was crowded with eager party-goers from dusk to dawn. "My aunt kept open house at Westover," Jimmy Audain remembered. "People knew how lavish she was in her entertainment and trespassed greatly on her generosity and good nature." But Kat did not care. "She was a born entertainer and hostess and while in the full course of her flight into hospitality, would count little the cost of the morrow."

In 1929, after Selden's tour of duty as *aide-de-camp* came to an end, the Humphreys built a house of their own near the Oak Bay waterfront. They lived there with their four children, Jim, their first child, born in 1918, and his three sisters, the youngest of whom, Judy, had been born only two years earlier. Kat made quite an impact on her son's schoolmates. "She was glamorous—*and* she wore heavy make-up," one of them recalled. "We thought she was a movie star."

A movie star was just what Kathleen wanted to be. Her marriage to Selden had become a series of bitter arguments. One visitor, who peeped into her pastel pink bedroom, noticed there was a drink stain on the wall "as if she had thrown it there." In 1930, only a year after they had moved into the sprawling California Spanish-style house, Selden Humphreys joined the ranks of discarded husbands. "A charming man, but weak as water," he was eventually shipped off to Shanghai with an annuity that paid him £20 a month and the promise of a further £300 to start a business. Meanwhile, Kathleen, determined to jump-start her long-abandoned theatrical career, went Hollywood.

She was forty years old, hardly the most propitious age to launch a career, and she had lost the girlish beauty that had distracted attention from her short neck and formidable chin. But nothing daunted, Kathleen lightened her hair and had herself photographed in vampish poses, wearing clinging black satin and a sultry expression. And then, with her portfolio under her arm and her younger daughters in tow, she set off for Beverly Hills.

Southern California suited her very well. "I have decided to *live* down here," she wrote to a Victoria friend early in 1931. "Simply love the place & feel so well." She settled in a house on Canon Drive, near the corner of Hollywood Boulevard and Rodeo Drive, and began to spend her money entertaining studio executives before whom she dangled the possibility that she might invest in their projects in return for a role.

"This won't be an absolute break from all my friends in Victoria as I shall always go back in the summer," Kathleen wrote. But she soon discovered that moving back to Victoria would present her with her only chance to break into the movies.

In 1927 the British government had voted to protect its own motion picture industry by establishing a quota system. By 1936, one out of every five films distributed and screened in Great Britain and throughout the Commonwealth would be required to meet the legislative definition of "British": that is, they must be made by a British subject or a British company, filmed in a studio within the British Commonwealth, and be based on a story written by a British subject. While established American studios, like Columbia and RKO, railed against the quota system, Kenneth J. Bishop saw it as an answer to prayer.

Bishop described himself as a man of many parts—actor, stage manager, film distributor, independent producer and owner of the wonder-dog Lightning. Others put it more simply: he was a promoter and a hustler. Born in England in 1893, he had spent upwards of twenty years on the fringes of the film industry in New York and Hollywood. He was quick to recognize Kathleen as a heaven-sent opportunity. Since he was a British subject, any film made by a company he controlled would meet at least one of the criteria. If he established a studio in Canada, then he need only look for a British writer, and any film he produced would sail through the quota barrier with its distribution throughout the Commonwealth virtually guaranteed.

On 30 July 1932 he launched Commonwealth Productions, a company registered in British Columbia, which had Bishop as its president and Kathleen Humphreys as one of its most prominent backers. An abandoned exhibition building on the Willows Fairground was fitted up as a sound stage, and in February 1933 production began on *The Mystery of Harlow Manor*, which would take advantage of the beauty of Hatley Park for its exterior scenes and the talents of Kathleen Humphreys in a small supporting role. Three months into production that project was shelved and work was begun on a more ambitious and expensive film, *The Crimson Paradise*, in which Kathleen invested $10,000 and in which she would be permitted to co-star.

The plot synopsis provided by Commonwealth Productions did not augur well for the film's success.

Youth, high spirits and a Boston night club is the combination that leads to the undoing of young Donald McLean [Hollywood actor Nick Stuart], a college boy who has just been granted his diploma as a civil engineer . . . Disowned by his father, he is thrown on his own resources with no notion of which way to turn.

The chance remark of a friend sends him to British Columbia—"The Crimson Paradise"—and in that glorious environment he discovers opportunities and a new outlook on life itself.

The scene changes to Victoria—the boy, broke, disheartened and as far as he can see, even worse off than he was in the city in which he was born. Then comes a change of luck. His ability as a fighter proves to be the lever that opens up the way to success. The success as a professional fighter procures for him an introduction to one Jasper Rennie, a lumberman in a large way of business and while Rennie's whole interest is centered in lumber, his daughter, Janet [Kathleen], is interested in nothing but Donald. The attraction is mutual, and it looks as though it only remained to be written "and they lived happily ever after."

Fate, however, had other ideas and the love story was not to end quite so easily for young Donald is put to work in the magnificent forests of British Columbia and there, in some of the most wonderful country that God ever made, he meets a girl [Hollywood actress Lucille Browne] so different from all other girls of his acquaintance; so different in mind, body, and habit of thought, that he does not even understand the enormous impression she has made on him, and it is not until the very end of the picture when he again meets Janet— who is herself the very charming product of a modern civilization— that he realizes how quickly he has slipped away from his old town life and how this new existence that he has been leading under Nature's own guidance, has called into being the full forces of real Love and concentrated every craving of human desire in Connie— this wild child of the woods—who has literally dropped out of the branches of a tree straight into the very centre of his heart.

Not a scenario designed to win critical applause, but then Commonwealth Productions was out to make money rather than produce works of art. And *The Crimson Paradise* did seem likely to turn a tidy profit, at least for Kenneth Bishop, who had risked none of his own capital. The production costs were underwritten by Kathleen, who eagerly anted-up an additional $20,000.

The film was shot on Dunsmuir property—at Hatley and on the Cowichan River—and Kathleen treated the crew to her legendary hospitality. "She fed everyone breakfast, lunch and supper," Mike Heppell, an eighteen-year-old local actor remembered. As well as providing sustenance, Kathleen provided most of the cast by coaxing and coercing friends and family into accepting small nonpaying roles. "She left no stone unturned," one bit player recalled. "She made it clear that it was their duty, if they had a grain of talent, to appear on the silver screen." Byrdie Audain's daughter, Laura, played "Janet's friend"; Robin Dunsmuir's daughter, Laura, was cast as "a cloak room girl," and Robin's son joined his second cousin, Jack Bryden, to play "Donald's friends." Even William Packe, Hatley's stately English butler, was pressed into service playing himself.

Ten weeks after the first film had been exposed, *The Crimson Paradise* was ready for its premiere. But just where it would be screened presented a problem. Local theatres were controlled by

American distribution companies and had little interest in encouraging British Columbia film production or in wasting theatre time on a picture that seemed unlikely to do good box office. Ivan Ackery, the manager of Victoria's Capitol Theatre, won Famous Players over by suggesting that the premiere take place late at night, after the regular feature.

On 14 December 1933 with the Capitol bathed in floodlights and decorated with Union Jacks, a tuxedo-clad Ackery welcomed the elite of Victoria to the premiere showing—at 11 P.M. The theatre's organist played the overture; the assembly sang "O Canada"; the premier of the province, T. D. Pattullo, gave a welcoming address; the mayor of the city extended his congratulations; Kenneth Bishop treated the audience to an enthusiastic address; the cast was introduced; Kathleen, glamorous in pale satin and white fur, staggered onstage, the victim of nerves and far too much champagne; Fred Wright sang a solo; and finally, close to midnight, the theatre dimmed and *The Crimson Paradise*, "Canada's First All Talking Motion Picture," flickered onto the screen.

"It was a real turkey," Ackery laughed. "So lousy it was good." Local newspaper reviews were kind. "Everyone who attended agreed that few pictures have ever been shown here with more beautiful outdoor scenes," one ventured, avoiding mention of the poor sound, rough editing and wooden acting.

The Crimson Paradise, playing on a double bill with an "Our Gang" comedy, lumbered through a three-day run, December 20, 21 and 22, before slinking out of town to play for a week at Vancouver's Pantages theatre, after which it disappeared, apparently forever.

As soon as *The Crimson Paradise* was completed, Bishop began production on *Secrets Of Chinatown*, a lurid tale of opium smuggling, which, he assured Kathleen, would make a great deal of money. But Commonwealth Productions was tottering on the brink of bankruptcy even as filming got under way. His other investors had let him down; could Kathleen advance him the money, Bishop pleaded. And Kathleen wrote yet another cheque.

Bishop's creditors were not nearly so understanding. In March 1934, Victoria lawyer Patrick Sinnott, representing a group of local people to whom Commonwealth Productions owed money, presented himself at the door of Kathleen's Oak Bay house. "I pointed out that economically the jig was up," Sinnott said. "I had some difficulty serving the bankruptcy papers. She didn't want to be served. But she poured me a drink and we parted friends."

Kathleen would pour a good many more drinks as the enormity of her loss slowly dawned on her. In total she had invested over $50,000—most of it advanced without the legal protection of a written contract. She pleaded with the bankruptcy court to grant her possession of the two films, but the judge decided that any profits they might generate should go to their creditors rather than their principal investor. Her $50,000 investment returned not so much as a penny.

It must have been galling to Kathleen that the man who had fleeced her of a small fortune escaped unscathed. Bishop had sold his interest in Commonwealth Productions before the axe fell. In 1935 he formed Central Films Limited, whose only purpose was to serve as a front for a series of "quota quickies" for Columbia Pictures and filmed in and around Victoria. Between 1935 and 1937 Bishop churned out a dozen of them, all uncompromisingly B-grade movies and all easily forgotten, except perhaps for his last two efforts, *Across the Border* and *Convicted*, which featured a very young Rita Hayworth in her first starring roles.

While Bishop bustled about Victoria making six films a year, Kathleen, reduced to relative poverty, moved into an apartment above the old stables at Hatley, where she spent several months before she managed to wheedle more money out of her mother. She rented the Audain's Oak Bay house, moved her furniture out of storage, settled comfortably in Ellora and began to entertain once again. She was living there in 1937 when her mother died.

———

Laura Dunsmuir's obituary did her proud. "She was a wonderful hostess, dispensing hospitality with rare graciousness and charm, exhibiting an unusual gift for remembering people, and at all times impressing one with her sincerity and genuine sympathy and friendliness," the *Colonist* mourned. "A great lover of flowers and aboriculture, she took a keen personal interest in the beautifying of the gardens at Hatley." That was how Laura would have wanted to be remembered—the province's greatest hostess, famous for her hospitality and renowned for her love of flowers.

She died in her eightieth year after having spent several years as a semi-invalid, confined to the second floor until a special elevator was installed to carry her downstairs. She had had a great deal of time to think about the problem James had left in her hands—deciding what should become of the fortune after her death. Laura dallied and delayed, finally signing her last will and testament on 9 July

1937, only a month before her death. She had been left little room for creativity. Not one member of the family could be trusted to take charge; and not one of them could afford to live at Hatley. And so, she left everything in the hands of trustees who were instructed to sell the estate, combine the monies realized from the sale with her other assets, invest the total and dole out the interest in nine equal shares—one to Robin's widow and her children, one to Byrdie's children, and one to each of her seven living daughters, Bessie, Maye, Elinor, Marion, Muriel, Kathleen and Dola.

From an estate valued at $2,334,903, more than half of which was held in Canada Savings Bonds, she left only $17,000 to charity, a rather parsimonious amount for a woman of whom the *Colonist* had said, "Her private benefactions were endless."

Other than that, some bequests to servants and a special provision that Robin's former wife, Maude, should continue to receive her $1,800 annuity, she left everything to her family.

Laura's trustees soon discovered that they were going to have a great deal of trouble finding a buyer who could afford the $260,000 at which Hatley was valued. Although James Dunsmuir had regarded the estate as a working farm, it fell far short of paying its way, requiring a subsidy of $1,500 a month to break even. In March 1938 Hatley was advertised in England in *Mayfair* and *Country Life*; and a short motion picture was filmed later that spring and dispatched to California. The latter brought a few nibbles from Culver City producers who recognized Hatley's potential as a movie studio but who were discouraged by its price tag. Meanwhile, the estate manager did what he could to increase Hatley's income. Milk, lambs, wool, wood, potatoes, apples, flowers and hay were sold off the estate; orchids from Laura's conservatory made their way to the city's florists. But still Hatley did not pay. In May 1939 John Graham decided to open the grounds to paying customers. The returns were disappointingly small. But that summer, Hatley entertained at least one visitor who fell quite in love with the place and could easily picture himself as feeling very much at home within the castle's walls.

—

On 29 May, King George VI and his wife Queen Elizabeth arrived in Victoria on their cross-Canada royal tour. The papers were full of Hatley during their visit, for a public auction of all the furnishings was to be held on 1 June. A private visit was quickly arranged. They strolled along the beach, collecting clamshells, enjoyed a quiet tea on the terrace and carried away fond memories of the castle by the sea.

Two years later, with war raging, bombs falling on London and an invasion still regarded as a very real possibility, the king found himself thinking about Hatley as a possible bolt-hole, if not for himself, at least for his family, in particular his brother Edward, the Duke of Windsor.

On 30 August 1941 the Canadian prime minister, Mackenzie King, who had reason to remember the Dunsmuirs from his years as deputy minister of labour, paid a courtesy call on the king at Balmoral. During the course of a far-ranging conversation, the subject drifted round to the Duke of Windsor. In 1936 George's older brother, Edward, had abdicated the throne to marry a twice-divorced American woman. Now, he was serving as the reluctant governor of the Bahamas, and both he and his wife had been less than discreet in accepting the friendships of shady Americans and wealthy pro-Nazi Europeans.

"I told the King I thought Nassau was not a good place for the Duke, that he was with a bad lot of Americans there," the prime minister confided to his diary. The king agreed, and soon the conversation shifted to Hatley. "At one stage, he asked me what had become of the Dunsmuir property," Mackenzie King wrote. He was able to supply him with the welcome information that no private purchaser had been found and that on 14 December 1940 the house and grounds had been acquired by the Department of National Defence as an extension of the nearby Esquimalt naval base. "I could see what he had in mind was the possibility of making a sort of Canadian residence for the King," the prime minister noted. But George was thinking of Hatley for his brother rather than himself. Hatley Park, protected from attack by a nearby coastal battery and reassuringly close to the naval base, would provide an admirably secure spot in which to keep the Windsors out of harm's way.

"I said that I would be glad to do anything I could to further Their Majesties wishes, that if at any time they wished me to give attention to any particular matter, word could be sent to me privately . . . and I would do my utmost to further their wishes," King wrote.

But the call never came. The Japanese entered the war that December. With enemy submarines reported to be lurking off the west coast and Victoria braced for imminent attack, Hatley could no longer be considered a safe haven. And so the Duke of Windsor never came to stay. Still, James Dunsmuir would have been most gratified had he known his country estate would be considered fit for a king, even if he was an ex-king.

—

That knowledge would have been cold comfort to the Dunsmuir girls. Hatley had been sold to the Department of Defence for a meagre $75,000—less than the amount spent to build the high stone wall that lined the roadside boundary of the estate. And the auction of the furnishings had been a sorry, sad affair. Laura's prized possessions were knocked down for prices her daughters must have found distressingly low—the dining room suite, so large that it could easily seat twenty, sold for $98; Laura's Steinway grand went for $500.

By the time the furniture was auctioned and Hatley was sold, Kathleen was long gone. Included in Laura's will was a provision that prohibited the trustees from paying Kathleen her share of the estate unless she maintained and educated her children to their satisfaction. By October 1937, just two months after her mother's death, Kathleen had decided that it might be prudent to put some distance between herself and the trustees. She held an auction of her own at Ellora, bade Victoria good-bye and took up residence in Switzerland. And there she might have stayed, sitting out the war in a neutral country. But as another European war loomed, she responded, once again, to duty's call. She moved to London, settled her youngest daughter, twelve-year-old Judy, in a school in Wales and prepared to roll up her sleeves. She organized and subsidized a mobile canteen at Aldershot. She became "one of the most active and loyal volunteers" at the Regent Street canteen at British Columbia House. She worked with the Canadian Legion and the Beaver Club. She felt wonderful.

Kathleen's older children followed her example. Her twenty-one year old son, Jim, joined the RAF. Her oldest daughter, Joan, worked at her mobile canteen and then enlisted in the Women's Army Transport Service, and fifteen-year-old Jill waited impatiently for the birthday that would allow her to do her part.

They were all in and out of London at the height of the blitz, when Jim Humphreys decided to marry. For Kathleen there was only one place in London worthy of her son's postnuptial celebration— the Café de Paris. Located 20 feet underground in the basement of the Rialto Cinema, it was billed as London's safest restaurant. During the 1920s, the patronage of Edward, Prince of Wales, had established the café as the smartest place in London, and the prince's glamour still hovered in the air, even though the tailcoats and dinner jackets of earlier years had been replaced by uniforms. And the café was home to the best band in the city, Ken "Snakehips" Johnson and his Caribbean swing ensemble.

Like Kathleen, actor John Mills and his wife, Mary, had cause to regard 8 March 1941 as a night to celebrate. "I booked a table at the Café de Paris," Mills remembered. "I was changing in the bedroom, and Mary was in the living-room shaking a cocktail for me . . . For no apparent reason I suddenly felt that the last thing I wanted to do was to go to the Café de Paris that evening." Instead, he and his wife went for a walk in Hyde Park.

Kathleen had no similar premonition. At ten o'clock that Saturday night, she and Jim, together with his new wife, were ensconced in the Café de Paris, drinking champagne. Snakehips struck up "Oh Johnny." Kathleen rose to her feet ready to dance. And the world exploded around her. A 50-kilo bomb had entered the air chute that vented the restaurant. The ceiling fell in; the lights went out; the room filled with fumes and smoke. It was "like someone's imagination of hell"—screams and moans—choking fumes—bodies knifed apart by shattered glass. Jim and his wife were injured. Kathleen was killed.

It was only after Kathleen's ashes were shipped home to Victoria to be interred in the family plot at Ross Bay Cemetery that someone remembered, with a chill creeping up his spine, that the Café de Paris had been modelled on the Palm Room of the *Lusitania*.

Twenty-four

Dola Frances Dunsmuir always felt like the odd girl out. "I was an afterthought," she used to say, by way of explaining the nine years that elapsed between the birth of Boy, her closest sibling, and her own arrival in 1903. "She did not fit in," her nephew, Jimmy Audain, observed. "And being half a generation younger than her brothers and sisters necessitated a special nursery regime for her sole benefit." Reason enough, perhaps, for the lack of enthusiasm with which Laura regarded her.

She was three years old when her family took up residence in Government House. And while her sisters Elinor and Marion and Muriel prepared to make their debut, she was isolated in the nursery suite under the care of her grim-faced, black-garbed nanny, Miss Easom.

Jimmy Audain was Dola's only playmate during the years she spent sequestered in the nursery at Government House. The son of her sister Byrdie, who was twenty-five years Dola's senior, Jimmy was two months older than his aunt; their relationship was much more that of brother and sister than aunt and nephew.

Dola was treated with "a certain disinterested tolerance" by the rest of the family, at least by everyone except her father, who doted on her and "spoiled her tremendously." He was fifty-two and close to retirement when she was born. And he found it easy to lavish on her the devoted attention more often found in delighted grandfathers. His older daughters had seen him as distant and stern—a punctual man who stood at the dining room door, his gold watch in hand, ready to bar entrance to any of his children who dared to arrive after the appointed hour. With Dola, he displayed an almost childish sense of humour. He particularly enjoyed treating Dola and Jimmy to an evening game of "bears," during which he would throw a giant polar bear rug over his shoulders and lumber menacingly around Government House.

Later, one of Dola's fondest memories would be of being dressed up in her Sunday best and going for a drive with her father. It was with Dola at his side that he had called at Craigdarroch to attempt to effect a reconciliation with his mother, only to be met on the castle's steps by a footman with the message that Joan was not at home.

Dola was six years old when the family moved to Hatley, and she was treated to the pampering that came with being a millionaire's daughter—a pony of her own in Hatley's stables and in "The Glen," a sunny clearing in the woods a few hundred feet from the main house, a charming log cabin built specially for Dola and her dolls. She was sent to the best schools—St. Margaret's in Victoria, Mills Seminary in Berkeley, and then on to Mademoiselle Ozanne's finishing school in Paris to be groomed for her introduction to London society.

But Dola, despite her advantages, remained painfully shy and desperately self-conscious about her dumpy, waistless shape. It did nothing to improve her morale when, during her years in Paris, she was taken up by her sister Moulie and Moulie's new husband, Edward Molyneux, who introduced her to the fashionably thin and terribly sophisticated members of their set. Poor Dola. With her hair straight and short, parted severely on the side and dragged across her head schoolgirl fashion, and wearing shapeless skirts and sweaters that did little to disguise her lumpiness, she appeared awkward and uncomfortable and ill at ease. She trudged along with Moulie and Edward when they took her on a tour of the battlefields. And she allowed herself to be coaxed to a Riviera beach, where she wrapped herself up in the largest towel she could find.

It was with some relief that she left Paris and escaped to London and the camaraderie of Jimmy Audain. The product of the right English public schools and a graduate of Sandhurst, he had followed his father into the army. By 1923 he had been commissioned a lieutenant in an elite cavalry regiment and was busy living the life of a dashing young officer-about-town. Laura was ensconced in a suite in a London hotel and labouring mightily to wedge the youngest Dunsmuir into society, with scant success.

Dola's "one all-consuming passion" was her love for the stage and all things theatrical. In London in the 1920s a young throaty-voiced American actress was taking the West End by storm. Tallulah Bankhead had achieved notoriety for appearing in roles that demanded she strip down to her crepe-de-chine underwear. "No criticism of Tallulah Bankhead's play is complete without reference to her display of lingerie," one reviewer grumbled. Causing even more comment and a certain amount of unease was a strange new phenomenon her appearances provoked. Hours before a performance, the street outside the theatre would become choked with crowds of young women eager to buy seats in the gallery and clamouring for a glimpse of her when she arrived at the theatre. "Well, well, girls will be boys," one commentator quipped, trying to account for Tallulah's appeal.

Tallulah was young, beautiful, free and wild. In an era of flaming youth, she was a one-woman conflagration. "Press on!" was her motto, and to Tallulah pressing on meant partying till dawn, never resting and trying anything—exotic drink and stimulating drugs, men with shady pasts and men of dubious preferences. And it meant flouting convention and saying anything that popped into her head, provided, of course, that it was outrageous. To the "gallery girls," most of whom were the daughters of conventional middle-class families, Tallulah represented dangerous new possibilities. They swooned at the thought of her, even while they knew that they would never dare to follow her example.

Dola burned to meet her. "Is she all right?" Dola would press her theatrical friends. "Does she need any money? Can I help her in any way?"

One spring night in 1925, after a performance of Noel Coward's *Fallen Angels* in which Tallulah appeared "impersonating to the life a joyless creature whose spiritual home was the gutter," Dola, emboldened by the presence of a tipsy Jimmy, stormed her dressing room, only to discover that Tallulah had already gone on to a party. They tracked her down to the Eiffel Tower, a notorious after-hours club in Soho. Barred by the doorman, Dola and Jimmy sent in a message, to which Tallulah, who must have heard tell of the rich girl who was her most constant admirer, sent a friendly reply. "Miss Bankhead regrets very much that her party is rather a rowdy one and she does not think Miss Dunsmuir would feel at her ease, so she asks that Miss Dunsmuir call around at her dressing-room on the morrow, and hopes that on that occasion Miss Dunsmuir will join her party."

The party Miss Dunsmuir joined would last for forty years. They became friends for life—Dola never letting a birthday pass without sending white flowers, Tallulah becoming increasingly dependent on Dola's devotion.

For two such different women their backgrounds were surprisingly similar. The Bankheads of Alabama were a comfortably well-off family, their prosperity based on their cotton lands and coal mines. Like the Dunsmuirs, they had risen to political prominence. And like Dola, Tallulah had been carefully schooled. But there the similarities ended, for while Dola was sweet-natured, shy and quiet, Tallulah was uninhibited, irrepressible and daring. At one party, early in her London career, she was introduced to a very proper titled gentleman whose noncommital expression suggested he had never heard of her. "What's the matter, dahling," Tallulah demanded. "Don't you recognize me with my clothes on?"

In concluding her 1952 autobiography, Tallulah struggled to explain what she described as "my plight; my philosophy." She settled on a poem by Edna St. Vincent Millay.

> My candle burns at both ends;
> It will not last the night;
> But ah, my foes, and oh, my friends—
> It gives a lovely light!

Being bathed in Tallulah's light became Dola's lifelong ambition. But first she felt duty-bound to make an attempt to live up to her mother's expectations. Laura had taken a house on Berkeley Square where she was preparing for the presentation at Court of her grand-daughters, Victoria Bromley and Laura Audain, and Dola not only participated in the festivities but also got herself engaged to Lieut.-Cmdr. Henry James Francis Cavendish, a member of a lesser branch of the distinguished Devonshire family.

They were married in Victoria on 11 August 1928 with Dola appearing radiantly happy hanging on the arm of her uniform-clad husband as they emerged from Christ Church Cathedral under an arch of crossed swords. She was twenty-five years old, and judging from the adoring looks she bestowed on the groom, very much in love. "Dish" was ten years Dola's senior. A naval hero, he had served with distinction during the war, being twice mentioned in dispatches and receiving the Distinguished Service Cross. But as successful husband material, Cavendish possessed a certain liability. He was, as Dola's Victoria friends could not help noticing, "a bit of a sissy." They settled in London, in Dola's "splendid digs" in Regent's Park.

Dish retired from the navy and busied himself by spending hours with his bookmaker. Dola amused herself by buying a half-interest in a London dress agency—an elegant thrift store that sold once-worn designer gowns. "I had more fun there than in my whole life," Dola said. "Dish and I sould go out to dinner at the Grosvenor or Claridges in London and sit comparing notes on which friends were wearing whose clothes."

In the winter of 1930 Tallulah accepted an offer from Paramount Pictures, which required her to leave London. She held farewell party at Southampton aboard the *Aquitania*. When the whistle sounded, warning well-wishers that the time had come to leave the ship, Tallulah begged her friends, "Oh, come with me! Do come with me!" Only one of them answered her plea; when the *Aquitania* sailed, Dola was still aboard.

She disembarked at Cherbourg, an expired passport rather than thoughts of Dish forcing her to reconsider her spontaneous decision. Almost a decade would pass before the right circumstances allowed her to become a permanent fixture in Tallulah's life. Meanwhile, she divorced Dish in 1934 and took a job in Molyneux's London fashion house. She was working there when she received word of her mother's death in 1937; and two years later, she was again behind the counter at Molyneux, on this occasion serving the Duchess of Kent, when a special messenger arrived to deliver a copy of the auction catalogue listing Hatley's contents.

It cannot have come as a complete surprise. Laura's will had stipulated that the furnishings be auctioned and had allowed her daughters six months to select and purchase from the estate anything they particularly desired. But still, Dola described herself as horrified as she perused the twenty-five page booklet listing her family's possessions—everything from "Lot 1. Pair Silver Snuffers" to "Lot 927. Books"—so much that the auctioneer had scheduled a sale extending over five days. By the time Dola received the catalogue, it was all over. And now the estate itself was for sale. Her only connection with her former home was the 23 acres she had acquired, partly as a gift from her father and partly by purchasing land from the estate, that lay between the main house and the coastal battery at Fort Rodd Hill.

Dola's desire to build a house on her land drew her back to Hatley and put her on the right side of the Atlantic when war broke out. She was wondering what on earth to do with herself when she received a summons from Tallulah.

During the 1930s, Tallulah had appeared in half a dozen undistinguished films and had auditioned for the part of Scarlett O'Hara in *Gone With the Wind*—a role she lost, some said, only because the Hollywood establishment was becoming increasingly wary of her exhibitionism, her unpredictability and her inability to resist a wisecrack, no matter how ill-advised. Interviewed by Hollywood gossip columnist Earl Wilson who asked, "Have you ever been mistaken for a man on the phone?" husky-voiced Tallulah replied, "No, dahling. Have you?"

Tallulah, who took little comfort in her own company, had developed a near-obsessive fear of being alone. She was desperate for friends, especially friends who could cope with the mad energy that drove her through the night—singing, drinking, talking, dancing, arguing. "A day *away* from Tallulah is like a month in the country," one exhausted party-goer exclaimed.

The thought that Tallulah needed her companionship would have been more than enough for Dola. "She had," Jimmy Audain remembered, "a weakness for lame dogs." She loved to feel needed, loved to hover over people, worrying about them, making sure they were all right. And more than that, she knew that a summons from Tallulah was not to be ignored.

Dola settled herself into "Windows," Tallulah's white brick house in Bedford Village, an hour and a half's drive from New York, which stood in a secluded 17-acre estate where Tallulah grew "chives for the vichyssoise and mint for the juleps." Staff came and went; guests came and stayed. Dola straddled both roles. She was Tallulah's friend, but she was also her unpaid and willing servant— her bartender, her nurse, her secretary, her maid, her cook. She ran Tallulah's bath; she helped deal with the mail; she scrambled eggs at three o'clock in the morning; and after the other guests had crept off to bed, she sat up, listening attentively, while Tallulah talked into the morning.

Because of Dola's obvious adoration and Tallulah's dare-devil approach to life—"Well, dahling," she once exclaimed to astonished listeners, "my parents warned me about men but they never mentioned a *word* about women"—many of their acquaintances presumed that their relationship was sexual. Tallulah, aware of the rumours, was quick to deny them. "I know what people think," she confided, "but I've never seen Dola in a slip." And that may have been true enough. Tallulah needed a friend, especially a financially independent friend, who was free to do as she liked and follow her anywhere; Dola needed someone to take care of.

On 5 February 1940, *The Little Foxes*, with Tallulah playing the role of Regina Giddens, began its national tour. Over the next four-teen months, the company travelled 25,000 miles and appeared in 104 cities. Tallulah never missed a performance. And for that physi-cal *tour de force*, Dola and her solicitous attention must be given some credit. But living in reflected glory was not without its toll. Dola began to drink heavily. For anyone who spent any time at all with Tallulah, alcohol was hard to avoid.

"I am," Tallulah declared, "the foe of moderation; the champion of excess." For Dola, those became words to live by. In the topsy-turvy, day for night world in which Tallulah spun, Dola was the pale moon, revolving around her. Tallulah drank anything she could raise to her lips; Dola's favourite tipple was warm gin—vast quantities of warm gin. A Victoria friend, who happened to be in New York when Dola and Tallulah were holed up in a New York hotel, was invited to a party. Putting her coat away in Dola's bedroom, she kicked over a bottle. "Don't worry about it," Dola assured her. "I just keep one open beside the bed. So handy for the morning. I can just lean over with a straw without getting out of bed."

Dola might have stayed with Tallulah indefinitely. But, in March 1941, after her sister Kathleen was killed in the Café de Paris, she decided that her three motherless nieces needed her even more. She returned to her little part of Hatley, ordered an addition to her house, the house she had christened "Dolaura" after her father's yacht, and prepared to provide a wartime home base for Kathleen's three daughters. She planted a flower garden, mothered stray dogs, and, after the attack on Pearl Harbor, prepared to do her part in the event of a Japanese invasion by enrolling in first-aid courses.

Tallulah visited when she could, and when she did the two women boosted Allied morale by holding liquid open houses at Dolaura for handsome young officers from the near-by naval base. After the war, with her nieces safe and settled, Dola returned to Tallulah.

It was a sad entourage. Tallulah was taking drugs—Tuinal, Benzedrine, Dexamyl, Dexedrine, morphine—anything to put her to sleep or wake her up—and all washed down by a daily quart of bourbon. And she was beginning to struggle for breath as her ciga-rette consumption, which had, since the 1920s, never fallen below 40 a day and now often reached as many as 150, began to make it-self felt. Dola, who was "never quite herself," had allowed her rela-tionship with Tallulah to degenerate into a drink-driven ritual—Dola nagging, Tallulah losing patience and slapping her, Dola marching to the telephone and pretending to call for a cab, while Tallulah growled, "The bitch isn't calling anyone."

As early as 1947, Dola's drinking had begun to give Tallulah concern. "If you drink as much as she does," Tallulah grumbled, "it should be soaked up with *something*! . . . Dola doesn't eat a thing. Just a peck here a peck there."

By 1959, Dola was done in. Feeling old and tired and suffering from cirrhosis of the liver, she retreated to Dolaura. But she always managed to summon up strength for Tallulah's visits. In 1964, Tallulah was wheezing from emphysema but determined to live up to the legend when she breezed through Canadian customs, declaring to the inspector who was about to open her suitcases, "Oh, you don't have to worry about that, Baby. Nothing in them but liquor and dope." It was a bravura performance. Both women knew that they were approaching the end. Sitting at the airport, after having taken leave of Dola, Tallulah broke down and cried. "I have a feeling that I'll never see Dola again," she sobbed. And she was right.

—

Dola Dunsmuir died on 8 December 1966. She was the last of James Dunsmuir's children to die, a fact that was noted in her obituary, as was her close friendship with Tallulah Bankhead and her particular fondness for flowers and dogs. Not much to sum up a life . . . And precious little to mark the end of a dynasty.

—

Notes

Abbreviations

BCARS	British Columbia Archives and Records Service
CCC	Craigdarroch Castle Collection
HBCA-PAM	Hudson's Bay Company Archives, Public Archives of Manitoba
LTO	Land Titles Office, British Columbia
NAC	National Archives of Canada
SRO	Scottish Records Office

Chapter One

Civil registration of birth did not become compulsory in Scotland until 1855, and no record of Robert Dunsmuir's baptism has been found. His 31 August 1825 birthdate appears on his memorial windows in St. Andrew's Presbyterian Church, Victoria.

Early years of the Ayrshire coal industry: Lebon, "The Development of the Ayrshire Coalfield"; Wilson, *The Ayrshire Hermit,* also makes specific references to the senior Robert Dunsmuir's career.

The elder Robert Dunsmuir's will, which includes an inventory of his estate, is held by the SRO.

Robert Dunsmuir and Jean Kirkland had at least seven children: Allan 1803-1847; James 1805-1832; Mary 1810-infancy; Mary 1814-?; Jean 1816-infancy; Jean (Gilmour) 1818-1856; Marion d. 1872.

Dunsmuir family gravestones: "Beattie's Pre-1855 gravestone inscriptions"; the inscriptions were reproduced in Porter, "Robert Dunsmuir—An Exercise in Genealogical Reconstruction."

The Census of Scotland, 1841, lists Jean Dunsmuir, aged thirteen, residing in Hurlford with Jean Hamilton, aged seventy.

The Kilmarnock Parish Registers give the birthdate of Joanna (Joan) Olive White as 22 July 1828. The date of Elizabeth Hamilton Dunsmuir's birth appears on her tombstone in Victoria's Ross Bay Cemetery; the date of her parents' marriage is in the Kilmarnock Parish Registers.

In the Gilmour/Landale correspondence see: Gilmour to Landale 5 and 7 December 1850; Landale to Gilmour 6 December 1850.

According to the Riccarton Parish Registers, Boyd Gilmour was born on 22 February

1814. By 1850, he and his wife, Jean, had five children: Jean born 18 March 1836; Joseph born 5 July 1840; Mary born 4 January 1843; Marion born 1 January 1847; and Boyd born 11 January 1849.

Reaction of Muir party to Fort Rupert: Andrew Muir's diary. The Fort Rupert affair: Dr. J. S. Helmcken's inquiry, Helmcken Papers. Muir's progress: Douglas to Barclay 7 February 1850, Fort Victoria Correspondence Outward, BCARS.

Short provisions and scurvy on the *Pekin*: letters exchanged by Gilmour and James Douglas; also Peter Skene Ogden to Andrew Barclay 2 July 1851, HBCA-PAM. Grounding of the *Pekin*: Ogden to W. F. Tolmie, cited Audain, *Coalmine to Castle.* Birth of Allan Columbia Gilmour: Riccarton Parish Registers. Crew's desertion: Douglas to Barclay 18 August 1851, Fort Victoria Correspondence Outward, BCARS.

Description of Fort Vancouver: Hussey, *History of Fort Vancouver.*

James Dunsmuir's birthdate: Dunsmuir family bible, BCARS.

Descriptions of Fort Rupert: Douglas to Barclay 16 November 1850 and 24 November 1851, Fort Victoria Correspondence Outward, BCARS. The hardships of the Dunsmuirs at Fort Rupert were underlined by a story first reported in Lugrin, *Pioneer Women*:

"They [the Indians] were charmed with the Dunsmuir baby, small James of the flaxen hair. Never a day passed that they did not seek admission within the fort for the purpose of purchasing him. . . . They wanted to adopt him into the tribe and to make him their chief. As day by day all of their offers were refused, they increased the price, bringing their richest pelts and most valued treasures, feeling that in the end his parents would consent to give him up."

After being snatched from his bed, the sleeping baby was found in an Indian lodge being passed from hand to hand around a circle of admiring native women.

This odd story has been included in almost every account of James's life, most recently in Bowen, *Three Dollar Dreams*. In fact, the kidnapping probably never happened. According to Brunvand, *The Vanishing Hitchhiker*, the most popular of all pioneer legends is known as "Goldilocks on the Oregon Trail," and usually begins "My great grandmother had this strange experience when she was a young girl on a wagon train going through Wyoming when an Indian chief wanted to adopt her." As in the Dunsmuir version, the child's blond hair is the attraction. The story, with its obvious racial overtones, appears only in white folklore, and as Brunvand points out, while "hundreds of different great-grandmothers are supposed to have had the same doubtful experience," no letters, diaries or other contemporary accounts have been found. Likewise, the story of Baby James's kidnapping was not mentioned in the Post Journal or in HBC correspondence.

Douglas's criticism of Gilmour: Douglas to Barclay 18 March 1852, Fort Victoria Correspondence Outward, BCARS; Douglas to Gilmour 16 February 1852, HBCA-PAM.

Adams brothers' work stoppage: Douglas to Barclay 6 October 1851, Fort Victoria Correspondence Outward, BCARS.

Discovery of Nanaimo coal: McKay's "Recollections: and Douglas's instructions to McKay 24 August 1852, Nanaimo Correspondence, BCARS.

Quality of Nanaimo coal: McKay to Douglas 16 September 1852, Nanaimo Correspondence, BCARS.

Gilmour's efforts on Newcastle Island: McKay to Douglas 9 April 1853. His efforts near Chase River: Douglas to McKay 6 May 1853; his success on Commercial Inlet: McKay to Douglas 18 May 1853. All Nanaimo Correspondence, BCARS.

Journal of the bore kept and worked by Robert Dunsmuir, 25 August 1852 to 21 December 1853, BCARS.

Miners' demands: Douglas to Barclay 11 August 1854, HBCA-PAM. Douglas's opinion of Gilmour: Douglas to Barclay 25 December 1854, HBCA-PAM.

The Gilmours left Vancouver Island in January 1855, a few days after Jean gave birth to their seventh child, John Gilmour, born Fort Victoria, 24 December 1854. They had been home for less than a year when Jean died of enteritis (death certificate, SRO). Boyd died 26 March 1869, six months before his nephew, Robert Dunsmuir, discovered the Wellington Seam.

The contract between Dunsmuir and the HBC was not finalized until 22 January 1856, Nanaimo Journal.

Dunsmuir's mine continued to operate during contract disputes because he employed native Indian colliers.

About Robinson: Vickers, "George Robinson." *Contretemps* between Dunsmuir and Robinson: Douglas to Stuart 14 January 1856, HBCA-PAM; Douglas to Robinson 18 June and 23 September 1857; Douglas to Stuart 18 June, 10 September and 27 November 1857, Fort Victoria Correspondence Outward, BCARS. Assessment of Robinson's activities: A. G. Dallas to Thomas Fraser 16 September 1860, HBCA-PAM.

Chapter Two

Description of Nanaimo and its residents: Mark Bate's reminiscences, *Nanaimo Free Press* 9 February to 18 May 1907.

Sale to the Vancouver Coal Company: Currie, "The Vancouver Company" and Articles of Conveyance, BCARS.

Benson's coal claim correspondence: Young to Benson 25 September 1863 and Benson to Young 1 December 1863, BCARS.

Dunsmuir's account of his discovery of the Wellington seam: reprinted in Langevin, *British Columbia*.

Letters exchanged about Dunsmuir & Diggle's acquisition of Section 5 and difficulties with Hughes: Dunsmuir, Diggle Coal Claim Correspondence, BCARS.

Tilly Smallbones's account is confirmed, in part, in Beresford, *Memoirs*.

Dunsmuir's need for American partners: Rickard, "A History of Coal Mining."

Biographical details about W. N. Diggle: in his Vertical File, BCARS.

Details of agreement between Dunsmuir and Diggle: Articles of Partnership 14 November 1871, BCARS. They were equal partners: Dunsmuir was mine manager while Diggle was sales agent. As well as an equal share of the profits, Dunsmuir was to receive a bonus of ten cents for each ton he raised, Diggle for each ton he sold.

Conveyance from Crown: Grant 27 January 1872, LTO. Sale by ten partners to Dunsmuir, Diggle and Farquhar: Indenture 9 February 1872, LTO.

Pacific Mail line contract: *Nanaimo Free Press* 7 August 1875 and 28 June 1876.

Statistics relating to prices and tonnage printed regularly in the *Nanaimo Free Press* and were reported annually in the Minister of Mines Report, *Sessional Papers*.

Reaction to Dunsmuir in Nanaimo and his civic career: *Nanaimo Free Press*, in particular 10 October, 11 November and 26 December 1874; 27 January 1875.

Town of Wellington and comments of residents: *Nanaimo Free Press* 29 May, 21 August and 27 November 1875; 31 May, 12 August and 23 September 1876.

Vipond's accident: *Nanaimo Free Press* 3 October 1874. Dunsmuir's comments: *Nanaimo Free Press* 3 March 1877.

Chapter Three

Dunsmuir's problems with Pacific Mail line: *Nanaimo Free Press* 28 June, 5 and 12 July 1876.

The strike was covered in detail by local newspapers, in particular the *Nanaimo Free Press* and the *Colonist*. Testimony taken in various legal actions arising from the strike was often reported verbatim. See also Houghton's "Report" for the role of the militia.

Letters written by Spalding and Dunsmuir: *Sessional Papers*, 1878.

Chapter Four

Statistics relating to colliery operations: *Sessional Papers*, 1878.

Bate's suspicions are recorded in his diary, BCARS.

Lawyer A. Roche Robertson conveyed the remaining shares in the Union mine to Dunsmuir, Diggle on 8 November 1880, LTO.

Charges against Berryman: *Colonist* 13 August and 4 October 1878.

Bryden's correspondence with the Vancouver Company: Bryden to Robins 26 February, 18 March and 9 April 1880. Letterbook, BCARS.

Coroner's inquest after fire of 1879: *Nanaimo Free Press* 26 and 30 April 1879; *Sessional Papers* 1879. Investigation into 1880 cave-in: *Sessional Papers* 1880.

The claim that the Wellington Colliery was producing profits of $500,000 a year is based, in part, on the length of time it took Dunsmuir to pay off the mortgage held by Diggle.

Chapter Five

Dunsmuir's original proposal: Dunsmuir, Diggle, E & N Railway terms, 1 September 1881, BCARS.

Of the 15,000 shares, Dunsmuir owned 7,450; Charles Crocker and his son Fred owned 3,750; Huntington and Stanford each owned 1,875; John Bryden owned 25, as did James Dunsmuir. MacLachlan, *The Esquimalt & Nanaimo Railway*.

The letters of introduction written by Gray 19 February 1882 and Trutch 18 February 1882 as well as Lorne's confidential report of 24 October 1882 are in Macdonald Papers, BCARS.

Lorne's Nanaimo visit: *Nanaimo Free Press* 25 October 1882. Dunsmuir's version of the Clements proposal and Lorne's visit: *Colonist* 22 January 1888.

House of Commons reaction to E & N contract: Myers, *Canadian Wealth*.

Election of 1882: *Nanaimo Free Press* 19, 22 and 26 July 1882; *Colonist* 25 July 1882.

Dunsmuir's 19 November 1883 letter to his constituents: reprinted *Colonist* 21 November 1883. Reaction to it: *Nanaimo Free Press* 24 November 1883.

O'Brian's opposition to Dunsmuir: *Westward Ho!* 8 May, 5 and 26 June, 14 and 16 July 1886; *Nanaimo Free Press* 26 May 1886.

O'Brian's telegram: Executive Council Papers, BCARS.

Raybould's death: *Nanaimo Free Press* 4 December 1886.

Chapter Six

Victoria history: Reksten, *More English*. Visitors' impressions of Victoria: *Colonist* 22 September 1880, 20 August 1886.

O'Reillys' reaction to the Dunsmuirs: P. O'Reilly to C. K. O'Reilly 26 December

1883; C. O'Reilly to C. K. O'Reilly 25 December 1883. Probate of O'Reilly's will provides an indication of his net worth. All O'Reilly Papers, BCARS.

Victoria Theatre: *Colonist* 1 April, 10 and 17 October, 11 November 1885. A mortgage in favour of Robert Dunsmuir was registered 3 August 1888, by which time the accrued interest was $5,706.30, LTO.

A notion persists that Dunsmuir lost the Victoria Theatre in a card game (*Colonist* 1 May 1955 and 27 March 1977). In fact, it passed to his widow, Joan, who sold it to Joseph Boscowitz on 9 May 1891 for $30,000, conveyance, LTO.

Last spike ceremonies and Macdonald's remarks: *Colonist* 14 and 15 August 1886; *Colonist* 10 August 1886.

The story of Joan and the tea kettle was related by her granddaughter: *Colonist* 1 May 1955.

Knighthood: State Book, Executive Council Papers, BCARS; Davie to Macdonald 22 June 1887, Macdonald Papers, BCARS.

Williams' career: Reksten, *Craigdarroch*.

Cost of Craigdarroch: *Victoria Times* 27 December 1888 and *Colonist* 1 January 1891 both estimated cost at $500,000; the city assessor estimated $185,000, *Colonist* 7 August 1898.

Chapter Seven

Dunsmuir and Vancouver charter: *Vancouver News Advertiser* 6 April 1887. Vancouver reaction to Dunsmuir's proposed ferry link: *Vancouver News Advertiser* 20 March 1887.

Portland News article: reprinted *Victoria Times* 24 December 1887; see also *Victoria Times* 27 December 1887.

Humphreys: Halleran, "Humphreys"; Journals of the Legislative Assembly; Wade, *Cariboo Road*; *Colonist* 4 December 1887.

By-election covered in detail by *Colonist* and *Victoria Times*.

Explosion reported in detail by newspapers in Victoria and Nanaimo. Morgan interview: *Colonist* 26 January 1888. The opinion of "a coal miner": *Colonist* 25 January 1888.

Explosion of 1884: Mines Report, 1884. Coroner's inquest: *Nanaimo Free Press* 12 July 1884.

Coroner's inquest, explosion of 1888: *Nanaimo Free Press* 4 and 11 February 1888.

Early reaction to Chinese employment in the mines: Lai, *Chinatowns*. Opinion of Hough and others: *Victoria Times* 7 February 1888.

Knights of Labor: Forer, *History of Labor Movement* and Brooks, *Toil and Trouble*. Opposition to Dunsmuir: *Victoria Times* 28 March 1888.

Chapter Eight

Dunsmuir's speech: *Colonist* 30 March 1888.

Griffin's trial: *Victoria Times* 14 November 1888; *Colonist* 15, 18, 29 and 30 November; 30 December 1888. His subsequent career: *Colonist* 23 July 1908.

Chapter Nine

Dunsmuir's letter to Trutch 22 February 1889: Robert Dunsmuir, Correspondence Outward,, BCARS.

Dunsmuir's meeting with miners' committee: *Colonist* 10 and 11 January 1889.

Dunsmuir's exchange with Humphreys: *Colonist* 15 February 1888.

Trutch's letter to Dunsmuir's widow: 29 April 1889, Trutch, Correspondence Outward, BCARS.

Dunsmuir's presentiment of death: *Nanaimo Free Press* 18 April 1889.

Chapter Ten

James Audain's biography of his uncle, *Alex Dunsmuir's Dilemma*, contains invented dialogue and imagined scenes, and cannot be used as a reliable source.

Held by the BCARS is a transcript of the sworn testimony taken in *Hopper v. Dunsmuir*. Unless otherwise indicated, that testimony provided the source of all direct quotations relating to Alex and his life in San Francisco. Other details were drawn from documentary evidence introduced in the trial as "exhibits."

Sworn testimony indicates Alex's drinking habits underwent a sudden change in 1886. Possibly he was sent on a downward spiral by the birth of a child he is said to have fathered—a son christened Robert after his grandfather, but whose very existence was considered so shameful that he was spirited away to Scotland and grew to adulthood sure that his father was Alex, but never knowing the identity of his mother.

The mother may have been Edna, but at twelve or thirteen, she seems too young. Or Josephine, but in her shadow-world a pregnancy would hardly seem so shameful. It may be that an unknown woman was the mother of Alex's child. Many years later, while giving evidence about Alex's life in San Francisco, James Dunsmuir alluded to "another woman" and the family's concern that she might have grounds for laying claim to Alexander's estate.

And it may be that there was no child at all. Perhaps the present-day Dunsmuirs who claim to be Alex's descendants are in the thrall of a romantic fiction, despite the strong family resemblance that lends credence to their claim. Records that might settle the issue are sealed until the year 2000, in CCC.

Chapter Eleven

Boyce's activities and the Wellington troubles received detailed coverage in *Victoria Times* and *Colonist*. See clipping file, CCC.

Chapter Twelve

James Harvey seems to have been well-liked in Nanaimo. His money problems probably stemmed from the difficulties trying to collect from his customers. Mortgage on Harvey's store and its conveyance to the lenders: Charge Book, LTO. Agnes Harvey's death: *Colonist* 17 September 1889. Harvey's death: *Nanaimo Free Press* 27 February and 10 March 1890.

Houghton's early career: Roy, "The Early Militia." His explorations for Douglas: Ormsby, "Exploratory Trip, 1864" and Norris, "Explorations." His election: Gosnell, "B.C.'s Strangest Election" and Wade, *Cariboo Road*. His marriage to Sophie: Brent, "My Life." Hugh Macdonald's opinion of Houghton: 8 July 1884, Macdonald Papers, BCARS; for other opinions see Morton, *Telegrams*. His death: *Montreal Star* 16 August 1898 and *Colonist* 14 August 1898.

Croft biographical information provided by John Croft. See also *Colonist* 29 July 1917. Details of Croft's property transactions, mortgages and rental agreements are from documents in the LTO. Chemainus property acquired 16 August 1883; mortgage in Robert Dunsmuir's favour registered 29 October 1886; Chemainus property conveyed to Robert Dunsmuir 21 January 1889. Esquimalt property acquired 12 November 1889; first lots sold 11 February 1890; $38,000 mortgage in favour of Pemberton Trust registered 14 February 1891; $20,000 mortgage in favour of Joan Dunsmuir registered 7 September 1892; Mary Croft leases property from Pemberton Trust 5 April 1895; Joan Dunsmuir conveys to Mary Croft 13 May 1907.

Exploits of Francis Bees Bourchier: *Colonist* 20 November 1894 and 13 April 1901.

Snowden's death certificate provides the cause and place of death.

About Sir Richard and Jessie Musgrave: information from Shane Jameson. The first Sir Richard: *Dictionary of National Biography, 1894*. His piscatorial prowess: *Cork Examiner* 8 March 1930. Victoria opinion of Sir Richard: Mrs. O'Reilly's letter, reprinted *Colonist* 17 September 1961.

Chapter Thirteen

Voyage aboard the *Thistle*: Log of the *Thistle*, BCARS.

Barrymore's comments: Eells, *Hedda and Louella*.

James's letter, direct quotations, description of incidents: *Hopper v. Dunsmuir*, BCARS.

Chapter Fourteen

Freeman: Mjelde, *Glory of the Seas*.

Edna's interview with the *Examiner* appeared 20 July 1899; the story of her dalliance with Sloan in Churchill, *Great White Way*. Edna was Hopper's third wife. In all, he went to the altar six times, earning the soubriquet "Husband of his Country." His fifth wife, Elda, became so irritated by Hopper's insistence on calling her Edna that she changed her name to Hedda. And after divorcing him in 1925, she became famous as Hollywood gossip columnist Hedda Hopper.

Chapter Fifteen

Unstable political situation: Gosnell, *History of British Columbia* and contemporary newspapers.

Dunsmuir's insistence he did not lead revolt: *Colonist* 6 March 1900.

Dunsmuir's acceptance in Ottawa: *Colonist* 29 January 1901 and *Province* 12 February 1901.

Chapter Sixteen

Dunsmuir's conflict-of-interest philosophy: *Province* 21 March 1901.

Little's attitude toward Chinese and Scottish miners: his testimony in *Report of the Royal Commission on Chinese and Japanese Immigration.*

Terry's letter and Dunsmuir's response: *Province* 6 February 1901.

Cumberland explosion: detailed coverage by newspapers in Nanaimo, Victoria and Vancouver. See, for example, *Province* 16, 18 and 20 February 1901; *Nanaimo Free Press* 18 February 1901. William Roy's interview: *Province* 19 February 1901.

Terry's meeting with Nanaimo miners: *Nanaimo Free Press* 25 February 1901. His letter to *Nanaimo Free Press* 1 March 1901.

Hawthornthwaite's speech and Dunsmuir's reaction: *Province* 12 March 1901.

Notice about sale of Wellington town lots: *Nanaimo Free Press* 21 August 1875. James Dunsmuir's offer of Ladysmith lots: *Colonist* 22 May 1901.

Dunsmuir's meeting with miners' delegation: *Province* 24 December 1901. King's proposed settlement of Alexandra dispute: *Province* 29 November 1901.

Closure of Extension: *Province* 11 March and 13 March 1903.

Baker's Cumberland meeting: *Colonist* 7 April and 14 April 1903.

Chapter Seventeen

Dunsmuir's statements of his policies: *Province* 13 January 1902 and *Colonist* 26 January 1902.

Criticism of Dunsmuir's meeting with Laurier: *Province* 8 May 1901. Dunsmuir's reply: *Colonist* 9 May 1901.

Dunsmuir's refutation of Bodwell's charges: *Province* 21 February 1901.

Dunsmuir's proposal to the Committee of Fifty: *Colonist* 4, 9, 10, and 21 May, 22 July 1899.

Dunsmuir's correspondence with Hubbard: *Colonist* 28 March and 8 April 1902; Wellington Colliery Letterbook, Buckham papers, BCARS.

Threat to Dunsmuir's life: *Colonist* 9 March 1902.

Dunsmuir's testimony before inquiry: *Colonist* 10 and 11 April 1902.

Chapter Eighteen

Continent-wide interest in will case: *New York Times* 10 November 1901.

Croft/Dunsmuir controversy: *Colonist* 15, 16 and 17 January 1902.

Testimony from *Hopper v. Dunsmuir.* The trial was covered in detail by newspapers in British Columbia and San Francisco.

Chapter Nineteen

Effie: Master in Lunacy papers, LTO. Her last days were described in a letter to the author from her great-nephew, Shane Jameson, who also provided information about Jessie Musgrave, Maude Chaplin, and Emily and Harry Burroughes.

Adele Astaire Cavendish: Thomas, *Fred Astaire.*

Mary Croft's affair was first mentioned by a former neighbour (Mrs. E. Harris) and confirmed by one of Mary's nephews. Photocopies of her letters were provided by John Croft. Biographical information on Matson: *Victoria Times* 2 November 1931 and *Colonist* 3 November 1931.

Edna Hopper: *Victoria Times* 10 February 1905, *San Francisco Examiner* 12 June 1910, *New York Times* 19 April 1953 and 15 December 1959, *Colonist* 19 November 1972.

Chapter Twenty

Laura's connection to Byrd family: genealogical research of Bill Murphy (North Carolina) provided to the author. Her father's status: U.S. Census 1860 and 1870.

Richardson's background: *Raleigh News and Observer* 21 April 1968; *National Cyclopaedia of Biography*; Campbell, *Why Did They Name It*; and Burton, *Richardson.*

Kathleen O'Reilly's comments: letter to her mother 26 December 1896, O'Reilly Papers, BCARS.

Duchess's visit: Bessie Dunsmuir's recollections, *Colonist* 1 May 1955.

Purchase agreement between Dunsmuir and PIC in Graham collection, BCARS. Terms of CPR sale: Indenture, Graham Collection, BCARS. Mayor's reaction: *Province* 28 March 1905.

Reaction to Dunsmuir's appointment: *Victoria Times* 12 May 1906.

Dunsmuir's early success as lieutenant-governor: *Colonist* 24 October 1906 and 25

May 1907; *Province* 20 June and 26 July 1906, 18 June 1907.

Williams's comments: *Province* 6 January 1908. Extra guards for lieutenant-governor: *Province* 16 January 1908. Oliver's research: *Province* 17 and 22 January 1908. Hawthornthwaite's remarks: *Province* 3 February 1908.

Stuart's home destroyed by fire: *Colonist* 24 August 1905. Biographical information: Vertical File, BCARS.

Hatley purchase, 26 November 1907 (242 acres); 10 April 1908 (250 acres); 3 January 1910 (200 acres): Indentures, LTO.

Fire aboard the *Thistle*: *Province* 27 May 1907 and *Colonist* 28 May 1907. The *Dolaura*: *Province* 28 March 1908 (also includes a description of Hatley).

Dunsmuir's meeting with the Kaiser: wide press coverage, for example, *Victoria Times* and *Province* 13 July 1908. Bessie Dunsmuir's recollection: *Colonist* 1 May 1955.

First report of sale to Canadian Northern: *Victoria Times* 2 May 1910. Terms: Indenture, Graham Collection, BCARS; and in evidence in the Supreme Court, *Victoria Times* 13 September 1911. Dunsmuir was reinvested $6 million in Canadian Northern 3 1/2 per cent debentures: *Victoria Times* 28 June 1910.

Mackenzie did in fact launch legal action. Dunsmuir's testimony regarding his having declared a dividend and his attitude to business in *Victoria Times* 13 September 1911.

On 13 September 1911, the Supreme Court decided in Dunsmuir's favour, *Victoria Times* 14 September 1911. Mackenzie appealed the decision. On 22 July 1913 the appeal court decided in Dunsmuir's favour, *Colonist* 23 July 1913.

Chapter Twenty-one

Robin's education: Audain, *Coalmine to Castle* and *Colonist*, 7 July 1899.

Willamette affair: Barraclough, Robin Dunsmuir, Vertical File, BCARS. Other suspicions: Buckham (handwritten notes), Buckham Papers, BCARS.

A circumspect version of Stuart's involvement in a personal recollection in Stuart, Vertical File, BCARS: "A very prominent man in political life had got a young lady in trouble, and, to avoid scandal, he asked his friend Roland Stuart to marry the girl. This Roland consented to do, married the girl in a very quiet ceremony, said good-bye, and that was that."

Rumours of Robin's paternity of the child later claimed as his sister, Dola: see notes, Chapter 24. The truth hardly matters. More to the point, Robin's character and behaviour were sufficient to encourage such rumours.

Pep Groos provided Laura's opinion of Maude. Robin's defence of Maude: *San Francisco Chronicle* 15 July 1909. His dalliance with Dorothy Russell: *San Francisco Chronicle* 25 March and 28 May 1910.

Robin's letter 30 March 1905 to James J. Hill, Minnesota Historical Society, copy BCARS.

Robin's Esquimalt property: LTO (acquires first parcel 10 April 1905; acquires second parcel 10 May 1906; house and land conveyed to Laura Dunsmuir 1 July 1909); and *Victoria Times* 11 January 1907 (Maclure design completed, cost $20,000).

Robin's Peruvian schemes: *Colonist* 16 December 1922; *Victoria Times*, 14 July and 27 September 1922. Incident on *Mauretania*: Audain, *Coalmine to Castle*.

Robin's obituary: *Vancouver Sun* 7 January 1929 and *Colonist* 8 January 1929.

James Audain's recollections of his uncle, Boy Dunsmuir: *Coalmine to Castle*, *Borrowed Life* and *Colonist* 1 February 1970.

Role of CMRs: Johnston, *2nd Canadian Mounted Rifles*. Reaction to Boy's death: *Colonist* 16 May 1915; Audain *Coalmine to Castle*; reminiscences of Mrs. G. Terry. The "Lusitania Riot" was widely covered in the local press: see, for example, *Colonist* 9 and 11 May 1915.

The *Dolaura* passed through several hands before being renamed *Valena* and seconded to the Admiralty in World War II. When last heard of, she was carrying displaced European Jews to Israel.

Chapter Twenty-two

Information about Byrdie and her sisters: James Audain, *Coalmine to Castle* and *Borrowed Life*.

Conditions Byrdie encountered in India: Allen, *Raj*.

According to James Dunsmuir's probate papers, Audain's annuity was dated 2 August 1906. By 1920 the capitalized value of the annuity was $30,908.

Purchase of Okanagan ranch: *Colonist* 27 and 28 March 1907. Sale of ranch: Weeks, "Steamboating."

Byrdie purchased Ellora property 12 August 1909 for $11,000. Over the next two years she added 3 acres to the original parcel, LTO.

Arthur Bromley: *Burke's Peerage* and *The Times* 9 May 1927. Marriage: *Colonist* 25 June 1904. Maye's obituary: *The Times* 21 September 1959.

Bessie's wedding: *The Times* 16 April 1907. Her death: *Victoria Times* 28 December 1962. Reminiscences of Bessie: Trevor Green and Pep Groos. See also *Debrett's Peerage*.

Girls' debut: *Colonist* 12 August 1906.

Some of Elinor's books are in the Craigdarroch Castle Library. Elinor's great niece, Kat McCann, provided reminiscences.

Muriel's marriage: *The Times* 24 October 1921. See also *Vogue* 1 January 1922. Vera Poncin, a former Molyneux model, provided her reminiscences and expressed her surprise at the marriage. Pronunciation of Molyneux: *Current Biography.* Nicolson's letter: Lees-Milne, *Nicolson.* Molyneux's subsequent career: Kennedy, *Times to Remember*; "Paris Personalities." Pep Groos provided information about Muriel's continuing good relationship with Molyneux.

Stevenson's death: *Victoria Times* 14 October 1922. Marion's death: *Colonist* 12 July 1952.

Chapter Twenty-three

Kathleen as a "popular amateur artist": *Vancouver Province* 14 November 1914.

Kathleen's wartime canteen: *Colonist*, 22 and 25 April, 7 May and 16 October 1915; 26 March 1916.

Kathleen's correspondence and comments about California are in her papers, lent to the author by Kat McCann.

Storyline of *The Crimson Paradise* is in the Souvenir Programme of 14 December 1933 among Kathleen's papers.

Bishop-produced Victoria films: Browne, *Motion Picture Production.*

Comments of Ivan Ackery and Patrick Sinnott: *Vancouver Province* 14 December 1973.

Terms of Laura's will: Probate Papers, BCARS.

Visit of George VI recalled by Betty Jenkins.

Bombing of the Café de Paris: widely reported, in particular *Vancouver Province* 10 March 1941 and *The Times* 10 March 1941.

Chapter Twenty-four

For more than a few Victorians who were contemporaries of Dola, her parentage remained in doubt. Gossip had it that she was the illegitimate child of one of the maids at Burleith, and that her father was Robin Dunsmuir. The basis for the rumour is obvious. After giving her husband twelve children over the first eighteen years of their marriage, Laura seems to have retired from the field after giving birth to a second son, Boy, in 1894. Nine years had passed and Laura was forty-five before Dola was born. See notes Chapter 22.

Audain's recollections of Dola: Audain, *Coalmine to Castle* and *Borrowed Life.*

Dola's comments: Young, "The Fabulous Dunsmuirs."

Tallulah anecdotes are scattered throughout the Bankhead biographies listed in Sources, as are references to Dola. Tallulah's comments about her "philosophy" are in her autobiography.

Dola's obituary: *Colonist* 11 December 1966.

Sources

Abbreviations

BCARS	British Columbia Archives and Records Service
CCC	Craigdarroch Castle Collection
HBCA-PAM	Hudson's Bay Company Archives, Public Archives of Manitoba
LTO	Land Titles Office, British Columbia
NAC	National Archives of Canada
SRO	Scottish Records Office

Newspapers

British Columbian
Irvine Valley News
Nanaimo Free Press
New York Times
Raleigh News and Observer
San Francisco Call
San Francisco Chronicle
San Francisco Examiner

The Times
Vancouver Daily World
Vancouver News Advertiser
Vancouver Province
Victoria Daily Colonist
Victoria Daily Standard
Victoria Daily Times
Westward Ho!

Documents and Manuscripts

Albion Iron Works. Minutes of Directors' Meetings. BCARS.
Attorney General's Papers. BCARS.
Bate, Mark. Director's Diary. BCARS.
Bryden, John. Letterbook. BCARS.
Buckham Papers (collected letterbooks, Wellington Collieries). BCARS.
Census, Canada, 1881, 1891.
_____, Scotland, 1841.
_____, United States, 1860, 1870.
Coal Claim Correspondence, R. Dunsmuir and W. N. Diggle, 1869–1871. BCARS.
Croft, John. Family Papers. Private collection.
Dunsmuir, Allan. Probate Papers. SRO.
Dunsmuir, Kathleen. Papers. Private collection.
Dunsmuir, Robert. Correspondence Outward. BCARS.
Dunsmuir, Robert (senior). Probate Papers. SRO.
Dunsmuir & Diggle. Dissolution of Partnership, 12 May 1881. BCARS.
Executive Council Papers. BCARS.
_____. Reports, State Book. BCARS.
Fort Victoria Correspondence Outward. BCARS.
Gilmour/Landale Correspondence. HBCA-PAM.

Graham Collection. BCARS.
Helmcken Papers. BCARS.
Hopper v. Dunsmuir Transcript. BCARS.
Houghton, Charles Frederick. Report of the Deputy Adjutant General re: Anticipated Riot. BCARS.
Kilmarnock Parish Registers. SRO.
King, William Lyon Mackenzie. Diaries. NAC.
Kirk Sessions, Riccarton and Kilmarnock. SRO.
Macdonald Papers [microfilm]. BCARS.
McKay, Joseph. "Recollections." BCARS.
Muir, Andrew. Diary, 9 November 1848 to 5 August 5 1850. BCARS.
Nanaimo Correspondence. James Douglas to Joseph McKay, August 1852 to September 1853. BCARS.
O'Reilly Papers. BCARS.
Riccarton Parish Registers. SRO.
Smallbones, Tilly. W. J. O'Neill to A. Wills, 1 December 1956. CCC.
Stuart, Capt. Charles Edward. Nanaimo Journal, August 1855 to March 1857. BCARS.
Trutch, Sir Joseph William. Correspondence Outward. BCARS.
Vertical Files. BCARS.

Published Sources

Allen, Charles. *Raj: A Scrapbook of British India 1877–1947*. London: André Deutch, 1977.

Audain, James. *Alex Dunsmuir's Dilemma*. Victoria: Sunnylane, 1964.

_____. *From Coalmine to Castle*. New York: Pageant, 1955.

_____. *My Borrowed Life*. Sidney: Gray's, 1962.

Bailey, Thomas A., and Paul B. Ryan. *The Lusitania Disaster*. New York: Macmillan, 1975.

Bankhead, Tallulah. *Tallulah*. New York: Harper, 1952.

Beresford, Lord Charles. *The Memoirs of Admiral Lord Charles Beresford*. London: Methuen, 1916.

Bowen, Lynne. *Boss Whistle*. Lantzville: Oolichan Books, 1982.

_____. *Three Dollar Dreams*. Lantzville: Oolichan Books, 1987.

Bowsfield, Hartwell, ed. *Fort Victoria Letters 1843–1851*. Winnipeg: Hudson's Bay Record Society, 1979.

Brent, Marie. "My Life . . . Marie Houghton Brent," *Report of the Okanagan Historical Society* 1966.

Brooks, Thomas R. *Toil and Trouble: A History of American Labor*. New York: Delacorte, 1964, 1971.

Browne, Colin. *Motion Picture Production in British Columbia: 1898–1946*. Victoria: B.C. Provincial Museum, 1979.

Brunvand, Jan Harold. *The Vanishing Hitchhiker: American Urban Legends and Their Meanings*. New York: Norton, 1981.

Burton, W. C. *H. Smith Richardson: Ideas into Action*. Greensboro: Smith Richardson Foundation, 1979.

Campbell, Hannah. *"Why Did They Name It . . .".* New York: Fleet, 1964.

Cheadle, W. B. *Cheadle's Journal of a Trip Across Canada 1862–1863*. Ed. A. G. Doughty and Gustave Lanctot. Ottawa, 1931.

Churchill, Allen. *The Great White Way*. New York: Dutton, 1962.

Current Biography. 1942. Currie, A. W. "The Vancouver Coal Mining Company." *Queen's Quarterly*. Spring 1963.

Department of Militia and Defence. *Report upon the suppression of the rebellion in the North-West Territories in 1885*. Ottawa, 1886.

Droste, C. L. (coll.), and W. H. Tatum (ed.). *The Lusitania Case*. London: Stephens, 1916, 1972.

Eells, George. *Hedda and Louella*. New York: Putnam's, 1972.

Forer, Philip S. *A History of the Labor Movement in the United States*. New York: International Publishers, 1947.

Gill, Brendan. *Tallulah*. New York: Holt, Rinehart & Winston, 1972.

Gosnell, R. E. "B.C.'s Strangest Parliamentary Election," *Vancouver Province* 11 March 1928.

_____. *A History of British Columbia*. Lewis Pub. Co., 1906.

Halleran, Michael. "Thomas Basil Humphreys" in *Dictionary of Canadian Biography*. Toronto: University of Toronto Press, 1982.

Hickey, Des, and Gus Smith. *Seven Days to Disaster*. London: Collins, 1981.

Hussey, John A. *The History of Fort Vancouver and Its Physical Structure*. Washington State Historical Association, 1957.

Israel, Lee. *Miss Tallulah Bankhead*. New York: Putnam's, 1972.

Johnston, Lt.-Col. G. Chambers. *The 2nd Canadian Mounted Rifles* Vernon: privately printed, n.d.

Kennedy, Rose. *Times to Remember*. New York: Doubleday, 1974.

Lai, David Chuenyan. *Chinatowns*. Vancouver: University of British Columbia Press, 1988.

Langevin, H. L. *British Columbia: Report of H. L. Langevin, Minister of Public Works*. Ottawa, 1872.

Lebon, John H. G. "The Development of the Ayrshire Coalfield," *Scottish Geographical Magazine* May 1933.

Lees-Milne, James. *Harold Nicolson: A Biography*. Toronto: Clarke Irwin, 1980.

Lewis, Oscar. *The Big Four*. New York: Knopf, 1959.

Lugrin, N. de B. *The Pioneer Women of Vancouver Island*. Victoria, 1928.

MacLachlan, Donald F. *The Esquimalt & Nanaimo Railway*. Victoria: B.C. Railway Historical Assoc., 1986.

Mills, John. *Up in the Clouds, Gentlemen Please*. London: Weidenfeld & Nicolson, 1980.

Mjelde, Michael J. *Glory of the Seas*. Middletown: Marine Historical Association, Wesleyan University Press, 1970.

Morton, Desmond, and R. H. Roy (eds.). *Telegrams of the North-West Campaign.* Toronto: Champlain Society, 1972.

Myers, Gustavus. *A History of Canadian Wealth.* Toronto: James Lewis & Samuel, 1914, reprint 1972.

National Cyclopaedia of Biography.

Norris, L. "The Explorations of Captain Houghton," *Report, Okanagan Historical Society,* Vol. 5.

Ormsby, Margaret L. "Captain Houghton's Exploratory Trip, 1864," *Report, Okanagan Historical Society,* 1949.

"Paris Personalities," *Good Housekeeping* June 1938.

Porter, Brian. "Robert Dunsmuir—An Exercise in Genealogical Reconstruction," *B.C. Genealogist* Summer 1981.

Ralston, H. Keith. "Miners and Managers: The Organization of Coal Production on Vancouver Island by the Hudson's Bay Company" in *The Company on the Coast.* Ed. E. Blanche Norcross. Nanaimo: Nanaimo Historical Society, 1983.

Reksten, Terry. *Craigdarroch: The Story of Dunsmuir Castle.* Victoria: Orca, 1988.
_____. *"More English Than the English": A Very Social History of Victoria.* Victoria: Orca, 1986.

Report of the Royal Commission on Chinese Immigration. Ottawa: Queen's Printer, 1885.

Report of the Royal Commission on Chinese and Japanese Immigration. Ottawa: King's Printer, 1902.

Rickard, T. A. "A History of Coal Mining in British Columbia," *The Miner.*

Roy, Patricia E. *A White Man's Province.* Vancouver: University of British Columbia Press, 1988.

Roy, Reginald H. "The Early Militia in British Columbia," *B.C. Historical Quarterly* 1954.

Sessional Papers. Contract—E & N Railway (1883).
_____. Correspondence—Wellington Strike (1878).
_____. Minister of Mines, Annual Reports, (1874–1898).

Smith, Colin. *Lusitania.* London: Longman, 1972.

Smith, Dorothy Blakey (ed.). *The Reminiscences of Doctor John Sebastian Helmcken.* Vancouver: University of British Columbia Press, 1975.

Thomas, Bob. *The Man, the Dancer: The Life of Fred Astaire.* New York: St. Martin's Press, 1984.

Tunney, Kieran. *Tallulah: Darling of the Gods.* London: Secker & Warburg, 1972.

Vickers, Randolph S. "George Robinson: Nanaimo Mine Agent," *The Beaver* Autumn, 1984.

Wade, Mark S. *The Cariboo Road.* Victoria: Haunted Bookshop, 1979.

Weeks, Joseph B. "Steamboating on Okanagan Lake," 6th Report, Okanagan Historical Society, 1935.

Wilson, M. *The Ayrshire Hermit.* Kilmarnock: A. C. Jonas, 1875.

Young, Patricia. "The Fabulous Dunsmuirs," *Chatelaine* September, October, November 1961.

Index

W

Y

Z

TERRY REKSTEN was born in England, grew up in Vancouver and was educated at the University of British Columbia and the University of Victoria. She is a full-time writer and lecturer. In 1985 she was named an Honorary Citizen of the City of Victoria in recognition of her writing and her work in heritage preservation.

Terry and her husband, Don, live near the sea in Oak Bay, B.C. *The Dunsmuir Saga* is her fourth book. Her previous books are *Rattenbury* (1978), *"More English than the English": A Very Social History of Victoria* (1986) and *Craigdarroch: The Story of Dunsmuir Castle* (1988).